SO-AAE-011

VRML

BROWSING AND BUILDING CYBERSPACE

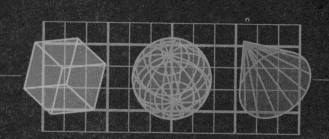

New Riders

VRML—Browsing and Building Cyberspace

By Mark Pesce

Published by:
New Riders Publishing
201 West 103rd Street
Indianapolis, IN 46290 USA

All rights reserved. No part of this book may be reproduced or transmitted in any form or by any means, electronic or mechanical, including photocopying, recording, or by any information storage and retrieval system, without written permission from the publisher, except for the inclusion of brief quotations in a review.

Copyright © 1995 by New Riders Publishing

Printed in the United States of America 2 3 4 5 6 7 8 9 0

CIP data available upon request

Warning and Disclaimer

This book is designed to provide information about Virtual Reality Modeling Language (VRML). Every effort has been made to make this book as complete and as accurate as possible, but no warranty or fitness is implied.

The information is provided on an "as is" basis. The author and New Riders Publishing shall have neither liability nor responsibility to any person or entity with respect to any loss or damages arising from the information contained in this book or from the use of the disks or programs that may accompany it.

Publisher	**Don Fowley**
Associate Publisher	**Tim Huddleston**
Marketing Manager	**Ray Robinson**
Acquisitions Manager	**Jim LeValley**
Managing Editor	**Tad Ringo**

Product Development Specialist
David Dwyer

Acquisitions Editor
Jim LeValley

Software Specialist
Steve Weiss

Production Editor
Sarah Kearns

Copy Editor
Amy Bezek

Technical Editor
Jan Hardenbergh

Assistant Marketing Manager
Tamara Apple

Acquisitions Coordinator
Stacey Beheler

Publisher's Assistant
Karen Opal

Cover Designer
Karen Ruggles

Book Designers
Paula Carroll
Sandra Schroeder

Manufacturing Coordinator
Paul Gilchrist

Production Manager
Kelly Dobbs

Production Team Supervisor
Laurie Casey

Illustrator
C. Scott Young

Graphic Image Specialists
Stephen Carlin, Jason Hand, Clint Lahnen,
Ryan Oldfather, Todd Wente

Production Analysts
Angela Bannan
Bobbi Satterfield
Mary Beth Wakefield

Production Team
Kim Cofer, Kevin Foltz, David Garratt,
Aleata Howard, Shawn MacDonald,
Joe Millay, Erika Millen, Brian-Kent Proffitt,
Beth Rago, Erich J. Richter, Christine Tyner,
Karen Walsh, Robert Wolf

Indexers
Bront Davis, Chris Cleveland

About the Author

Mark Pesce is a cyberspace researcher and theorist. After spending a decade working in data communications, he left Shiva Corporation in 1991 to found Ono-Sendai Corporation, an early virtual reality company. After leaving Ono-Sendai in 1993, Mr. Pesce began work on *Labyrinth*, the prototype for Virtual Reality Modeling Language. As moderator of the VRML mailing list on the Internet, Mr. Pesce works to ensure that VRML remains an open standard and grows into a fully interactive cyberspace. An established writer, he is a frequent contributor to magazines such as *WIRED*, *Mondo 2000*, and *Morph's Outpost*. This is his first book.

Trademark Acknowledgments

All terms mentioned in this book that are known to be trademarks or service marks have been appropriately capitalized. New Riders Publishing cannot attest to the accuracy of this information. Use of a term in this book should not be regarded as affecting the validity of any trademark or service mark.

Dedication

For:
Frances Veronica Pesce
Donald Lewis Pesce
Judith Ann Quandt

Contents at a Glance

Table of Contents

7 Intermediate VRML   129

8 Advanced VRML and Server Scripts   167

Part III: Project 188   209

9 Homesteading Cyberspace   211

13 VRML: The Next Generation   313

Afterword: The World-song   326

Part V: Appendixes   327

A VRML: The Virtual Reality
Modeling Language Version 1.0 Specification   329

Preface: The Earth-Garden

In June of 1995, the second Interactive Media Festival opened its doors to the world. Twenty-one exhibits—from Europe, Asia, and America—filled Los Angeles' Variety Arts Center with a new vision of the possibilities of human-centered computing.

Two of the exhibits at the Festival captivated the imaginations of everyone involved. *The Tele-Garden* (http://www.usc.edu/dept/garden/), created by researchers at the University of Southern California, connected a robot's arm to the World Wide Web. This robot tended a 6' diameter garden, in which one could plant seeds, water them, and tend to other gardening tasks like weeding. Individuals and communities would take turns caring for the garden—sharing the chores globally for a local space—and together created a verdant, well-manicured garden within the Web.

Finally, the most remarkable entry—and perhaps the most incredible piece of computing I've ever seen—was *T_Vision* (http://www.artcom.de/projects/terra/), produced by Berlin's ART+COM. It looks simple enough; using a beach ball-sized trackball, you can control and manipulate an image of the Earth projected on a large monitor in front of you. T_Vision includes an implicit level of detail—as you zoom in, features resolve. It's possible to go from 200,000 miles above the Earth down to about 200' above the Kurfurstendam in Berlin, all in a series of 22 steps of progressive resolution. While that's impressive, it's not much different from work others have done, except for the fact that T_Vision is *live*. Satellite data from around the Earth —updated every hour—is coordinated in the T_Vision database to create an integrated view of the Earth as it is right now.

T_Vision spans the entire planet, but most of the database is incomplete. There's about 20 billion characters of topological data in it already, and perhaps another trillion characters that would define the basic features of the surface of the Earth in detail. ART+COM doesn't have the resources for that project; instead they're looking for ways to integrate their system with existing databases to improve T_Vision's ability to deliver a visualization of the whole planet. It's the millennial equivalent of the "big blue marble" we saw for the first time when the Apollo astronauts photographed the Earth on their way to the Moon.

I gave a lecture at the Festival, talking about the applications of VRML. I noted that The Tele-Garden, T_Vision, and VRML are perfectly orthogonal—each, when fully articulated, provides something that makes the other more complete. Together, they provide a framework for planetary management in the 21st century.

VRML is here, and its applications are practically endless. I wrote this book because I have an agenda, beyond getting VRML out into the hands of everyone who wants to use it. I want to see the Earth in VRML before the end of the decade, T_Vision extended to the level of the individual household, and The Tele-Garden spread over the surface of the planet.

Cyberspace is a great medium for planetary management. It lets you view the whole picture, and helps you to understand the relationships between the different components of complex systems, such as the planet's ecology. VRML is the language of cyberspace, and it seems fitting that the first book we write in this language should be the Story of the World. It will be written by many hands, sung in many tongues, and will stretch out—like a great canvas—to cover the whole planet.

This book is about how to make that happen.

Mark Pesce

June 1995

Acknowledgments

This book, like VRML, was a group effort. They say that while success has many fathers, defeat is an orphan; as this book is completed, I count many people who should be passing out cigars.

VRML is a history of people who believed in a vision, people like Linda Jacobson, Timothy Childs, and Peter Rothman, who gave these ideas their exposure and some room to grow. Others, like Tim Berners-Lee, Dave Raggett, and Robert Callieau, who, as founders of the World Wide Web community, created an environment where crazy ideas like VRML could take root, grow, and finally blossom.

As we formed that community, I found Brian Behlendorf, Gavin Bell, Rikk Carey, Paul Strauss, Tamara Munzner, Don Brutzman, Kevin Goldsmith, and Jan Hardenbergh (who also served as technical reviewer of this manuscript) all eager to share in the work before us. As we moved from specification to products, Robert Weideman, Stepan and Georg Pachikov, David Smith, and Konstantin Guericke contributed by creating great products that used VRML.

Jerry Michalski, managing editor of *Release 1.0*, recognized VRML early on, and helped to popularize it. I'd like to thank him and the whole staff at EDVentures. Others such as Ben Delaney, Robert Gelman, Michael Miller, Jared Sanberg, Erik Davis, Azeem Azar, Dan Duncan, Dave Blackburn, and Louis Brill helped to get the word out. The staff at the Interactive Media Festival—Hal Josephson, Lisa Goldman, David Lewis, Melanie Cornwell, Pamela Coddington, Jamie Cherry, Denise DeCecco, Victor Friedberg, Debbie Giusti, Mark Gunson, and Annette Loudon—made a commitment to VRML that gave it a place in the public eye. Many thanks to all!

Some of the times in the last year have been very lean; before VRML was recognized as a useful innovation, body and soul maintenance fell on the shoulders of friends and business colleagues like Marina Berlin, James Curnow, Robert French, Brian French, Linda Fleming, Daniel Lynch, John Miller, Constanze Kensinger, Kevin McGee, Rosey Machado, Darr Aley, Elizabeth George, Mark Owen, David Levine, Gordon Fuller, Dr. Steven Corey, Lisa Signorelli, William Desjardins, Elizabeth McLindon, Jonathan Wenocur, Keith Kahla, Ronan Hallowell, Phillip Harrington, Rhiannon MacBride, Casey Caston, Brenda Laurel, Paul Godwin (who engineered the VOCE recording on the CD-ROM), Chris Morin, Logos, Betsy De Fries, Neil Redding, Neil Haldar, Tom Aley, Gabriel Lawrence, Robert Powers, Brett Leonard, Georg Gerber, Coco Conn, Brian Blau, Zane Vella, Kit Galloway, Sherri Rabinowitz, William Enright, John Louch, William Martens, Dan Mapes, Claudia Lemeraux, Cyberlab 7, Will Kreith, Chip Bayers, Julie Petersen, WIRED/HOTWIRED, Queen Mu, Wes Thomas, MONDO 2000, Wendy Govier, Rico Zapatelli, Jim Lovette, Dev Inder, John Bates, Mark Stahlman, Denise Caruso, Marty Tenenbaum, Joy Pesce, Servan Keondjian, Kate Seekings, and Dr. Stuart Brorson.

The Virtual Reality Modeling Nerds—or vermin, as they like to be called—were invaluable as a resource: Michael Boehm, Thomas Caleshu, Michael Gernstein, Richard Gilligan, Todd Goldenbaum, Adam Gould, Jeffrey Gray, Ian Kallen, Daniel Kegel, Vojislav Lalich-Petrich, Jeannine Parker, Steven Piaseki, Jim Race, Jeff Sherwood, and James Waldrop (who also contributed some source code).

The folks at New Riders Publishing have been an enormous help getting this book together, keeping me on schedule, and smoothing out any obstacles that I've encountered. After Jim LeValley contacted me about doing a book on VRML—a show of faith long before most people had heard of it—I met with Don Fowley to strike a deal. David Dwyer contributed to the manuscript with his insightful commentary, and Sarah Kearns provided copy editing. I am grateful to all of them for their hard work and enthusiasm on this project.

The four contributors to this manuscript—Tim Berners-Lee, Clay Graham, Michael Gough, and Mark Meadows—have my deep thanks and respect for their well-thought-out additions to this work.

My artists—Greg Jacobson, Kevin Hughes, and C. Scott Young— have given this book a unique and wonderful look, taking my ideas, sketches, and e-mail, and translating them into the graphics that adorn the volume, inside and out. All have been deeply involved in VRML from the earliest days; this is a coming home in many ways, and I thank them as we all return together. David Bauman, tirelessly cleaning up after my mistakes and overzealous planning, also gets a big tip o' the hat.

Finally, three individuals have been absolutely essential in the creation and refinement of the ideas as they appear in this manuscript: Peter Kennard, who continually stretched my mind with his visions of cyberspace; Owen Rowley for his patience and deep wisdom; and Tony Parisi for his collaborative genius and down-to-earth attitude. Without them, none of this would have happened.

Of course, any list of acknowledgments for *VRML* must remain incomplete. I apologize to those whom I have neglected to thank for their singular efforts in a global task.

Foreword

The Web is often described as the space consisting of all network accessible information.

The word "space" is used in an abstract way, but people seem to feel more at home in a hyperspace when it has some of the properties of the real space they are used to. Frans Koesel's early Web of the Vatican Library's exhibit of the Renaissance in Rome, apart from being filled with beautiful pictures, was a success because it kept to a geographical metaphor. The visitor could look at a map of the museum site, take a "bus" to a pavilion, or enter halls and rooms. Introductory text was provided on this journey, so that by the time the visitor was staring at an illuminated manuscript, he or she had some idea of what it was all about.

Virtual reality takes the whole process further, using three dimensions to connect directly with our brains' abilities to handle spatial data with power and familiarity. It is so natural for us to be immersed in a three-dimensional space that we might expect more of the warp and weft of the Web to provide the basic navigation between its resources, woven in VRML rather than HTML.

In May of 1994, the First International WWW Conference was held at CERN in Geneva, Switzerland. At that conference, David Raggett and I held a small "birds of a feather" session in order to kick the Web in the direction of 3D. We felt that although few users had the power of 3D workstations, it was time we had a common language for at least describing simple 3D scenes. The idea was that different representations of 3D and 2D objects could be mixed within one scene. According to its ability for handling each object, a browser program would be able to choose a representation that it could handle, compromising between speed and resolution. Mark Pesce—the author of this book, and already a dabbler in 3D hyperspace—was there, and rapidly formed a small group of enthusiasts to follow up the idea, under Dave's "VRML" label. The result seems to have met with almost universal acceptance. Only a year later, there is a specification to which everyone can design. The World Wide Web Consortium will be working with Mark to ensure that a well-defined standard exists, both at its current level and in the future.

Less than a year after the first conference, the third WWW conference was held in Darmstadt, Germany. A packed plenary session was thrilled by demonstrations of fly-throughs of 3D scenes painted in VRML. Kevin Hughes, a graphic artist and early Web pioneer, rose to his feet and declared the beginning of a new era.

Mark is to be congratulated on his balancing of vision and practicality to make this big step so cleanly. A new era does not come without a certain amount of hard work.

Tim Berners-Lee

Cambridge, Massachusetts, 1995

Introduction:
Cyberspace Begins

This book is about cyberspace. That word gets used a lot these days, so much that it's come to mean almost nothing at all. Everything from the telephone to full virtual reality systems announces itself as the "latest innovation in cyberspace." By now, most people think that all electric communication—everything after the telegraph—is cyberspace.

William Gibson, who coined the word in his short story, "Burning Chrome," gave a picturesque definition of cyberspace in his epochal science fiction novel, *Neuromancer*:

> "Cyberspace. A consensual hallucination experienced daily by billions of legitimate operators, in every nation, by children being taught mathematical concepts... A graphic representation of data abstracted from the banks of every computer in the human system. Unthinkable complexity. Lines of light ranged in the nonspace of the mind, clusters and constellations of data. Like city lights, receding..."

It seems innocent enough, but these few words had an enormous impact. You could almost hear the collective sound as researchers at NASA, the University of North Carolina, and other laboratories scattered all across the world slapped their hands to their heads and said, "*That's* what we're doing!"

Gibson painted a picture—literally—evoking the image of a computer network that you could see. This global cyberspace—which he called the *matrix*—was nothing less than every computer on the Earth contributing to a collective visualization, a shared delusion.

In the early 1980s, when Gibson thought up and wrote out most of these ideas, few people had heard of the Internet. Still confined to a few universities and U.S. Military contractors, it showed few signs that it would mushroom—almost overnight—into the incredible garden of knowledge and community that it has become.

The early Internet was quite difficult to use, but who cared? Almost no one used it. For 20 years, services like CompuServe and Telenet have provided global networking for their customers, but, until 1990, very few people took advantage of them. As people jumped online, it became clear that the Internet interfaces designed for programming wizards only confounded the lawyers, doctors, and executives who now needed to share information on a global scale.

All of this has begun to change. Part of the recent explosion of Internet use—and very probably the cause of it—has been a radical reformation of the ways people can access the riches available through it. New services, like America Online, have created interfaces that anyone can use if he or she knows how to operate a computer. They hide a cryptic and confusing array of services and destinations behind an easy-to-use interface. All of this has made it possible for another generation of "infonauts" to take the Internet where it hadn't gone before—into the minds and hearts of average people. This book is written for them.

The most recent of all of the great innovations on the "information superhighway" happened just a few years ago when the World Wide Web came onto the scene, tying all of the Internet's computers and resources together into a patchwork mosaic of text, images, movies, and sounds. The World Wide Web (often shortened to "the Web") created a brand new type of publishing: the *home page*. The home page was your face in the Web, something you could create to reflect what you were interested in—photos of the children, the sound of a cat's meow (the White House has Socks' meow on its home page), or an essay written about O.J. Simpson. And more, you could link your home page to the home pages of your friends, your favorite band, or your congressman. Soon the Web looked more like a gigantic family album than a newspaper or an endless shopping mall. The Internet had begun to reflect the richness and emotion that make us human.

For a very long time, human beings have been creating spaces to live in, or adapting existing spaces for their own needs. The thirty thousand year-old caves at Lascaux testify to the antiquity of human creation, shaping a natural environment with symbol and myth to create sacred space. Our first architecture created sacred space. As we entered history, Egyptians and Mayans built pyramids, Greeks the Acropolis, and Chinese the Forbidden City. Our civilizations define themselves with architecture; we know of a few civilizations, like the Anasazi, only through their incredible ruins.

If space and place are so important to our humanity, to our civilization—and civilization begins with cities—then the Internet, which is a reflection of humanity, should be as expressive with architecture as it is with text. We should be able to create Gibson's cyberspace and, in so doing, create a place where we can build one city or one hundred million. This is now possible.

A new technology, the *Virtual Reality Modeling Language* (VRML), brings architecture, space, and place to the World Wide Web. Using VRML, you can create a "living room" in cyberspace as easily as you can create a home page, and fill it with the objects of your life—a piano with your photos, a television that plays videos of the kids' last birthday parties, a telephone upon which people can leave messages for you...

This may all sound like some crazy science-fiction movie, closer to *Lawnmower Man* than *WIRED* magazine, but it's an absolutely predictable improvement. The Internet gave us text—lines in one dimension, while the Web gave us pages—spread out in two dimensions. VRML gives us three dimensions to play within, to communicate, to create. In the same way that prose, painting, and sculpture all coexist, all of these technologies cooperate together to produce something greater than any alone. Imagine architecture with no text, or text with no images, or images with no space. We use all of our senses together; the Internet is just beginning to reflect that.

It's easy to use VRML to create a place in cyberspace. That's why I wrote this book. I promise that if you read through the text, you'll find out that there are a number of painless ways to create a VRML "home world" in the Web. Tools developed especially for use with VRML make it a lot easier to create a home world than a home page. You won't even have to learn VRML if you don't want to—the tools don't require that you learn how VRML works before you turn out rich worlds. I'll teach you every shortcut I know to get you up and creating in a hurry. That's what people care most about—creating and sharing.

So why does this matter? Why should you care that the Web has a three-dimensional interface on it? There are a number of reasons. First, without space, we're lost. Surfing the Internet is a nice turn of a phrase, but most of the time none of us know where we're going, or how to get back there again. Stumbling through cyberspace might be a more apt analogy. If we can bring space into this Internet-without-place, it will become possible to give directions to places within the Web just as we do in the real world. The clumsy "http://www.vrml.org/" becomes, "the third building on the right." Which would you remember? (One of my British friends says that the Brits navigate through space not by street names, as Americans do, but by the names of pubs. Whatever works.)

Second, it becomes possible to take things that are very abstract—like a database containing six trillion characters of information—and create interfaces to them that don't overwhelm or confuse their users. One VRML project took an artificial life ecology, where tiny computer programs acting like living organisms were born, ate (each other), bred, and died—and created a window onto this world. Until VRML had been used to open a vista to this environment, it was quite difficult for the project's creator to explain what was happening within the computer's simulated ecosystem. Suddenly, people could see the organisms grow and migrate; they immediately understood.

Finally, we can take the real world and bring it to anyone, anywhere. In my native city of San Francisco, we're beginning a project of modeling the entire city in VRML—and then making it accessible on the Web. When it's done, people in Paris or Tokyo can tour San Francisco in cyberspace, plan their vacations, or study the city's history. San Franciscans will be able to use it as a super "Yellow Pages," where you can actually find out more about a business by remembering where it is. Our spatial memory is quite often much better than our literal memory, and this will be a major improvement to the community infrastructure in the city. Sometime within the next few years, it will be possible to bring up a VRML space of most of the major public arenas across the United States, to check your seating for that concert or sporting event.

If you can visit The Meadowlands in cyberspace, why not your sister's home? She can show you the new kitchen layout, or the new sofa. In the late 20th century, we live everywhere, pretty much all at once. Families drift apart spatially and start trading electronic mail to maintain their bonds. Already people create Web-based birth announcements, Mother's Day cards, and holiday greetings; why not the "family homestead in cyberspace," which changes to reflect the seasons, family events, and the tides of time? The Internet really ought to look a little bit more like a grandmother's house—loaded with knickknacks, cozy, and warm.

The text is divided into four main parts, each encompassing a direction of the compass, starting in the East. This book was composed (for the most part) in New England, where the sun rises over the Atlantic Ocean. Starting in the East then, we work with watery metaphors. The first part, "Colonizing Cyberspace," covers the history of communications in "Charting the Current," and concludes with a guided tour of VRML *browsers* (a browser is a computer program that enables you to view and interact with VRML worlds).

Next, we move to the South (covering the compass points in a clockwise fashion), which is where we get our heat, our fire, and hot weather. The language of VRML, as bits flying across the wires, is covered in the second section of the book, "The Complete VRML Primer." It starts off with a basic discussion of three-dimensional graphics. For many people, VRML is the first time they've used 3D graphics themselves. *Jurassic Park* aside, it's not very difficult, and some basic examples will demystify a lot of computer hocus-pocus about graphics and virtual reality. Then, in a step-by-step fashion, you'll learn how to construct a model of the solar system—really!—using VRML. By the end of the primer, you'll have a solar clock as accurate as any you'll find in the world.

Go West, young man! And so we do, moving to the uncharted plains of cyberspace. Here, in the heart of the book, "Project 188" shows how to set up your own homestead in cyberspace. We take a real house (located in Cambridge, Massachusetts) and detail the entire process of creating a set of VRML models—using software designed specifically for this purpose—and publishing these models on the World Wide Web. Whether you build an imaginative space, or take the real and put it into cyberspace, the process is largely the same, and "Project 188" will give you all the information you need to do the job well.

Finally, the North—land of cold and blustery winds. In these airy zones of the intellect, we'll take "The Road to Know Where." We'll move into the heady issues, like how to optimize VRML for publishing the Web, how to write a VRML browser—if you so desire—and where VRML is going from here. One chapter, "The Cyberspace Style Guide," presents guidelines for cyberspace design that will help you to create the kind of environment people will enjoy and visit again and again.

A road map immediately following this Introduction suggests several paths you can take through this book; some of you will want to skip the technical details, and others will eat them up. To each his or her own!

Cyberspace is going to be a big, rich place. Coke and Pepsi, IBM and Apple, and Ford and Chevy will all be using it to sell you on their next toys—turn the tables around, and build your living room next to their showrooms. We've a lot to share with each other, and cyberspace is big—infinitely big, actually—so there's more than enough room for every creation any of us can dream up. Gibson's vision is on the verge of coming true, and you— the first readers of this book—are like the Sooners, who, over a hundred years ago, took the best parts of Oklahoma because *they got there first.* Cultures are located in our heads, not the land— there will be a Fifth Avenue of cyberspace, a Rodeo Drive, a Kurfurstendam. The choice spots belong to the pioneers who get to the new lands first, and turn the black silence of undeveloped cyberspace into a true reflection of human creativity.

Good luck, and without further ado, here we go...

A Road Map to VRML

This book has been written for a broad audience. Everyone from a novice Web user to an accomplished programmer will find some part of this book relevant.

Of course, some of you may not want to read the whole text—after all, that's so dreadfully linear—but with this road map, you can chart your own course through this book.

All of the paths take you through the first three chapters; these provide context—the history of the Internet, the Web, and VRML—and then transition into a basic explanation of how VRML operates.

The Novice Path

The *novice path* is designed for individuals who are not familiar with the Web or VRML; skipping the technical sections, it moves through VRML browsers and directly into VRML tools. This is a good first path for people who want to get up and running right away:

Chapter 1   *Charting the Current*

Chapter 2   *The VRML Equinox*

Chapter 3   *How VRML Works*

Chapter 4   *Sailing Through Cyberspace: Using VRML Browsers*

Chapter 5   *3D Graphics Primer*

Chapter 9   *Homesteading Cyberspace*

The Hacker's Path

The *hacker's path* is for individuals who have a wealth of experience in the Web and 3D graphics. It covers the VRML Primer and the important technical publishing issues. If you want to write a VRML browser or VRML authoring tools, this is the best path to a quick start. In addition, if you're setting up a Web server for VRML, you'll find the information you'll need in these chapters:

Chapter 1   *Charting the Current*

Chapter 2   *The VRML Equinox*

Chapter 3   *How VRML Works*

Chapter 4   *Sailing Through Cyberspace: Using VRML Browsers*

Chapter 6   *An Introduction to VRML*

Chapter 7   *Intermediate VRML*

Chapter 8   *Advanced VRML and Server Scripts*

Chapter 10   *VRML Optimization and Publishing Issues*

Chapter 11   *How to Write a VRML Browser*

Chapter 13   *VRML: The Next Generation*

The Designer's Path

The *designer's path* is a shortcut for individuals who may be designing their own VRML site, professionally or for any other reason. It covers the basics of VRML, 3D graphics, the tools, and publishing issues, and concludes with a discussion of style and design in cyberspace:

Chapter 1   *Charting the Current*

Chapter 2   *The VRML Equinox*

Chapter 3   *How VRML Works*

Chapter 4   *Sailing Through Cyberspace: Using VRML Browsers*

Chapter 5   *3D Graphics Primer*

Chapter 9   *Homesteading Cyberspace*

Chapter 10   *VRML Optimization and Publishing Issues*

Chapter 12   *The Cyberspace Style Guide*

While these paths will provide you with a more direct route to the answers you need, I hope you'll take an opportunity to read the book from cover to cover; there are plenty of useful suggestions scattered throughout the text.

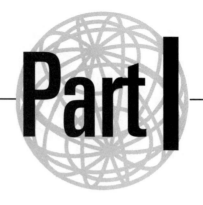

Part I

Colonizing Cyberspace

BROWSING AND BUILDING CYBERSPACE

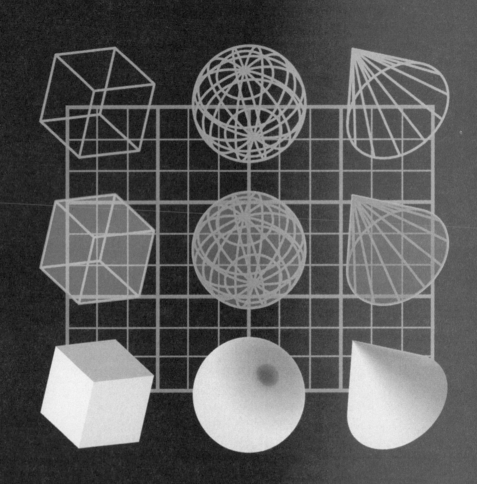

Chapter 1

Charting the Current

Cyberspace is the unexplored country.

When the European sailors ventured forth during the 15th century, their primary task was to develop accurate maps of the currents of sea and air, and chart the lands they found on their journeys. They returned, and these maps—jealously guarded by greedy sovereigns—passed to the next voyager, and so grew in accuracy and detail.

The explosive growth of computers, the Internet, and the World Wide Web is like the discovery of a new world, populated by the content of our own imaginations. It's possible to quickly become overwhelmed by the rapid progress in each of these technologies, and easy to forget that in each of them, we see a reflection of ourselves.

Understanding Media

The latest of these innovations, *Virtual Reality Modeling Language* (VRML) has itself achieved sudden and overwhelming popularity. Well before companies had released any VRML "browsers" or VRML editors, the press and the Web community began to act like kids on Christmas Eve, filled with expectations—visions of cyber-plums dancing in their heads. To many it seemed like the beginning of the cyberspace revolution, but it's actually very easy to trace the path that leads to VRML. It's the story of human communication.

Communicating Imagination

Since the dawn of consciousness in *Homo sapiens*, we've been expressing our thoughts and feelings to each other. That is the largest part of our success as a species; because we communicate, our ideas can outlive us. In the oral era—before the Sumerian invention of cuneiform—we kept our learning in mythic forms. Myths are a shorthand, encompassing a universe of meaning in just a few words. Myths are the stories before history.

In this age, we think of mythology as unscientific, irrational, unreasonable. Myths are none of these things—they are a human attempt to speak about things for which there are no words: the joy of birth, the valor and honor of heroic deeds, the mystery of death.

Finally, the dawn of human communication brought us imagination. Myths are never literal. The figurative power of mythology casts this *as* that, not this *is* that. The ancients understood their imaginations, and understood their myths as the essential forms of those imaginations.

Imagination Electrified

In the hundreds of thousands of years since ancient time, we've gotten better and better at our forms of communication. We invented writing, which extended our ability to retain information to vast quantities of information. Take a look at a cuneiform tablet or hieroglyphic monolith—you're looking at the high technology of the 20th century, B.C.E., and the ancients felt the same wonderment looking upon those marks that we get when we stare at the rainbow of exposed silicon on a memory chip or microprocessor.

It took hundreds of thousands of years to get to writing, but only a few thousand to get to the *Phoenician alpha-beta* (phonetic alphabet), and a few thousand more to get to the printing press. When Gutenberg printed his first *Bible*, he lit a fire that transformed all of civilization from a primarily oral and aural culture to a literate and visual culture. The human riches of poetry, drama, and song became the fertile grounds of mathematics, physics, and biology. These fields had existed before the invention of printing, but now any individual could share Newton's thoughts, or Harvey's or Linneas'. To stand on the shoulders of giants meant to prop oneself up on a shelf of books. These individuals might then write books; Plato and Democritus would influence Voltaire, who would then influence Rousseau, who would then influence Thomas Paine, Benjamin Franklin, and Thomas Jefferson. In this way, the explosion of knowledge in our modern era began.

Franklin himself studied physics avidly; his electricity experiments became known worldwide. Half a century later, Samuel Morse, who studied the works of Franklin, Volta, and Ampere, would develop a device that used electricity to send words, as fast as a beam of light. He called it the *telegraph*, Latin for "distant writing."

All of a sudden, everything changed. For the first time in human history, messages arrived immediately. With this, all media took on a new form; we saw the birth of the modern newspaper, which thrived on news reports from distant lands brought to one's hometown through the magic of telegraphy. The telegram itself acquired a magical and foreboding quality—to receive one was akin to being struck by lightning, and could announce the visitation of a rich supply of either good or bad fortune.

The telegraph defines the Victorian era; Great Britain used the telegraph to give form and backbone to their colonial policies.

India was mapped and railed and telegraphed by the British—this gave them an indomitable hold on the people of that nation. This hold continued unchecked until the press reported—via telegraph—the actions of a single man, Mahatma Ghandi. With little more than a pure heart and publicity, Ghandi brought the British empire to its end.

Electronic Computing

Even before the beginning of the electric era, we constructed enormous machinery, such as textile mills and locomotives. This machinery augmented human power, making possible tasks that would otherwise require an army of slaves or serfs. Despite this, the machinery was unreliable and often dangerous to the people who worked with it, because it had no understanding of itself, no mechanism to monitor its progress, no sensors to detect problems. James Watt, who perfected the modern steam engine, invented a device called the "governor"—govern in its original sense means *monitor* rather than *control*. The governor regulated the output of the engine and kept it in balance, so that it would not destroy itself from its own fires. Watt created a system that took its own past results and fed these outputs back into the system (hence the term *feedback*), to create a system that could self-regulate.

A few years later, Charles Babbage and Ada Lovelace prototyped the "difference engine," which could perform numerical calculations and, along much the same lines, feed intermediate calculations back into the engine to further modify its outputs. This machine is considered the forerunner of the modern computer.

A hundred years later, Alan Turing used this peculiar quality of the "thinking machine" to break the codes used by the German High Command in the Second World War. The Germans used a device, called ENIGMA, which could generate a "scrambling code" that was used to encrypt messages sent to submarines, spies, and so forth. The code could quickly be changed, and although the British captured one of the ENIGMA encoders, the Germans quickly modified the design to prevent backward engineering. Turing, a mathematician and computing theorist, developed a set of logical steps that could, within a few hours, "break the code" of the ENIGMA and render the messages readable. It is believed that this breakthrough considerably shortened the duration of the war.

Turing relied upon the essential mutability of his computer—which was not much like what we consider a computer today—it could change itself, recharacterize its inputs and outputs, based upon its own inputs and outputs. The computer could make decisions, could change its behavior, and act as if it were, in some small way, conscious. At about the same time, working at Princeton, John Von Neumann developed the basics of the architecture used by almost all computers—an arithmetic unit, a decision unit, and a memory unit. These three units functioned together, each modifying the content and behavior of the other, creating the paradigm for modern computing.

After the war, the still-young field of electronics coupled with the brand-new discipline of computer science to create the electronic computer. These computers were used to automate huge decision-making tasks like the U.S. Census.

It's taken about forty years, but computers have now become completely ubiquitous; we rely on a computer to keep the wheels of our automobiles from locking up in a skid—they talk to each other and adjust their own behavior. We use them in microwave ovens to cook our food just right. We use them in our bombs to make sure they hit their designated targets, and nothing else.

Computing Communication

The essential nature of the computer is as a simulator. The computer knows nothing of itself—it is nearly completely innocent, but, when filled with rules and data and sensations provided by a scientist, a nurse, or a video game player, the computer creates a *simulation*—an understanding of a situation—and then uses its rules to bring that simulation forward in time. Will this steel be strong enough? Will this patient survive? Will I make it to the next level of DOOM?

Yet, isolated, cut off from the outside world, computers are very poor simulation engines. Simulation is based in reality, or an approximation of reality. The more communication you have with the real world, the more believable, the more accurate, and the more thrilling your simulation is likely to be.

Your weatherperson works with simulations all of the time. A network of satellites, communicating with ground stations, and supercomputers that attempt to simulate future weather conditions, create the forecast you read in the newspaper or see on the television. In a vacuum—without that sophisticated infrastructure of electronic eyes and brains—that forecast wouldn't be very accurate. Even with the best information, the forecasts can be off base, but the accuracy of a near-term forecast has gone way up, primarily because we have a network of computers that communicate what they know (or predict) about the weather to each other.

To facilitate this coordination, to improve the quality of our simulations, we have taught the computers to talk to each other, so that they can act in concert, each modifying the others through a complex relationship of messages and behaviors. It's a *society of machines*, a society built upon communication and cooperation in a group context. In essence, we're imparting to our machines some of the basic attributes that make us social animals. We've only just started to do this—the Internet has been around for a quarter-century—but, as this society of machines evolves into a social ecology, we'll no longer think of computers as isolated. We'll think of them in concert, each like a neuron in a brain.

There is a natural—and surprisingly circular—progression at work through these ages. First, man communicates his imagination, then imagination is electrified with the telegraph. Next, mutability becomes the quality of electronic computing, and the loop closes with computer communication. It looks like figure 1.1.

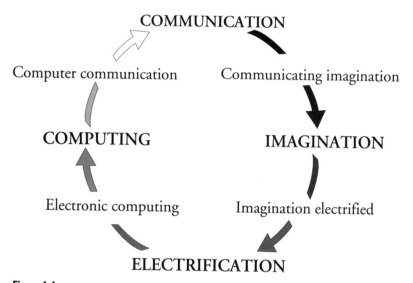

Figure 1.1

The circle of communication.

We can see that we're about to come full circle, back into the era of the communication of the imagination. That's what cyberspace is really all about. The content of cyberspace—what we put there—is our imagination. Cyberspace is the shared imagination, using electronic computing communications.

Cyberspace stands above this wheel of media, using all of them.

A Great Design Criterion

The Internet we know today started as a fallout shelter for computers.

In the late 1960s, the U.S. Department of Defense began a detailed investigation of methodologies to protect military computing systems in the event of nuclear war. These systems—mostly very large and well-guarded—were rapidly becoming the backbone of the nation's defense strategy. Using these machines in a coordinated fashion would produce a more accurate simulation of the defense posture of the United States, as well as the attack posture of its enemies.

This communications network, at once a great strength, had a very natural Achille's heel—cut the cables and the computers would stop talking. In the event of war—real war, with multi-megaton blasts over major cities and military installations—the defense computing network would quickly collapse, and with it America's ability to simulate and monitor any threats.

Further, the burgeoning military-industrial complex had given the U.S. armed forces a vast array of incompatible hardware. Computers from IBM, Univac, Sperry, and Burroughs all fit into the defense infrastructure. They couldn't talk to each other, though, so the defense planners were faced with a choice: either all of the computers in America's defense infrastructure would have to be of the same design—and from the same company, most likely—or they would need a way to make many heterogeneous systems talk to one another. The planners opted for the latter solution, paving the way for a network of many types of machines, all speaking the same language or protocol.

The planners now moved from the design to the prototyping stage. On October 27, 1969, two computers began talking to each other across a line leased from the telephone company. This network was named ARPAnet after the agency that funded it—the Advanced Research Projects Agency. ARPAnet used an "abstract" protocol—tied to no particular computer hardware or software—that later became known as *Internet Protocol* (IP).

Internet Protocol got its name because it allowed sites that already had networks—rare except in high-end military environments—to provide a "gateway" into a "network of networks," or an internetwork. The Internet has always been a collection of individual networks that have agreed to speak the same protocol with respect to each other, in much the same way that all of the states in the United States enforce the same laws with respect to the national government. A state has broad powers internally—as long as they do not violate conditions laid down in the Constitution—but is strictly regulated in how it deals with its neighbors. The Internet is a greater ocean composed of a sea of networks, island states.

The computers could send messages to each other across the Internet. A message on the Internet is called a *packet*, and it is the basic unit of communication. Computers communicate with each other seamlessly because these packets direct themselves— just as letters do in the Post Office—through the network. This is called *routing*. Using routing, the computer simply puts the packet onto the Internet, and the Internet ensures that it is delivered. The path between two computers is unimportant, as far as the computers are concerned. That path can be very complex, and it can even change in the middle of a conversation between two computers.

In the middle of a war, three computers—in Pasadena, Colorado Springs, and Cambridge, for example—might be assigned to tracking and targeting incoming missiles. If the computer in Colorado Springs suddenly went off the Net because of a 20-megaton explosion in its immediate vicinity, ARPAnet would dynamically adapt to the change in routing patterns, and send the packets for the computers in Pasadena and Cambridge (for as long as they lasted) over a different path, to other computers kept around for contingencies such as this. ARPAnet observed itself, monitored its own behavior, and fed its behavior back into itself, to recover from network failures.

To ARPAnet, nuclear war is no more than a bunch of routing errors that it could immediately correct.

Through years of trial and error, network planners have learned that whatever can happen to a network will happen. This means that disaster planning is the primary activity of a network designer, and nuclear war is clearly the ultimate disaster. When ARPAnet solved this worst-case in disaster planning, it gave itself the best possible recommendation as a reliable networking methodology. Internet Protocol, built on this foundation, slowly grew to become the dominant networking paradigm. The Internet ate network after network, adding them to its domain and giving all of the computers within its breadth the ability to talk to each other in a standardized, universal, fault-tolerant manner. These advantages prompted network administrators and planners worldwide to adopt IP as their long-term networking solution. Over the last decade, most networks have integrated into the Internet.

In short, nuclear war is a great design criterion for networks.

Computer-Centered Communication

While the Internet made it easy for computers to communicate with each other, its designers paid very little attention to the humans who would use it to communicate through those computers. Internet comes from an age where very few computers had interactive qualities; most of them ran in a "batch" mode. You gave the computer a set of commands, usually in the form of a stack of punched cards, and came back later—a few minutes, hours, or days later—to look at the results of your commands. Most of these commands had been designed around the computer, making it easy to "parse" or translate those commands into operations the computer could then execute. Very few people knew how to do this, and they were the white-coated "priesthood" of computing, the guardian of its terrible secret: computers had poorly designed interfaces, which made them extremely difficult to use. A bad interface disguised itself as sophisticated.

Over the last thirty years, we've moved from the sophisticated to the intuitive computer interface. Perhaps the most important thing we've learned is this: the easier it is to use a computer, the harder it is to design an interface for it. Developing applications for the Macintosh, which led the ease-of-use movement in computing, was many times more difficult than for its competitor, the IBM PC. Every operation had to be thought through from the user's perspective, and that takes a lot of up-front design work.

The priesthood claimed computers were too sophisticated for most people to learn or use. In truth, the computers were spectacularly stupid, so much so that we would have to learn baby-speak—the computer's control language—to have any conversation with them at all. Most people found this unacceptable. The few who could tolerate the endless error messages, the burps and whines and diaper-changing of infantile computer interfaces, had good jobs managing the informational infrastructure of big companies or big governments.

The Internet inherited this user interface legacy; most commands were completely cryptic, like "ftp 192.100.81.101," "rlogin 92.2.3.1," or "ping 172.27.31.30." A lot of this was the legacy of Unix, a cryptic operating system itself. As is commonplace in Unix, most of these Internet-related commands had dozens of options—ways to massage the computers into successful, happy communication. Very few people knew them all, and even the most expert occasionally consulted a manual.

More than that, there was no Internet "road map." Many computers with many different types of resources sprouted up all over ARPAnet. Keeping track of any of these resources—which could move or change without warning—became almost impossible. The Internet then added the *Domain Naming Service* (DNS), which morphed the computer's address into its name; for example, "192.80.57.1" became the more sensible "shiva.com," and "192.100.81.101" became "ns.netcom.com." Service naming helped—you could move a computer around, but keep its name the same, and folks could find it again. You could also move the service to another computer, and then map the name to that new computer; no one would be the wiser.

Still, enormous feats of memory were called for, and a legion of system administrators answered the call. Although it's generally thought that these "sysops" maintained the physical and software infrastructures on computers, they also functioned as the agents of community memory. The system administrator remembered where you put things, such as your accounting records, the test data, or your user surveys. Few others cared enough to learn Internet's difficult interfaces. Only sysops knew exactly where your files were, once they got sucked into the Internet. The sysops had a tidy little empire, managing the memory of cyberspace.

Despite this, the Internet proved to be very useful for many people, and the amount of information that could be accessed through it grew dramatically through the second half of the 1980s. Soon, even sysops lost track of the whole Internet universe, and began to specialize, each focusing on their own areas of expertise. The threads of community memory had begun to unravel; but within a few years, they'd be sewn into a new mosaic.

The Web That Ate the Net

The ARPAnet proved very useful for the research organizations and universities that had access to it, so much so that by 1987, the U.S. government divided ARPAnet into two zones, or domains. MILnet, as the name implies, handled secure military communications, while NSFnet, sponsored by the National Science Foundation, oversaw the development of Internet infrastructure for academia.

Before this decade, the Internet was used by only a few million people, but with the birth of NSFnet came many new commercial and educational Internet users. Most of these individuals used electronic mail systems, which provided an Internet without the unnecessary sophistications of Internet interfaces. Using electronic mail is easy—compared to file transfer or remote access—and often desktop software seamlessly integrates with it. People use electronic mail on the Internet because they don't have to think about the Internet to use it. The popular conception of the Internet as a big postal service has remained constant through the last several years.

Despite its difficulties, the total content of the Internet constantly grew into a small universe of documents, images, applications, and so forth that could be retrieved through it. Without any way to navigate or grasp any sense of the totality of the Internet, most of these resources lay underutilized, discovered by only a few people.

This problem was confronted a man by the name of Tim Berners-Lee. In the 1980s, Berners-Lee worked as a software engineer at the European Center for Particle Physics (CERN) in Geneva, Switzerland. CERN has the world's largest atom smasher—a huge ring that looped out from CERN, under the Alps, and back again. Scientists from all over Europe reserve time on CERN's accelerator to conduct experiments on particle physics and the basic construction of the universe.

The scientists, located at universities all across Europe, rarely wanted to travel to CERN to perform their experiments, and then return to receive the results of those experiments. Using the Internet, it was possible to send those results back to the researchers electronically. Berners-Lee realized, however, that they lacked context—how did this week's experiment by researchers in Milan relate to last month's experiment by researchers in Copenhagen relate to next year's experiments by researchers at Oxford?

The idea of linking different sets of data to show their relations with respect to each other—something we call *hypertext* or, more often these days, *hypermedia*—has been around for almost thirty years. Douglas Englebart, a researcher at *Stanford Research Institute* (SRI) in Menlo Park, California, demonstrated the first practical hypertext system in 1969. With Englebart's system, it was possible to group various items and link them together. Englebart demonstrated a hypertext shopping list; using a mouse—something else he invented while inventing hypertext—he could reorganize his shopping list or connect it to other documents within his computer. The ability to connect two items together is the essential feature of hypertext, and is called *linking*. He could link "butter" to the document "2 sticks, Land-o-Lakes, $0.79," or group "butter," "milk," and "cheese" into a "dairy" group. The system was very basic, but it demonstrated all of the features essential to hypermedia systems.

Hypermedia systems languished; a command-line is unfriendly to hypermedia, and until the late 1980s, most computers graced us with command-line interfaces. Hypercard, the first widely popular hypermedia application, showed the power of a contextual environment—how sharing and linking documents can create a whole greater than the sum of the parts—but Hypercard lacked support for networking. You could read the hypermedia version of *Jurassic Park* years before the novel made it to the screen, but you couldn't click on a link and check out the collection of the paleontology department at the University of Montana. Static hypermedia—constructed once and stubbornly persistent in the face of a rapidly changing world—proved only marginally useful.

Berners-Lee suspected that a hypermedia system fit for the physicists of CERN would have to tie together all of the information related to their discipline, wherever it resided—at CERN, Princeton, Stanford, Oxford, or wherever. In 1989, he developed a prototype of a hypermedia system that could fit the entire Internet into its scope; this system came to be called the *World Wide Web* (WWW).

The World Wide Web effectively turns the Internet into the equivalent of a large computer disk drive, or series of drives. These "virtual disk drives" have names—they are the names of the computers on the Internet. Within these computers, the World Wide Web can access various documents—images, sounds, text—using a file name. Together these components create a unique name for any resource on the Internet, and are called *Uniform Resource Locators* or URLs (pronounced "U-R-L" or "earl").

The innovations that Berners-Lee added to the Internet to create the World Wide Web had two fundamental dimensions: connectivity and interface. He invented a new protocol for the computers to speak as they exchanged hypermedia documents. This *Hypertext Transfer Protocol* (HTTP) made it very easy for any computer on the Internet to safely offer up its collection of documents into the greater whole; using HTTP, a computer that asked for a file from another computer would know, when it received the file, if it was a picture, a movie, or a spoken word. With this feature of HTTP, the Internet began to reflect an important truth—retrieving a file's data is almost useless unless you know what kind of data it is. In a sea of Web documents, it's impossible to know in advance what a document is—it could be almost anything—but the Web understands "data types" and passes that information along.

Once the data has been retrieved through the Web, Berners-Lee knew it would be necessary to display that data in a way that would be universal and consistent. Like the Internet itself, the Web needed to be independent of any computer upon it, yet all of these computers used differing systems to format data for presentation. The Macintosh used QuickDraw, Silicon Graphics' workstations used OpenGL, and IBM PCs used a number of incompatible solutions. The Web needed a standard interface language so that if a researcher in Chicago created a Web document for use at a laboratory in Toronto, it wouldn't be necessary to consider what computer the document would be displayed upon. PostScript, used in most laser printers, runs on most computers, but is difficult to use to show how one set of data links to another. Something new was needed—something that could reflect the capabilities of the Web as a medium.

For this reason, Berners-Lee and others developed the *Hypertext Markup Language* (HTML). HTML is a subset of the *Structured Generalized Markup Language* (SGML), which has been in use for about 20 years. Using HTML, an individual can create a hypermedia document that looks pretty much the same on any computer, anywhere in the world. For example:

```
<Title>VRML-Browsing and Building Cyberspace</Title>
VRML-Browsing and Building Cyberspace
```

This very basic HTML file creates a document whose title is "VRML–Browsing and Building Cyberspace." The content of the document is simply that same text.

HTML made it easy to reference or "link" documents together—even documents with widely varying data types like text and movies—so that a researcher could link a set of experimental test results with other relevant experiments, scientific papers, images, and so forth. We can change this document so that it links to my home page on the Web by using the "anchor" tag, which links one document to another:

```
<Title>VRML-Browsing and Building Cyberspace</Title>
<A HREF="http://hyperreal.com/~mpesce">
VRML-Browsing and Building Cyberspace
</A>
```

Clicking on the text within a Web browser will cause the browser to "jump to" my home page.

HTML provided an interface to the Internet that hid the cryptic commands behind the URL; the Internet, following the rest of computing, thus became a comfortable journey of pointing and clicking around a set of hypermedia documents with a mouse. It wasn't perfect—its major drawback was a lack of places to go—but it provided so much, for so little, that it was an immediate success in the academic community.

In the United States, researchers at the *National Center for Supercomputer Applications* (NCSA) found the World Wide Web to be a potent tool for sharing information over the Internet. NCSA has a mandate from the U.S. government to research and prototype tools for collaboration, developing interfaces that enable researchers to co-annotate and co-author documents. The Web, with its inherent features of linkage and supple interface, appealed to them immediately.

In early 1993, the developers at NCSA—Marc Andreesen, the founder of Netscape Communications Corporation, among them—took the World Wide Web and again extended it in the two dimensions that had proven so fruitful for Berners-Lee: interface and connectivity. For the interface, they added the ability to put images inside an HTML page, and beyond this, they created the *image map.* An image map "knows" when and where a user's mouse-click occurs, and sends that information out across the Web as part of a request for more information. Imagine a map of the Earth, and clicking on Cambridge, Massachusetts, then finding yourself at MIT's home page. This was a small improvement that yielded enormous benefits. They also added forms; HTML forms, like normal business forms, have places where a Web user can enter data within a Web page—perhaps to supply a mailing address or credit card number—and send back to a Web server for processing. This opened the Web up to two-way communication; you could change the way a Web site behaved by information you provided on a form.

The engineers at NCSA also added a mechanism to make the Web more active. Web pages usually are static—they almost never change. Yet the real world changes all the time. To tie the static world of Web pages into the dynamic world of real data, NCSA created the *Common Gateway Interface* (CGI). CGI created a dynamic Web; a document doesn't have to exist before you see it on the screen—many are created on-demand, in response to a specific request. This means that databases, control programs, and other useful applications can be integrated into the World Wide Web with only very minor modifications.

In July of 1993, NCSA released their World Wide Web server, and a Web "browser," which they called NCSA *Mosaic.*

NCSA's Mosaic is without question the most influential application ever developed for a computer. It made the Internet accessible to anyone who knew how to use a computer; the few hundred thousand who knew the ins and outs of the Internet suddenly became the tens of millions who knew how to use a word processor or spreadsheet. Mosaic was actually substantially easier to use than the other applications people had been trained to use, so people adopted it rapidly. At least two million people used it on a day-to-day basis in the first year after it was released.

With more Web users, the Internet began to see an explosive growth in Web servers. Only about 300 Web servers existed worldwide in October of 1993. Within a year, that number had grown to about 10,000. It's predicted that there will be at least 100,000 by October of 1995.

Just eighteen months after its introduction, Mosaic or an equivalent Web browser was in day-to-day use on almost every machine on the Internet. The reason for this is easy to identify: Mosaic increased the usability of the Internet by several orders of magnitude—no more commands; just point and click and you're off.

The real lesson of NCSA Mosaic is simple: increased usability always translates into increased usage. So, over the course of 1994 and 1995, the ivory towers of the Internet came tumbling down, and the hordes of individuals who had only experienced electronic mail suddenly found themselves in an amazing universe of sights, sounds, and creative collaborations.

Something else happened—unexpected, but wonderful: people began to create their own corners of the Internet, graced with their own style, sensibilities, and ideas. Authoring documents in HTML was not rocket science—although it still required some knowledge of computers to do it well—so hundreds of thousands of people rushed into the Web to create a human presence there. No longer just corporate data or science reports, the Web better articulates the entire range of human experience than any communications technology that preceded it. People fall in love with the expressiveness of the Web, and so they use it, add to it, and talk about it endlessly. In less than two years, World Wide Web protocols have become the dominant form of communication over the Internet—the Web has eaten the Net.

There's No There There

The World Wide Web has created the perception of a unified Internet; it's quite impossible to tell where Web data comes from—across the street or across the world. With HTML, it all looks pretty much the same. There are conventions of style and layout—many pioneered by Kevin Hughes when the Web was still very young—that have begun to look like a universal interface to the global information repository. It's not perfect, but the Web grows richer and increasingly more useful. Periodicals like *TIME*, *WIRED*, and *OMNI* are accessible through the Web, and the United States Library of Congress, the largest book repository in the world, has begun to provide its texts across the Web.

The major issue confronting the first users of the Web concerned locating relevant data. In a sea of information, unbound to any system of organization, how can one find anything?

CERN started to tackle this problem by creating the WWW Meta-index, a Web page that contained a partial listing of the resources available on the Web, categorized by subject. CERN had a dedicated staff of Web "librarians" who kept the list of subjects and sites up to date in the Web's early days. As the Web started growing uncontrollably, however, this list first became unusable—too big and only approximately accurate—and later became obsolete. There simply weren't enough librarians to track the growth of the Web.

Other indexes, such as YAHOO, sprang up, offering access thousands of categories of data. YAHOO offered two interfaces. One of these was a subject catalog, similar to a library's, but with hyperlinks, and so much easier to use. YAHOO also provided a search interface, using HTML's forms capability. Just tell YAHOO what you wanted to look for and—presto!—you'd have a page of links to relevant entries inside YAHOO's database.

Even YAHOO, while quite powerful, limits the range of possibilities to the domain of YAHOO's knowledge. With the Web doubling in size every four months (as of late-1995), any attempt to collate or map the entire content of the Web seems beyond the task of human beings. Computers have thus stepped in to do the dirty work of exhaustively searching the Web, charting its growth, and keeping indices of its content. Lycos, a "Web crawler" developed at Carnegie-Mellon University, uses fuzzy logic-based query capabilities, combined with an extensive database of Web content (Lycos comes closest to "knowing" the entire content of the Web), to provide an approximately exhaustive search of the Web. Other popular tools, such as InfoSeek, have made the job of finding relevance within the context-free Web much easier.

Presuming one could find the way to an interesting page within the Web, the next problem lay in finding the way back to that page. Early on, Mosaic adopted the "bookmark" interface, which maintained a list of URLs as a document, but Web users quickly found that this list could grow into thousands of entries. Even at just a few additions a day, any "hotlist" would quickly outgrow the limited human abilities of searching and sorting. Eventually, hotlists can grow so big that they need hotlists themselves.

All of this endless indexing and organizing points to a basic fact about the nature of the World Wide Web. The Web is "hyper-space;" that is, every "anchor" is directly linked to another point in the Web. You don't have to travel through anything as you cruise the Web; in short, there's no *there* there. While that's no problem for the computers—hyperspace comes naturally to them—it's a big problem for people, who have no sense of how to understand hyperspace. It eludes rational thought.

The best example of this is the ever-faithful URL. Perhaps the most useful construct in the history of the Internet, at its heart it's something built for computers and designed around what they can understand. To refer people to my home page in the Web, I tell them, "go to http://hyperreal.com/~mpesce"—and then I have to write it down for them, because they'll never remember it.

A URL is a message to the computer; as human beings, we have no hook to hang it on. Human beings don't think about things like URLs, or even lists. We think in very concrete terms, and always use the real world as our guide—it's all we know. If I told someone, "Go to Market Street, down to Third, make a right, and take Third down to Bryant Street," that they'd understand. It's still a set of directions, but it makes sense because it speaks to things human beings are very familiar with.

The Web creates an abstract knowledge space; useful, but hardly human. We can't grow to rely on hotlists and search facilities forever—they aren't the way we work. We have to teach our computers to present information with a human focus: we search, explore, and accidentally stumble upon truth. Rarely can we search every possibility, and absorb an entire field of knowledge in search of one fact. We need a Web that we can stumble through, using our intuition *and* our intellect as guides.

Consider a trip to the library. How many of us have gone into the building looking for a specific title, and come out with another, more relevant text—one we never even knew we were looking for—that lay beside it or on another shelf nearby? Accident and chaos are critical to learning; we reinforce our own ignorance if we confine ourselves to the well-known.

Most of us cruise around the Web like drunks on a random walk. We often find things that are interesting, sometimes find things that are relevant, but never know what we might be missing. The Web indexes, as useful as they are, will only tell you what the computer considers relevant, and that's because the Web is still centered around the computer, not around the human. When humans can organize the Web *on their own terms*, we'll have an information environment closer to the real world.

The Web needs to be more human. It's good, but still makes us conform to the way it works. We need to turn the tables, and make it conform to the way we think and feel. The Web must become an accidental, explorative, intuitive environment; it's the single most important component in expanding individual human understanding.

Start Making Sense

With the development of multitasking operating systems in the early 1960s, which enabled the computer to execute several simultaneous tasks, scientists began to prototype new interfaces that could put these new capabilities to good use. One of these individuals was a graduate student at the Massachusetts Institute of Technology by the name of Ivan Sutherland. For his doctoral thesis, Sutherland developed the first interactive drawing and design program, *SketchPad*, within which users could draw, paint, and transform computer-generated images, all in real-time. Using a light pen, icons, and windows—all radical innovations to the human-computer interface—Sutherland's design completely revisioned how people thought of computers. They could now augment human creativity as effortlessly as they could do the payroll.

Sutherland moved from MIT to the University of Utah in the mid-60s, and, over several years, invented all of the major components of what we today call *virtual reality* (VR)—body tracking, the head-mounted display, and real-time three-dimensional graphics processors, to name but a few. It all seemed very "far out" in 1968, but the U.S. Defense Department understood the power of simulation—as generals have for thousands of years—and Sutherland's work laid the foundation for both the field of interactive computer graphics and real-time simulation systems.

It may well be that by the end of the millennium, Sutherland will be remembered as the individual who most helped to shape computing in the 20th century. The innovations that most of us will be using day-to-day in the 21st century—interactive computer graphics, human-centered computer interfaces, and virtual reality—were first conceived of and created by Sutherland.

Systems capable of real-time simulation remained far too expensive for commercial or personal use through the 1960s and 1970s. The microprocessor revolution, which began to encroach on mainframe systems in the early 1980s, brought simulation into the high-end of commercial viability. NASA's Ames Research

Center began the *Virtual Interface Environment Workstation* (VIEW) project in 1982, and Scott Fisher, Scott Foster, Elizabeth Wenzel, and Warren Robinett (among many others) brought Sutherland's work into the age of workstations. Capitalizing on new developments in low-power, lightweight liquid crystal displays, the group created the modern head-mounted display. A gentleman named Jaron Lanier, working with Thomas Zimmerman of Stanford University, developed the DataGlove. The *DataGlove* is, as the name would suggest, a glove-like device that fits over the hand and then tracks its motion. The head-mounted display, in conjunction with the DataGlove, enables individuals to experience *immersion,* the sense of being placed inside a simulated environment. The head-mount and the DataGlove caused as great a revisioning of interface as Sutherland's work had twenty years before.

At the heart of this lay a complete paradigm shift in computing. Sensuality, which had never been thought of as a component of computing, suddenly became the important ingredient in inter-face design. Brenda Laurel, in her seminal work, *Computers as Theater,* structured an interface based upon Aristotelian poetics.

According to Laurel, the computer is like a stage set with actors. The dramatic arc (exposition, inciting incident, rising action, crisis, climax, falling action, and denouement) appeals to our *emotions,* rather than our intellect, and is the most effective way to design a user interface. The overwhelming popularity of games like DOOM and Myst clearly indicate that a well-constructed stage and plot—even a simplistic one—can create a compelling, emotional interface.

In order to make computers clear to our minds, we have to teach them to speak to our hearts. Drama, music, and architecture (the shape of a place) all have important places in computing.

Virtual reality has not lived up to the promises originally made a decade ago. Now that the hyperbole about virtual reality has abated, researchers understand that virtual reality is a methodology, not an end point. The visions of disembodied travel through a sensually vacuous space have evolved into a set of techniques for making interfaces more human-centered.

What we've learned through all of this trial and error is that *sensuality makes sense.* If you can present data sensually, it will make more sense to the user. Technologies like three-dimensional displays, body tracking, and spatialized audio, combined with dramatic narrative techniques, create an experience that conforms to human expectations. Instead of looking at a list of numbers, why not turn it into a mountain range you can fly through, or a crescendo of sound? Instead of a keyboard, why not send the computer hand gestures? We've found that if we can use the computer in our heads—our cerebral cortex—we can often find things that the computer would never notice or consider significant.

Bringing this back to the Web, imagine an Internet interface where data sources—books, sounds, movies—could be represented naturally, as they are in the real world, with real-world metaphors. People *can* remember real-world metaphors, because they make sense. We have an intrinsic, biological understanding of the real world. If we didn't, when we got out of bed in the morning, we'd immediately fall and hit the floor. We organize our lives sensually—think of your record collection or your books—and need to bring that same technique to the Internet if we ever hope to be able to use it to our fullest capacity.

The last twenty-five years have seen a continuing set of improvements to the Internet in two areas: connectivity and interface. We've moved from a world of gurus and impossibly cryptic interfaces into an era of point-and-click browsing. This alone has been enough to completely change how people thought of the Internet, and how they used it.

Immediately before us lies a transition as significant as all those that preceded it. We're about to make the Internet a human space—habitable, hospitable, intuitive, and warm. The Internet has been a space of the intellect; we're about to make it a place for the heart.

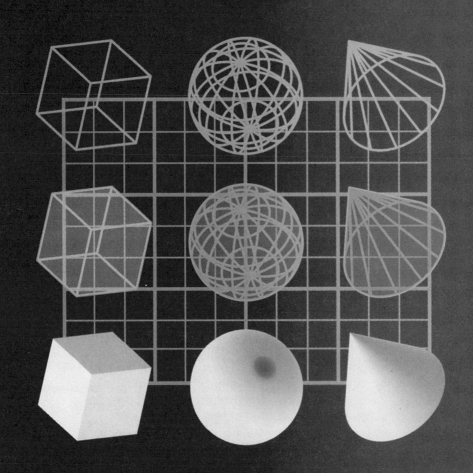

Chapter 2

The VRML Equinox

The World Wide Web is the quintessence of collaboration; as a tool, it inspires the coming together and juxtaposition of disparate pieces into an integrated whole. The software foundation of the Web has evolved similarly—sharing has been the driving force behind the rapid development and propagation of Web-based technologies. First, CERN created "libraries" of the World Wide Web source code; NCSA Mosaic has always been available (in its Unix incarnations) in source code form, so that anyone could freely modify the functionality to suit specific needs. The presumption is that these enhancements would in turn be returned to the community—as does happen—and that would broaden and accelerate the entire developmental process of the Web. Within the Internet, and specifically within the Web, *a resource shared is a resource squared.*

In October of 1993, I downloaded NCSA's Mosaic program, along with their World Wide Web server application. The server, NCSA *httpd*, allows a Unix workstation to act as a Web server; this means it can respond to requests made of it by Web browsers.

Both Mosaic and httpd are relatively easy to install on a Unix workstation, and within a few hours I had my very own Web site. I spent many hours that fall surfing the Web—small enough that it seemed possible to visit every site—and it quickly became clear that the global hypermedia system we'd been promised for years by Ted Nelson had finally come to pass. Unfortunately, Nelson's vision for *Xanadu*, a comprehensive hypermedia system, never came to pass. In development for almost 20 years, "Project Xanadu" collapsed into a wreck of finger pointing and name calling after Autodesk Corporation withdrew the project's financial backing in 1993.

Amazing as it was—I had an epiphany that has never really ended—I immediately sensed that the Web needed a three-dimensional interface. The text and pictures made for a pretty place, but was it really useful? If I had the Library of Congress, with hundreds of millions of volumes in its collection, how could I browse through it on a screenful of text? The Louvre was one of the first major Web sites, but even it was reduced to images glued to a Web page.

Architecture is art; space and place are essential to our civilization, our language, and our being. If we were really building the global info-organism—something I recognized from the moment I got onto the Web—we'd need to make it as sensually rich as human experience is. Text is a very recent thing; the printed word has five hundred years of history behind it. Compare that with half a million years of human language. What would the Web be if we couldn't recreate the cave paintings of Lascaux? Or Chartes Cathedral? Or Frank Lloyd Wright's Fallingwater?

We are creatures of sensation; here in the West we depend upon our eyes to tell us most of our stories. But we have ears to hear, skin to touch, space to move through. Bringing that to our Web would make it more human, and more like ourselves. If we want our global mind to be a mirror for our being, shouldn't it be perfectly clear?

With this in mind, I knew we could bring the Web out from the flat text and images into a new sensuality that would be more fluid, expressive, and emotional. I set to work.

Fortunately, the Web, built upon source code that I could download and compile on my own computer, lent itself to rapid modification for specific purposes. Within a few months, I had the basic designs for a three-dimensional Web browser completed—but only in my head. I needed some help to write the actual code because a 3D Web browser would need a new language—the equivalent of HTML—to serve as the bedrock of cyberspace. HTML is well suited for text, and can, when pressed, even work with images. Cyberspace defines the layout of complex objects in a three-dimensional environment, which was completely beyond HTML's capabilities. I knew I'd need to create a new language, one that could speak to the Web and cyberspace simultaneously. I could design the language all day long, but I didn't know how to implement it.

Enter Tony Parisi. In December of 1993, Tony moved to San Francisco with his wife, Marina Berlin, to start a new life in the promised land of Northern California. Tony is seven days older than me (we see a lot of things the same way as a result), and has a strong background in desktop software. At Lotus Development, he helped write the Microsoft Windows version of *Lotus 1-2-3*. When I met him, he was developing new computer languages and user interfaces as a Principal Engineer for Belmont Research Corporation.

As Tony says, he stepped off the plane and into cyberspace. On New Year's Day 1994, sitting among the packing boxes in his new apartment, I gave him the full indoctrination—about the Web (best thing since sliced bread), about virtual reality (the essence of VR is communication and experience, not reality and immersion), and about the importance—as I saw it—of bringing them both together. We're both excitable Italian-American kids; before we knew it, we were working out the details of the design of a 3D interface to the Web.

At the time, Tony thought he'd humor me. It wouldn't take very much effort, and it would be a neat hack, *if* we could pull it off. In mid-January, my day job as a consultant vaporized when the contracting company suddenly collapsed—this happens all the time in Silicon Valley—and I found myself with some free time.

I had my hands on another important piece: a very nice 3D renderer (a *renderer* draws 3D objects onto the computer screen) called *Reality Lab*, from a British start-up company named Rendermorphics. A few weeks before I met Tony, I was introduced to Servan Keondjian and Kate Seekings, the founders of Rendermorphics. Although I had no money to pay for a Reality Lab license, they believed in my still-forming vision for a 3D Web, and let me use their rendering library at no charge. (Rendermorphics was acquired by Microsoft in February of 1995 and Reality Lab is now a core component of Microsoft Windows.)

For his part, Tony wrote a *parser* (a computer language translator), which converted a text file into a set of objects that the computer could understand and manipulate. As I defined this language, he learned a lot about three-dimensional graphics—polygons, normals, shading, and lighting—and I learned a lot about parsers. It was a great collaboration.

By February 14th, 1994, we had created an application that would go across the Web to fetch a 3D object—a banana, of all things!—which would then be displayed in a window on the computer screen. I could move my mouse over the banana, click on it, and—ABRAHADABRA!—NCSA Mosaic launched and loaded my home page on the Web. We had successfully created a 3D interface to the Web. Even more, we could click on a link in Mosaic and have it fetch a 3D object, then Mosaic would launch our application, in which the object would be displayed. We could go from the 2D Web in HTML to the 3D Web and back again!

We named our embryonic little program *Labyrinth*, because it took a twisty place that had no space—the World Wide Web—and gave it depth.

Later in February, while searching the Web pages at CERN about the World Wide Web Project (all of the people developing Web software pooling their knowledge and resources), I noticed that Tim Berners-Lee had a number of pages talking about using virtual reality with the Web. I sent him electronic mail—excitedly sharing what Tony and I had done—and in March I found myself invited to the First International Conference on the World Wide Web at CERN, in Geneva, Switzerland, to present our work.

The air in Geneva that May seemed charged with electricity. The First International Conference on the World Wide Web gathered up the world's Web developers into a four-day whirlwind of conferences, lectures, and informal meetings. Everyone shared their own work, and took delight in everyone else's. Most of the attendees had academic backgrounds and concerns—this early on, the Web had no commercial focus. Despite diverse backgrounds, we all had something in common—the sense that something amazing was taking place in our midst. *This was it.* We'd been dreaming of the Web for years—a way to share our knowledge, everywhere, all at once. Not once did anyone suggest that the Web would soon change the whole world. That was a given.

The conference was filled up months in advance. Even so, people came to Geneva hoping to sneak into one of the sessions. It was standing room only as Tim Berners-Lee gave his keynote, speaking eloquently about the need of a constitution for cyberspace. He was followed by Dr. David Chaum, who talked about privacy and secure electronic voting, then demonstrated his DigiCash system publicly for the first time. The emphasis on security seemed quite appropriate. *Finally*, we had something worth protecting.

CERN had just one machine set up for electronic mail access! With 350 webheads, this created a tiny crisis. I came to CERN an hour before the conference opened each morning, so I could grab my turn at the terminal set up for that purpose. One morning, as I walked in, I saw conferees from Japan talking with Italians,

French, and Germans in murdered English. For a wonderful moment, I felt like I'd been transported to Starfleet Academy. This made *sense*—the nations of the Earth working together to create an infrastructure for sharing knowledge.

On the second day of the conference, Berners-Lee and David Raggett, one of the primary forces behind HTML's development, held a "birds-of-a-feather" on "Virtual Reality Markup Languages and the World Wide Web." (*Birds-of-a-feather sessions*, often called "BOFs," are informal meetings of individuals interested in a particular topic.) Raggett had given serious thought to a platform-independent standard for 3D in the Web, and his proposals helped to shape all of the work that followed. The acronym he coined—"VRML"—stuck, although "markup" was later modified to the more appropriate "modeling."

At that session, I met Brian Behlendorf, the Unix system administrator for *WIRED* magazine, and the technical brains behind *HOTWIRED*. He, too, seemed very interested in getting a real 3D Web language specified and into people's hands. He'd just finished a course on computer graphics at UC Berkeley; through the course, he'd come to realize the power 3D graphics gave to human communication. Brian wanted to see VRML happen, and sweet-talked *WIRED* into volunteering their considerable connectivity and computing resources to help create a standard for a VRML.

On the final day of the conference, at the "Advanced Topics" session, I presented a paper simply titled, "Cyberspace." I'd hastily rewritten some of my slides to use the acronym VRML wherever appropriate. In the demonstration that followed the session, people got their first taste of a 3D Web—I showed my cyber-banana, linked to the paper on cyberspace. It seemed appropriate.

The Web teaches an open philosophy of sharing and development. There are no barriers and no prejudices (ideally)—just an open forum for the discussion and development of ideas and applications. We wanted to repeat the success of the Web, so we approached the Internet and Web communities, saying, "Come help us design the 3D language for the Web—come help us design VRML." We set up a *list-server* (a program that forwards mail sent to it to a list of "subscribers") on *WIRED*'s computers, and a Web site that outlined our focus and goals.

I expected that only 50 or 100 people would be interested in such an esoteric effort. I was way off base. Within a week, we had well over two thousand people who had subscribed to the mailing list we set up to coordinate the effort. We'd struck a chord, and the whole Internet began to vibrate in response. (That week I got more electronic mail than any other period in my life. One morning I woke up to find 750 messages in my mailbox!)

The development time Tony Parisi and I had put into Labyrinth had helped us to define the issues important in VRML; all that work (just a man-month between us) could be set aside, for a more complete solution—something that could be as expressive as a professional 3D designer would want. Labyrinth was a good beginning, but little more than a demonstration of what the eventual capabilities of VRML should be. While *Jurassic Park* might not have been possible on most of 1994's computers, we knew we needed something with commercial potential and room to grow, otherwise we'd be considered some "hacker's project," garnering little interest outside of academia.

I don't believe in reinventing wheels. The last thing the world needs is another computer language—something else people have to adopt and learn and master. Wouldn't it be more appropriate, I thought, to adapt an existing computer language, one designed by graphics professionals? We could take it and modify it to understand the Web, to link with it. I posed this question to the members of the community forming to define VRML. With so many experts in computer graphics—some with twenty years experience or more—finding an existing solution that could do the job well should have been easy enough.

In fact, we soon discovered several candidates that would fit the task. The *Object Oriented Geometry Language* (OOGL) from the Geometry Center at the University of Minnesota, the *Cyberspace Development Format* (CDF) from Autodesk, and the *Manchester Scene Description Language* (MSDL) from the University of Manchester in Great Britain are but a few of the languages presented as potential VRML nominees.

The first suggestion I heard—from Clay Graham, a virtual architect of enormous talent and growing reputation—turned out to be the winner. A programming library, *Open Inventor*, from Silicon Graphics (a high-end workstation manufacturer), used for rapid prototyping of 3D applications, had a scene description language and file format rich enough for commercial quality applications. It could grow—you could add your own features to it, and most importantly, it had been time-tested in commercial production environments. *It was debugged.*

We debated the merits of each of the candidates for a month, but a consensus quickly developed around Open Inventor. I traveled down to SGI, where I was introduced to Rikk Carey and Open Inventor's principle designers, Paul Strauss and Gavin Bell. Gavin had been active on the discussion, serving as an incredible resource, answering questions about Open Inventor, proposing extensions to it, and speaking, on his own, about SGI's plans for Open Inventor.

The Web community is a community committed to open standards. We could not adopt a standard owned by any company. SGI had to be committed to putting Open Inventor's file format into the public domain, without restriction, so that the Web community could build upon it, free from the fear of lawsuits or royalties. The folks at SGI understood this. They wanted to see Open Inventor, even as VRML, succeed. We all knew that if it did, SGI would make a lot of hardware sales, and that SGI would have the inside track on VRML development. At the same time, many man-years of effort had gone into Open Inventor; SGI had made a serious investment in their technology. To just hand it over to the

Web community seemed a questionable idea at best, and lunacy at worst.

But Rikk believed. He worked out the legal particulars within SGI, and later that summer, the subset of Open Inventor that became the core of the VRML 1.0 specification was placed into the public domain.

Now that we had a language, we had to face a number of difficult decisions. How would we extend this language to meet the requirements of the Web? How could we produce a scene description that would have consistent performance across a wide range of computers? How could we allow for interactivity?

All of these questions, fraught with pitfalls, obsessed the VRML community throughout the summer and into the fall of 1994. Perhaps the most important consideration, interactivity, was completely left out of the first specification—distributed simulation is among the most difficult of all problems in computer science. The problem is this: if I'm on a computer running Microsoft Windows and you're on an Apple Macintosh, and I "hand" you an object in cyberspace, what do you know about that object? The two computers are very different, and really have no language in common. We'd need an equivalent of HTML for behavior—a generic way of describing how things happen. We had zero possibility of addressing this problem in the next year or five.

In the end, the VRML community took its cue from the Web. The Web had no interactivity, but it was still very useful, and quite perfectly of captivating the imaginations of the Internet's users.

On the 17th of October, 1994, at the Second International Conference on the World Wide Web in Chicago, Tony Parisi and Gavin Bell presented the draft specification for VRML 1.0. It needed a number of small refinements, but covered all of the bases. People could begin to design tools—browsers and editors —that conformed to the specification, and knew that these tools would interoperate.

The VRML session was another standing-room-only event. Mark Andreesen, now vice president of the recently formed Netscape Communications Corporation, sat in the back of the room, wildly scribbling notes. People from NASA and NCSA realized that they already had Open Inventor-capable machines, and were a stone's throw away from VRML. People talked about future directions and argued out points of architecture and design; the session's allotted time came and went, so the event evolved into the second VRML "birds-of-a-feather" meeting, concluding in dinner for all of the VRML die-hards.

After the fall Web conference, Paul Strauss and Gavin Bell set to work on QvLib, a "quick" VRML parser written in C++, using SGI's base of Open Inventor source code. This was another major gift from SGI; they turned over source code developed by SGI employees for use by the Web community. QvLib reads in the VRML files (that's what a parser does) and produces a set of objects that can be manipulated by the computer.

In December of 1994, QvLib was made available on several computer platforms. The stage was set—*anyone* could now implement a VRML browser.

One of VRML's biggest assets came along accidentally. There are many different 3D scene description languages, none of which interoperate. It's necessary to convert from one to another as you move from application to application. Every time a conversion happens, some important data gets lost. Yet, a designer will often use several different programs when creating a 3D scene, so 3D file conversions are very common. Companies began to look to VRML as a "metafile data format" or universal interchange format for 3D data. Using VRML, a designer could create an object in Caligari trueSpace, place it into a scene in 3D Studio, and render it in SoftImage, all without converting it from one format to another.

In January of 1995, Robert Weideman of Template Graphics Software—who resold Open Inventor for non-SGI platforms—

convinced SGI that they should build a VRML Web browser. SGI would design the browser and TGS would translate it to other platforms; that began the development of WebSpace. At the same time, Tony Parisi formed his own company, Intervista, and began development of his own VRML browser, WorldView.

VRML was gathering a head of steam, fueled by the 2.2 billion dollar marketing engine of Silicon Graphics, which sought and got endorsements from Ford, Netscape, Digital, and many other companies, hoping to make VRML a Web *fait accompli*. Each of these organizations saw how VRML could be used to sell cars, Web servers, or computers—there wasn't much hard sell. Cyberspace sold itself.

In fact, the press reacted so favorably that several reporters "jumped the gun" and announced the existence of WebSpace and VRML before the worldwide launch date of April 3, 1995. On that date, termed "Day Zero" by Kevin Hughes, most of America learned about VRML for the first time. SGI made a worldwide press announcement and front page (of the business section) all over the country.

The first weeks after that announcement were a heady time; reporters clamored to know everything about the technology that seemed destined to evolve into cyberspace. *NEWSWEEK* ran a two-page article on a technology just under two months old. But, now that VRML browsers like WebSpace were ready for prime time, I didn't need to talk about what it would be like—I could sit a reporter in front of a computer and *show them how VRML worked.*

The overwhelming response and welcoming of the technology made it clear that VRML was at the right place at the right time with the right approach. Two weeks later, in Darmstadt, Germany, at the Third International Conference on the World Wide Web, VRML evolved from an embryonic technology into a hotbed of Web development. I gave the keynote speech on "Developer's

Day," and later fielded questions from researchers interested in making VRML browsers or VRML Web sites.

Because VRML uses the existing Web infrastructure, and because SGI had already spent considerable time developing Open Inventor tools (quickly adapted to support VRML), at least fifty VRML sites appeared within the first week after Day Zero, and a few hundred appeared within the first month. Soon people began to talk about their *next* Web site—in VRML, of course. This transition—as important as the end of winter and the beginning of spring—is called the VRML (now pronounced "vermal") Equinox.

From its birth in February of 1994 to its acceptance in the heart of the Web community in April of 1995, VRML had been preparing for a rocket ship ride. Fasten your seatbelts, and prepare for liftoff.

Next stop, cyberspace.

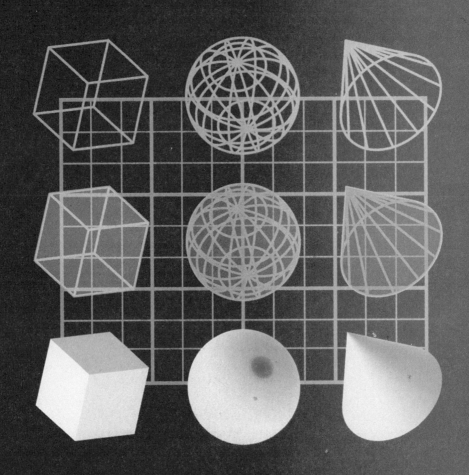

Chapter 3

How VRML Works

To understand how a VRML browser operates, it's a good idea to have some background on how VRML files work, and how the Web operates in general.

The World Wide Web is built out of two core components—browsers and servers. They're complementary parts of a greater whole. The browsers request information from Web servers, based upon the actions of the browser's user—for example, a user clicking on a link in a Web document. This generates a request that is sent to the appropriate server.

The server, upon receiving the request, interprets it and attempts to fulfill the request by returning a document that corresponds to the request made by the browser. When the reply is transmitted to the browser, some additional information is sent along with the document. This information, called *content type*, lets the browser know what kind of information it's receiving. Content type is very important—without it, a Web browser would never know the difference between a text document, which is just characters, or an image, which is a long run of binary data. The browser needs to know the content type of a document in order to display it correctly.

For example, Netscape *Navigator* version 1.1 has the ability to play audio files of several formats, including AIFF and AU formats. It can't play MPEG audio or QuickTime formats, however. How does it tell one sound from another? Each of them are identified with a content type. These content types are in a format specified by *Multimedia Internet Mail Extensions* (MIME), and are often called MIME types. The MIME type for AIFF files is audio/aiff, while the MIME type for MPEG audio files is audio/mpeg. These MIME types are returned as document content types by Web servers when fulfilling a request.

If a Web browser can't display a content type it receives from a Web server, most often it will ask the user what to do with the data sent in reply. When this happens to Netscape Navigator, you see a pop-up dialog that says "Unknown file type blah/fooby." Netscape then asks you what to do with the file: cancel it, save it to disk, or configure a "helper application" that will receive the data.

Using highly sophisticated data communications technology, we've been able to eavesdrop on the communication between a Web browser and a Web server. The conversation goes like this:

Web Browser: Excuse me, Mr. Server, do you have the file "important.wrl?"

Web Server: Yep... It's about 100,000 characters, two weeks old, and it's VRML—you want it?

WB: Yeah, I guess so. Send it along, please.

WS: Here it is...<send send send send send send send>....done!

WB: Thanks!

VRML documents require no change to the way Web servers operate; that's a good thing, because it means that it's very easy for people to add VRML to existing Web sites. The one change that has to be made is practically insignificant—you have to tell the Web server that VRML documents have an *extension*—a file ending—of "wrl," and that the MIME type of VRML documents is x-world/x-vrml. With this information, the Web server can detect VRML documents, and can inform a browser that a VRML document is being transmitted.

That's the *only* change that is required to make a Web server VRML-capable, and one reason why VRML has become so popular, especially with Web server administrators.

Central to the concept of VRML is the *world*, or VRML document. This world should be thought of as a scene, rather than a large, monolithic environment, like Earth.

As in theater, the VRML scene has a fixed number of items of specific types and qualities. For instance, Samuel Beckett's play *Waiting for Godot* specifies a sparse stage—the only set decoration is a tree in center rear stage. That's a simple layout, and would be a very simple VRML document. A more complicated set, such as Eugene O'Neill's *Long Day's Journey into Night*, might contain the drawing room of the Tyrone household, crowded with furniture and memorabilia. A VRML document describing this stage set would be correspondingly larger.

Beyond describing the content and layout of a world, the VRML document can also include "linkages" or "anchors" to other Web documents. This means that you click on an object in a VRML world and play a QuickTime movie or hear a sound view PostScript document. All of the same linking that you find in the Web today are present in VRML as well.

Taking our example a bit further, the tree on the set of *Godot* could be linked to the script of the play. Or, the items in the Tyrone residence could be linked into the lines for the various characters. This linking capability makes VRML very powerful; an object, or even any part of an object, in a VRML world can be linked to any object available in the Web. Even more, it's possible to link VRML worlds together. Just as it's possible to travel from page to page in the Web by clicking, you can travel—it's called *teleporting*—from world to world.

Each VRML scene has a "point of view," which is called a *camera*. (The stage metaphor gets a lot of work in VRML.) You see the scene through the eye of the camera. It's also possible to predefine *viewpoints*, which are VRML's equivalent of "scenic areas"—where the world's creator has created several points of view. In WebSpace and WorldView, it's possible to go directly to any viewpoint, without traveling through any intervening space, by making a menu selection. This can be a great convenience, especially on slower computers, where traveling through the world can be a painfully slow process. For example, if you create a walkthrough of a famous museum like the Louvre in Paris, you might create viewpoints in front of some of their famous works like the *Mona Lisa*, so visitors can "jump" directly to those points of interest.

The first step in viewing a VRML document is retrieving the document itself. The document request comes from a Web browser—either a VRML browser or an HTML browser. Some VRML browsers can't get documents on their own; these browsers need help from another Web browser. They send their request to the Web browser, and the Web browser sends the request on to its intended recipient, acting a bit like a delivery service (see fig. 3.1).

The Web server that receives the request for a VRML document attempts to fulfill the request with a reply (see fig. 3.2). As we saw earlier, the reply has a content type; in this case, the content type is x-world/x-vrml, because it's a VRML document. This reply goes back to the VRML browser. If the request was made through another Web browser, the reply goes to that browser, and then gets sent back to the VRML browser.

Once the document has been received by the VRML browser, it's *parsed*—that is, read in and understood by the browser. From this parsed description, the *renderer*, which acts like the stage director, creates visible representations of the objects described in the

VRML documents and displays them. Now you've got a VRML world on your display, ready to be examined. All browsers feature some interface for navigation, so that you can move the scene's camera throughout the world.

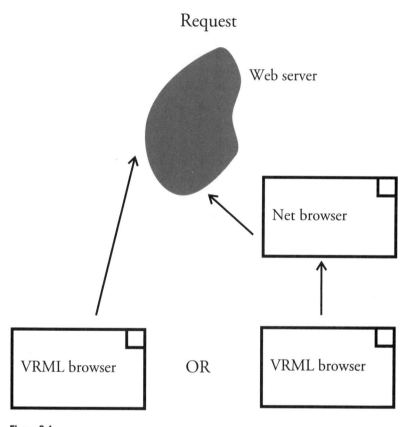

Figure 3.1

A VRML browser requesting a VRML document.

A VRML world can be *distributed*—that is, it can be spread across the Web in many different places. In the same way that an HTML page can be composed of text from one place and images from another, a VRML world can specify that some of its scene comes from *this* place, while other objects come from *that* place.

For example, I might be a VRML shopbuilder; I design spaces for retail use in cyberspace. If I were a real shopbuilder, I'd have a crew of my own (my own VRML objects) and I'd subcontract the sheetwall to someone, the painting to someone else, and the cabinet work to yet another individual. I've distributed the work; even though the shop is my creation, I've borrowed talent from other places to make the job a success. Distributed VRML is a bit like subcontracting—you reference other people's work out on the Web, but it's included in your world.

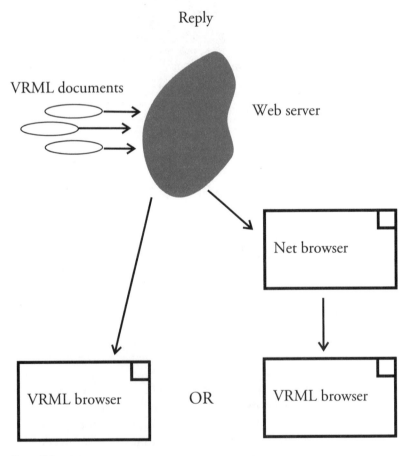

Figure 3.2

A VRML browser receiving a VRML document.

This means that VRML files often load in stages; first the basic scene description is loaded, and then—if this refers to *nested* (scene within a scene) descriptions—the browser loads these after the basic scene has been loaded. Computer speeds aren't ever quite as fast as we would like, and neither are modems quite as capable as the demands we make upon them. For this reason, there is almost always some delay involved in loading a VRML world—it rarely appears immediately, or all at once.

VRML has the ability to show you where objects will appear before they've been downloaded. Before the object appears, it's shown as an empty box of the correct dimension (called a *bounding box*), which is replaced by the actual object when it has read in. Called *lazy loading*, it allows the VRML browser to take its time—when it has no choice, that is—loading the scene from several different places while still giving you an accurate indication of what the scene will look like when it's fully loaded.

This means that you don't need to wait for an entire VRML world to load onto your computer before you navigate through it—the world will load while you sift through the pieces you've already received. In a rich VRML world with hundreds of objects, this can be a very important feature.

When a VRML browser loads a VRML document, it *parses*—that is, interprets—the document. A specific feature in VRML, called WWWInline, instructs the VRML browser to retrieve an additional VRML document. The browser thinks that the additional VRML document is actually *within* the original document—that it's all just one document and one world. Figure 3.3 demonstrates how the browser takes the VRML document and uses information within it to retrieve other documents.

Links in VRML work in precisely the same way as they do within HTML. A browser will try to display any data that it retrieves through the Web. VRML browsers can only display VRML data—unlike Netscape Navigator, they can't display HTML or images, only three-dimensional objects. Frequently, when navigating through a VRML world, clicking on a link will bring up an application that is designed for the data type. Clicking on a link to a PostScript document might launch Adobe Illustrator, or a link on a QuickTime movie might launch the QuickTime movie player. These companion viewers are called *helper applications*, because they provide some functionality that the browser doesn't have itself.

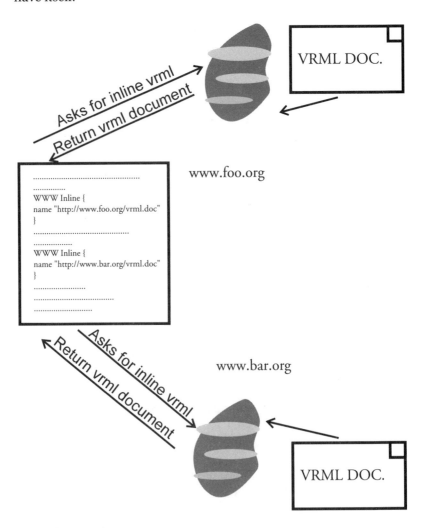

Figure 3.3

Distributed VRML with inline VRML documents.

One of the most useful features of the Web is *server scripting,* little programs that are executed on a Web server in response to a request for a document. The reply gets generated at the time of the request, however, so it can contain highly dynamic data, like the current time, temperature, or a stock price. There are many examples of HTML documents generated with server scripts; the Weather Page at Michigan State University (*http://rs560.cl.msu.edu/weather/*) is an excellent example of a document composed from real-world dynamic data.

VRML can be generated on-the-fly, too. Clay Graham, who develops VRML applications at Silicon Graphics, a computer manufacturer, has developed a server script to display the company's current stock price in VRML, using dynamic data and three-dimensions to produce a very readable financial "thermometer." The final example in Part 2, "The Complete VRML Primer," shows how you can write a server script to create an orrey (a type of planetarium) that displays the current astronomical time.

Those are the basic features of VRML. Now that you understand how Web browsers talk to Web servers, and how VRML browsers parse and display VRML documents, let's move on to the next chapter, "Sailing Through Cyberspace: Using VRML Browsers," and set sail in our cyberspace ships.

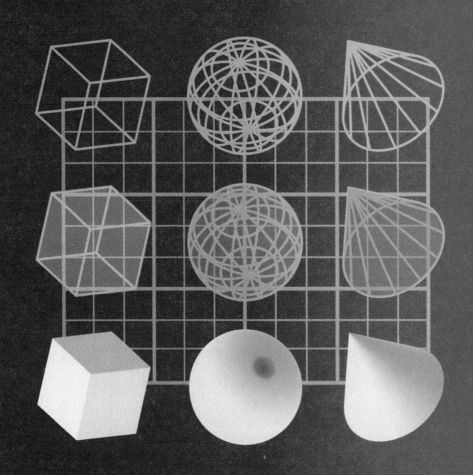

Chapter 4

Sailing Through Cyberspace: Using VRML Browsers

If cyberspace is a sea on which we set sail to discover new lands, then our craft is the VRML browser application. The *browser* interprets the VRML worlds and makes them visible on a computer. It's as though the bow of your cyber-spacecraft is the monitor on your computer; what you see through it is what's out there, in cyberspace.

In this chapter, we'll use three of the more popular VRML browsers, each of which has a very different feel. We'll use each of them to tour a particular site in cyberspace. This way, you'll get a feeling for the browsers themselves, while at the same time tour some large-scale VRML projects.

Sailboats, Powerboats, and Tugboats: Three Flavors of VRML Browsers

Each of the VRML browsers we'll examine integrate with the Web and with HTML—the language of Web pages—quite differently. There are three basic approaches: helper applications, stand-alone applications, and integrated applications. These approaches are discussed in the next sections.

Helper Applications

A *helper application* is sort of like a motorcycle sidecar; it can't go anywhere on its own, but it can be used in conjunction with another application to provide additional capabilities. You may already be familiar with helper applications, especially if you use a Web browser like Netscape Navigator. That application comes with an audio player that is used to play sounds retrieved from across the Web. The audio player can't get the files itself—it doesn't know how to use the Web. It instead talks to Navigator directly.

VRML browsers that work as helper applications are more sophisticated than the average helper application. They can receive information from a Web browser, like the audio player—click on a link in a Web document, and you may well find yourself within a VRML browser—but they can also make requests to the Web browser. The conversation goes something like this:

Web Browser: Hey, VRML helper application! I've got a world for you to display!

VRML Helper Application: Oh! OK. Here it is... Oh... Wait... Could you retrieve this Web document for me?

WB: Here you go!

VHA: Thanks, got it!

[...]

VHA: Hey, could you display this Web page?

WB: Sure thing. *(Web browser displays new page)*

[...]

WB: Could you display this world?

VHA: Absolutely. *(VRML browser displays a new world)*

[...etc...etc...etc...]

There's quite a bit of two-way communication between VRML helper applications and Web browsers. This means that, in general, a Web browser application must be running while a VRML helper application is being used.

Stand-Alone Applications

The second class of VRML browsers are fully equipped Web browsers; this means that they need no help from any other application to display VRML files. Such *stand-alone applications* are network-aware. They understand how to use the Web *protocols*—the languages the computers use to speak to one another—to retrieve documents across the Web. As of this writing, no stand-alone VRML browsers display any other data type than VRML. Because VRML can link to all Web data types, including HTML, sound, movies, and so forth, it's necessary to pass these files off to their own helper applications, just as Netscape Navigator does. When a VRML browser encounters a link to an HTML document, it will launch an HTML browser in order to display it. In this case, the stand-alone applications behave as if they are helper applications.

Strictly speaking, no helper applications are required to work with a stand-alone VRML browser application. If you want to experience the richness of the entire Web, however, and not just the VRML parts of it, you'll still need to have an HTML browser and a full complement of other helper applications.

Integrated Applications

Over the last few years, there's been a trend toward all-in-one desktop applications. These applications include everything you might need to do business in a small office—a word processor, spreadsheet, database, electronic mail, and so forth. These *integrated applications* make it quite easy for inexperienced computer users to produce sophisticated documents—linking correspondence to financial reports to accounts receivable—with a minimum of training. They've proven to be popular with the computer-phobic, and even Microsoft Office, which is a bundle of separate applications, has started to develop an umbrella that binds all of its pieces together into a whole.

Along the same lines, the developers of Web browsers have seen how novice Internet users are overwhelmed by the sheer number of helper applications needed to produce a satisfying Web experience. Audio players, movie players, image viewers—the user needs to correctly install and configure all of these and more, before much of the Web's richness becomes accessible. This is well beyond the abilities of most people.

For this reason, the newest trend in Web browsers is the integrated browser. An integrated browser understands many different data types—HTML and AIFF, TIFF, and MPEG—and requires very little user configuration. The latest crop of Web browsers has integrated VRML browsers. This means that it's possible to click on a link to a VRML world from within an HTML document and, rather than going to a separate application, the application opens a window onto the VRML world. Within an integrated browser application, HTML and VRML documents can be open simultaneously. Using VRML and HTML together provides some very powerful capabilities—like the capability to simultaneously browse the "stacks" of a virtual library while, at the same time, looking through any books you might find.

Here Come the Browsers

The three VRML browsers in release at the time this book was written—TGS' *WebSpace*, Intervista's *WorldView*, and Quarterdeck's *QMosaic*—each operate quite differently. The way you move around the world—called *navigation*—is implemented with differing metaphors within each browser; each one represents an instance of a helper application, a stand-alone application, and an integrated application, respectively. The discussion of each browser will begin with some history and an examination of the browser's interface, while looking at a very simple VRML model. From there, we'll up the ante, and use the browser to take a look at a real location in cyberspace, so you can get a feel for how each performs.

When this book was written, these browsers were still in development. Some of the features we talk about here may be implemented in different ways than will be demonstrated.

Template Graphics Software's WebSpace

Partners with SGI in the development of WebSpace, TGS' implementation of its VRML browser, brings SGI's interface to other platforms, including Microsoft Windows and SUN Microsystems Solaris. As with the SGI version, the Windows version of WebSpace is a helper application, unable to perform any network communications by itself. The SGI version of WebSpace is designed to run well with Netscape Navigator for IRIX; the TGS version will operate with either Netscape Navigator for Microsoft Windows or Spyglass' Enhanced NCSA Mosaic.

If you're using Netscape Navigator to launch WebSpace, you'll have to make sure that Navigator is set up to launch WebSpace when it loads a VRML file from the Web. This means that you'll have to go to the "Helper Applications" section of the "Preferences" dialog box under the "Options" menu, and do two things: add a new MIME type, and configure that MIME type to automatically launch WebSpace.

To add a new MIME type, make sure the "Set Preferences On:" drop-down menu is set to "Helper Applications." Click on the button "New Type;" when the dialog box pops up, set the field "Mime Type:" to **x-world**, and the field "Mime SubType:" to **x-vrml**. The dialog box should look like figure 4.1.

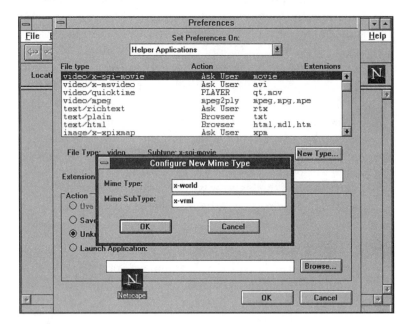

Figure 4.1

Creating a new MIME type in Netscape Navigator.

Once this is done, select the entry you've just created in the list of MIME entries in the upper half of the Preferences screen. Set the "Extensions:" field to **wrl**—this is the standard extension for VRML world files. Within the "Action" area at the bottom of the screen, select the "Launch Application:" radio button, and then type the path to your copy of WebSpace (you can also hit the "Browse" button to locate it). The "Preferences" dialog box will now look like figure 4.2.

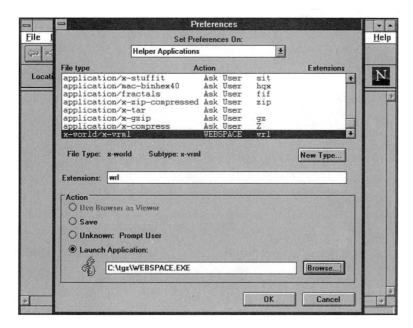

Figure 4.2

Configuring WebSpace as a Netscape helper application.

It's necessary to launch your Web browser *before* running WebSpace. When WebSpace starts up, it looks for a Web browser—Netscape Navigator or Enhanced NCSA Mosaic—to "register." If WebSpace doesn't find a Web browser with which to register itself, it won't be able to retrieve documents through the Web. Furthermore, you should always quit WebSpace before you quit your Web browser. If you don't, WebSpace may think it's registered to speak with an application that isn't running—a condition that can cause a crash of WebSpace or even Windows.

One of the elemental VRML models is the toy gun, gun.wrl. Open your Web browser, then open WebSpace. Under the "Open File" item of the "File" menu, find and open gun.wrl (which is on the CD-ROM). You'll see what is shown in figure 4.3.

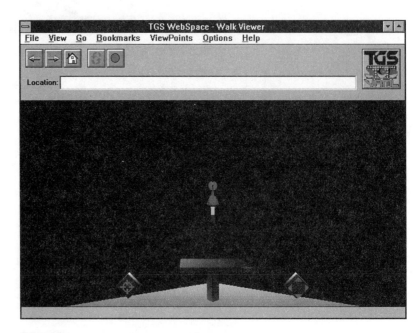

Figure 4.3
WebSpace displaying the VRML file gun.wrl.

This is the gun with the barrel pointing toward you. Bang—you're zapped!

WebSpace offers two different ways to get around in cyberspace—Walk Mode and Examiner Mode. Each of them has its own pluses and minuses. This file opens into Walk Mode, which is a bit like a cyberspace golf cart. At the bottom of the WebSpace screen, you can see a handlebar, with diamond-shaped controls to the right and left (see fig. 4.4). The handlebar itself has two parts; the left portion is used for steering, and the right portion of the handle is a knob used for looking up and down—technically known as *pitch*.

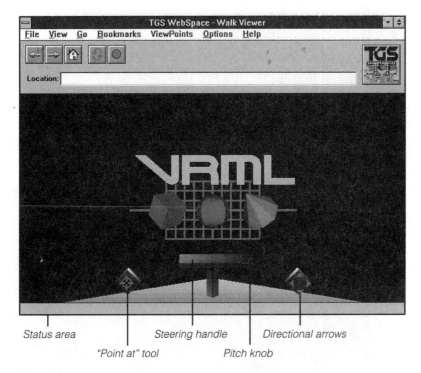

Status area   Steering handle   Directional arrows

"Point at" tool   Pitch knob

Figure 4.4

User interface features of WebSpace (Walk Mode).

The diamond containing the crosshairs, on the left side of the handlebar, is the seek tool. If you click on it, and then click on something in the scene, you'll move half the distance toward the object you've clicked on, as well as moving that object to the center of the view.

The diamond on the right side of the handlebar is the arrow pad. You can press on one of the arrows within the pad, and you'll move in the direction indicated by the arrow.

Finally, at the very bottom of the screen is the status area, which displays informational messages about the browser's status or the contents of a scene. For example, if you have your mouse over a VRML object that is linked to some other Web document, you'll see the link information displayed in this area.

The handlebar is your steering wheel and accelerator petal, all in one. To use it, click in the center of the bar—where the T joins—and, holding down the mouse button, roll the mouse forward (away from you). You'll see the bar bend forward, as if under pressure from you, and you'll see the gun come closer (see fig. 4.5).

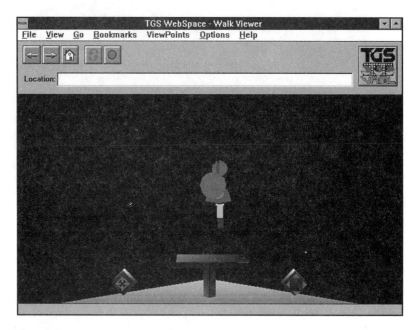

Figure 4.5
Using the WebSpace steering wheel to move into or out of a scene.

That might be a little too close for comfort. Click the mouse in the center of the bar once again, and roll the mouse back (pull it toward you). The gun moves away again.

This handlebar is also a steering knob. You can steer right or left by pulling the mouse right or left as you hold down the button (see fig. 4.6).

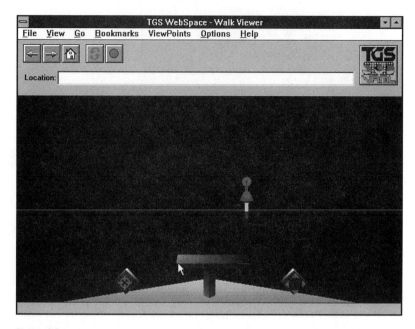

Figure 4.6

Using the WebSpace steering bar to move right or left through a scene.

Finally, by clicking and dragging on the pitch knob, you can look up or down (see fig. 4.7).

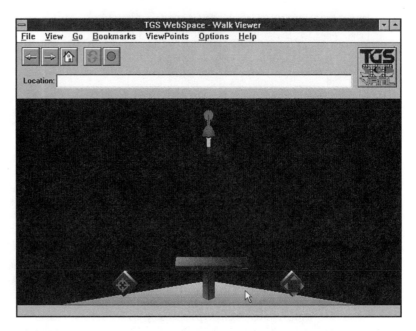

Figure 4.7

Using the WebSpace pitch bar to look up or down in a scene.

In worlds that have a single object, like gun.wrl, WebSpace provides Examiner Mode. In this mode, the handlebar is replaced by a sphere and a dial, which look like figure 4.8.

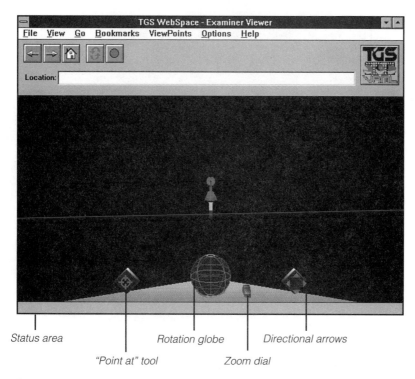

Status area — "Point at" tool — Rotation globe — Zoom dial — Directional arrows

Figure 4.8

User interface features of WebSpace (Examine Mode).

The sphere can be manipulated by the mouse to change the orientation of an object on display. If you click on the sphere at its center on the right-hand side and pull left, you'll see that the gun spins around as well (see fig. 4.9).

Figure 4.9

Using the Examine Mode sphere tool to rotate a scene.

The dial is used to bring the object closer or move it farther away, as shown in figure 4.10.

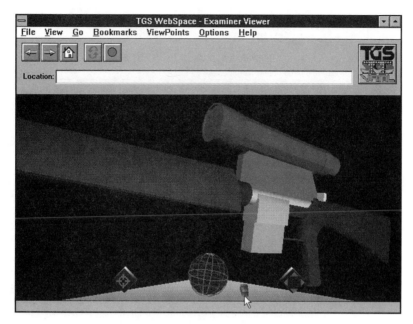

Figure 4.10
Using the Examine Mode dial to move into or out of a scene.

The seek tool and directional arrows work in exactly the same manner in either mode.

WebSpace in WAXWeb

David Blair, an avant-garde filmmaker and director of the critically acclaimed *WAX or the Discovery of Television Among the Bees*, spent a year developing an interactive film in VRML using his cinematic film as a starting point. Working with Tom Meyer, a brilliant artist and hacker from Brown University, the pair have created *WAXWeb*, which they hail as the "future of television." You can decide for yourself. First, inside your Web browser, go to WAXWeb's home page at http://bug.village.virginia.edu/ (see fig. 4.11).

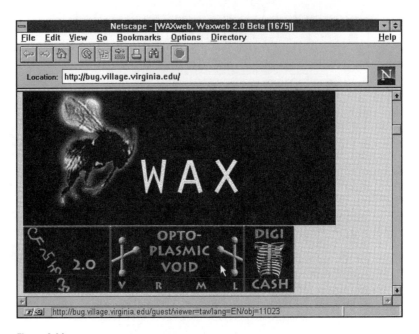

Figure 4.11
WAXWeb's home page.

Now, follow the links into the "Optoplasmic Void" (David has a weird sense of humor) and—why look! Your VRML browser has launched into a VRML view of WAXWeb (see fig. 4.12). Every VRML model in WAXWeb has links back into it. You can identify links in WebSpace because linked objects turn orange when the mouse is put over them.

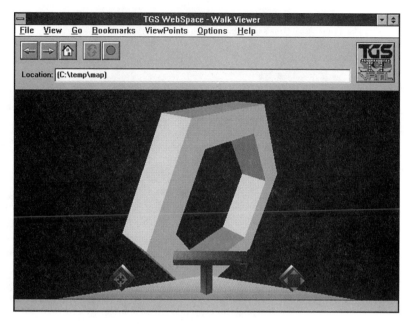

Figure 4.12

The VRML entry world within WAXWeb.

In WAXWeb, the content is simultaneously delivered in HTML and VRML; there are no more pages or spaces, but rather a combination of both, delivered together, to create something greater than the sum of the parts. Many of the 900 VRML objects in WAXWeb are fragments of the "language of the dead," which looks much like a roman alphabet, with a few extra strokes thrown in to confuse the eye (see fig. 4.13).

Figure 4.13

The "language of the dead" in WAXWeb.

WAXWeb generates VRML "phrases" in the language of the dead, and each of the letters in one of these phrases links to more HTML and VRML documents. It's all created on-the-fly, at the computer's whim, so it's hard to predict what your experience with WAXWeb will be, but it's likely to be strangely satisfying. WAXWeb is so big, so linked, and so strangely familiar, you might find yourself spending a lot of time mining its jewels.

Intervista WorldView

Perhaps the most straightforward of all VRML browsers, Intervista WorldView is a stand-alone VRML application. Nonetheless, if you plan on launching it from Netscape, you'll need to repeat the steps outlined above concerning how to configure WebSpace with Netscape. Simply substitute WorldView for WebSpace in the choice of Netscape helper applications, and you'll be ready to run WorldView, either by itself or from Netscape.

When WorldView is installed, the install program determines whether there are any valid Web browsers that it can launch if it loads an HTML document. If so, the Web browser will automatically be launched by WorldView if and when needed.

When you launch WorldView, you'll see the startup world—Earth from space. The interface is very straightforward, as shown in figure 4.14.

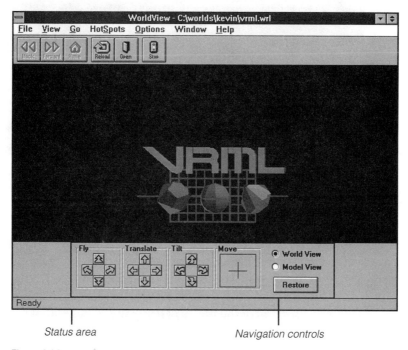

Figure 4.14
User interface details of WorldView.

The buttons in the upper left-hand portion of the screen correspond to the buttons you'd find in a normal Web browser—Backward, Forward, Home, Reload, and Open. The lower area of the screen contains the navigation panel, used to move yourself around the world (see fig. 4.15). The navigation panel is a relocatable window. If you click the mouse in the area outside any of the panel's controls and drag, the navigation panel will move.

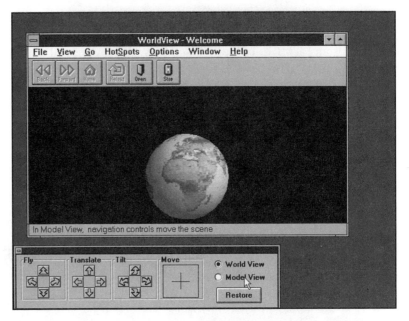

Figure 4.15
WorldView's navigation panel detaches from the main window.

The controls on the navigation panel are very straightforward. You can move around—in and out, left and right—by using the Move control area. Press the mouse down in the center of the Move control's crosshairs, and drag the mouse around. You'll see the Earth move. The Fly and Tilt controls act just as described. There's help on all of the buttons; if you don't know what something does, just hold the pointer over it and hint text will appear.

One of the models that best demonstrates WorldView is the New College's vrmLab. Created by Jeff Sonstein, this model resembles a mini-Acropolis. From the "File" menu, load vrmlab.wrl (on the CD-ROM) and you'll see what is shown in figure 4.16.

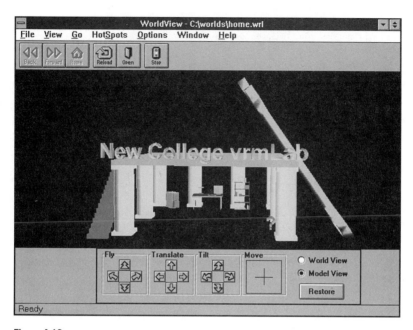

Figure 4.16

The New College vrmLab.

WorldView has two navigation modes, which are roughly analogous to the two metaphors used in WebSpace: World View and Model View. In World View, you move yourself around, or change your orientation. In Model View, you do the same to the model. For example, in World View, clicking on the Fly Forward button brings the model closer, but in Model View, it moves away—because the model itself is flying forward, and then away from you!

Links within VRML objects in the Web are shown by changing the cursor to a finger pointer. VRML includes the capability to attach text to a link so that users can have some idea of where they'll be going if they click on the link. Putting the cursor over the bottom drawer of the filing cabinet looks like what is shown in figure 4.17.

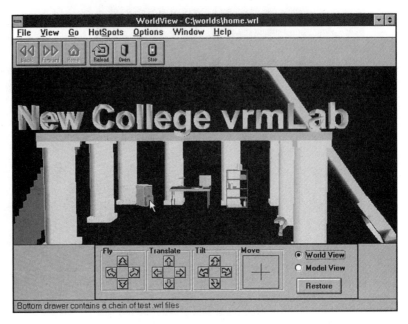

Figure 4.17
Descriptive text can be associated with a link.

Click on the filing cabinet—make sure you're on the Net—and WorldView will load another world (see fig. 4.18).

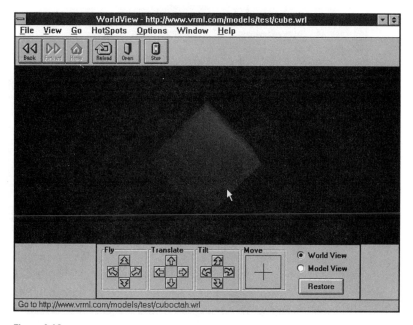

Figure 4.18

VRML links can transport you from world to world.

This world is part of a set of basic VRML test objects. You can click through a zoo of basic solids—squares, tetrahedrals, icosohedrals, and so forth.

WebFX and Quarterdeck QMosaic

Paper Software's WebFX is a VRML viewer that actually embeds itself within popular Internet browsers. When used with Quarterdeck's QMosaic, the result is an all-in-one integrated HTML/VRML browser application. This means that no configuration is required to use it as a VRML browser, or in conjunction with a Web browser. All of these components are within the framework of a single application.

Because it has one foot in HTML and one foot in VRML, QMosaic looks like a normal Web browser. It has an excellent facility for managing bookmarks, and uses a filing cabinet metaphor to keep links well organized. When you launch QMosaic, you'll see a ho-hum Web browser, as shown in figure 4.19.

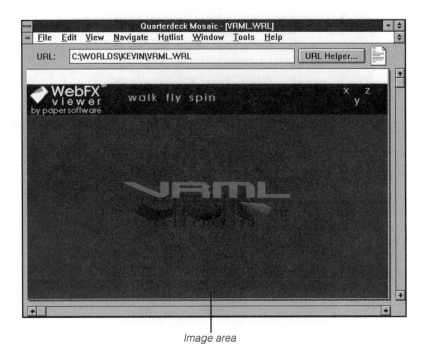

Image area

Figure 4.19

The QMosaic interface.

One of the HTML documents on the included CD-ROM is a copy
of the VRML 1.0 specification. If you open the file spec.htm, using
the "Open" item in the "File" menu (click on the "Browse" button
to bring up the file selection), you'll see a normal-looking Web
document, as shown in figure 4.20.

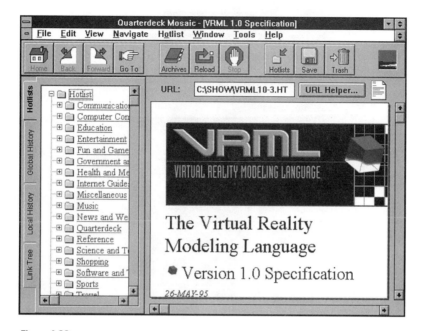

Figure 4.20

The VRML 1.0 Specification in QMosaic.

If you click on the VRML logo banner at the top of the document, however, you'll see that this is no ordinary Web browser—the logo links to a VRML version of the logo, so the browser soon looks like figure 4.21.

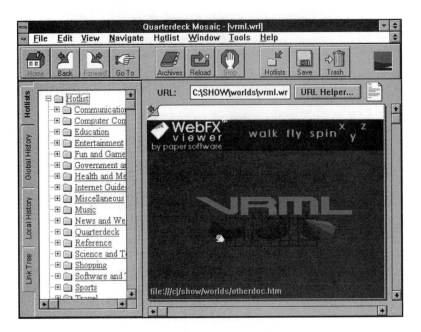

Figure 4.21
The VRML browser is inside QMosaic.

WebFX is a VRML browser that lives inside QMosaic. The browser itself is very easy to use; just the right and left mouse buttons are required. The entire area of the VRML browser's window is used for navigation. Click on the mouse's left button in the center of that area, and push the mouse away from you. You'll see the VRML logo approach. If you pull the mouse toward you—again, with the mouse button held down—the object moves away. Moving the mouse left or right moves you left and right. The right mouse button is used for object manipulation. Click it, hold it down, and you can drag the logo or spin it around, as shown in figure 4.22.

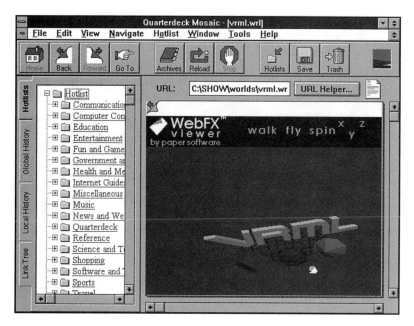

Figure 4.22
Using direct manipulation to navigate in WebFX.

If you click on a VRML object with the right mouse button, you'll
get a menu of options for WebFX (see fig. 4.23). You can add
cursor crosshairs, change the display style, and add on-screen
help. Paper Software is marketing embedded versions of WebFX
for most popular Web browsers, including Netscape. Check out
Paper's home page at www.paperinc.com to download the latest
versions of WebFX.

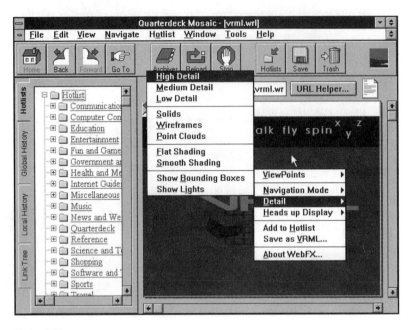

Figure 4.23
The WebFX options menu.

There's quite a set of available options; you can adjust them to create the WebFX environment that best meets your needs and the requirements of the scene.

Let's Get Lost

One thing you'll find quite often in VRML is that you'll go ripping through a scene and out into the boundless "black silence" of undeveloped cyberspace. If you're lucky, you can just back up and find yourself back in the scene. On the other hand, if you've gone so far that you can't see anything at all, you'll need to radically change your point of view to bring you back into the stage of visible objects. Fortunately, each of these VRML browsers enables you to reset your point of view to the "entry" point— where you started from. In WebSpace, selecting "Entry View" under the "Views" menu brings you back to your starting point. In WorldView, selecting "Restore Viewpoint" under the "View" menu will get you back. In QMosaic, the right mouse button brings up the VRML options menu. The first menu item, "Viewpoints"—which is a menu itself—has the "Entry View" as its first item.

And if all else fails, you can always reload the scene. Each of the browsers has a button labeled "Reload"—occasionally shown by a circular arrow icon—which will reload the scene and place you at the entry point.

Speeding It Up and Slowing It Down

You'll find—especially if you're on a slower computer—that larger scenes render much more slowly than smaller scenes, which makes sense, but doesn't make it any more enjoyable when you were expecting virtual reality and get something that looks like a slow sideshow. It's possible to tell the browser to fall back to various rendering schemes that take less computing power. While WebSpace doesn't allow this to take place, both WorldView and QMosaic can create images with high quality, low quality, or in wireframe mode. (The differences between these image types are explained in the next chapter, "3D Graphics Primer.")

The "View" menu in WorldView has a variety of options that can increase image quality or rendering speed—"Wireframe" is the fastest, while "Phong" is almost painfully slow, except on very capable computers.

QMosaic's VRML options menu—accessible through the right mouse button—has a "Detail" submenu with several options that affect rendering speed, including "Wireframe," "Solid," "Flat Shading," and "Smooth Shading." Wireframe is faster than solid rendering, and flat shading will be faster than smooth.

This concludes our tour of VRML browsers. You've gotten a taste of VRML as we've toured these models and, hopefully, your head is buzzing with ideas. In the next chapters, we'll discuss the specifics behind VRML—how it defines worlds and links within the Web.

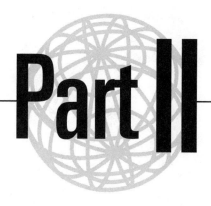

Part II

The Complete VRML Primer

BROWSING AND BUILDING CYBERSPACE

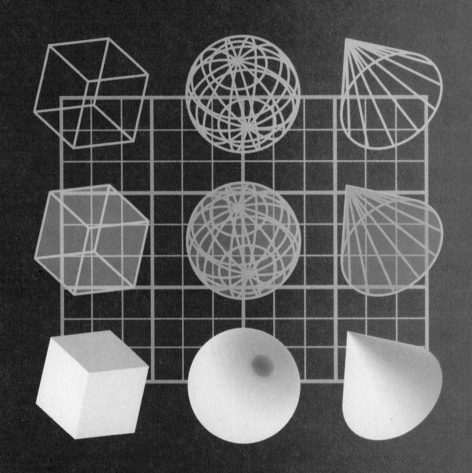

Chapter 5

3D Graphics Primer

Many of the readers of this book have enjoyed three-dimensional graphics—in films like *Terminator 2* or *Jurassic Park*, or in video games like *Tempest* or *Donkey Kong Country*—but chances are, you don't have any idea what powers the creative magic behind them. If so, this primer is written for you; it will help you to understand the basic components of three-dimensional graphics, and how we use a computer to create realistic images.

How Does the Computer Represent the Real World in 3D?

If you played with Tinker Toys as a child—or perhaps as an adult, playing with your children—you already have an intuitive understanding for how the computer conceptualizes 3D graphics. In the Tinker Toy set, you have spokes and wheels; the wheels are joint points, where spokes are joined together. The spokes and wheels create frames, outlines of structures like buildings, rocket ships, boats, and so forth.

In the computer-generated world of 3D graphics, the computer uses *points*—which are analogous to the Tinker Toy wheels—and links these points together to create the frameworks of objects.

The collection of points used to create an object is called a *point cloud* because, when you remove the framework that connects the points together, it looks like a cloud of points, floating in space. Almost all computer-generated objects begin as point clouds.

In the next step toward realism, the computer links the points together, creating a framework for the object. Now the object begins to look real, but hollow—very much like the superstructure of a building before the walls and floors have been added. This is known as a *wireframe* rendering of an object.

After the frame has been created, a skin—called a *surface*—is applied to the object. The surface can have many qualities; like the coat of paint on an automobile, it can be flat, shiny, or reflective, any color of the rainbow, and might even have racing stripes or a decal. The surface makes the object appear solid—even though it's hollow all the way through—and, with a creative surface design, the object can look impressively realistic.

In the real-world, objects are visible because they either emit or reflect light—you can see your car in the driveway because sunlight reflects off it and toward your eyes. In order to create a realistic view of an object, the computer must light the object using a computer-generated light source. Once the object has been lit, it is *shaded*. Each surface of an object reflects light differently, and the computer must calculate the shading for every surface of the object.

Now you have an object that looks very much as it would in the real world; the degree of realism is generally proportional to the amount of computing done to create a view of the object. Each dinosaur in *Jurassic Park* took thousands of hours to create, render, and animate; using tools on the CD-ROM, however, you can be building 3D worlds in just a few minutes.

Any understanding of 3D graphics must begin with place—where things are.

A Place for Everything

Everything in the world has a *position*—the place where it is. Think of your living room: in one corner is a sofa, and opposite it—in most homes—sits the television set. These positions are important because they define relationships, associations, and possibilities. You are about a foot away from this book as you read it; any less and the page would be blurry, too much more and the print would be too small.

In addition to position, the physical world has three dimensions, which we call width, height, and depth. *Width* is the quality of an object as it spreads from side to side; *height* is its characteristic as it spans above and below us; and *depth* is its characteristic as it comes toward or recedes away from us.

The world of the computer is a realm of pure mathematics. The computer doesn't understand width or what that might imply; instead we use the variable *x*. For height, we use the variable *y*, and for depth we use the variable *z*. To the computer, x, y, and z are as meaningful as width, height, and depth are for us. They are often represented as lines coming together to form one corner of a cube, as shown in figure 5.1.

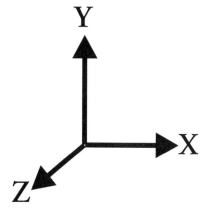

Figure 5.1

Width, height, and depth represented as x, y, and z.

Yaw, Pitch, and Roll

Let's go back to your living room again. You've placed the television set on the other side of the room from the sofa. Did you place it so that the picture tube points toward the sofa—or perhaps so that the picture shines against the wall? In either case, the television is in the same location, but its *orientation* has changed. In the real world, every object has a position and an orientation, and these are independent attributes. Think of a traffic light hanging in the middle of an intersection—its location is not particularly important, but its orientation certainly is.

Orientation is represented—again—using three values, because we can twist an object through three dimensions of orientation. These orientations are called *yaw*, *pitch*, and *roll*; each of these corresponds to orientation in x, y, and z, respectively (see fig. 5.2).

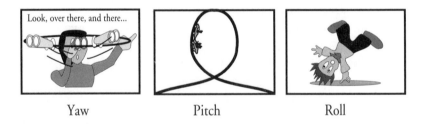

Yaw   Pitch   Roll

Figure 5.2

The three types of orientation: spinning (yaw), looping (pitch), and cartwheeling (roll).

Take a child's top as an example; it might wobble a bit, but basically it spins around and around. This spinning is called *yawing*. If you sat in a swivel chair and spun around, you'd be changing your orientation in yaw.

A roller coaster—especially the newer models—always lifts you up an incredible ramp, until it dips you down into a screaming terror. This lifting up and dropping down is called *pitching*. If you've been on one of the newer coasters that do a full loop-de-loop, you've been through the entire circle of pitch.

Finally, consider doing a cartwheel; you put your hands out to your side, and roll your body. In the end, you'll finish in the same position from which you began and, if you've done it well, you'll neither spin nor bounce—that is, yaw or pitch—as you make the movement. This change in orientation is called *roll*.

Yaw, pitch, and roll are circular motions; if you yaw far enough—spin in an entire circle—you'll end up back where you started. Because these motions have that circular quality, they're measured in degrees. A complete circle has 360 degrees, so a loop-de-loop on a roller coaster puts you through 360 degrees of pitch.

We often collect the x, y, and z of location with the yaw, pitch, and roll of orientation, and together call them *six degrees of freedom*. That means that in the 3D computer world, six different values are required to completely specify the location and orientation of an object.

Polygons

As we mentioned in the introduction to this chapter, the computer creates an object out of a cloud of points; these points are then connected together into a frame, and this frame is then covered with a surface. These surfaces are made up of objects known as *polygons*.

A *polygon* is the basic building block of a computer-generated 3D world. It can be thought of as a surface—a surface that is perfectly flat and infinitely thin. You already know how to identify some polygons; for example, a polygon composed of three points (from the point cloud) would be a triangle, four points would create a quadrilateral, five a pentagon, six a hexagon, and so forth. A polygon can be very complex, with hundreds or thousands of points, but it must have some area inside of it, so a line (two points) is not a polygon. Some examples of simple polygons are shown in figure 5.3.

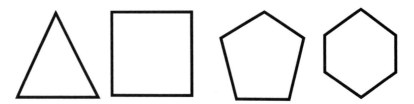

Figure 5.3

Examples of simple polygons.

Computers particularly like triangles; it's very easy for a computer to "color in" the interior of a triangular area, but it is often very difficult for a computer to fill an irregularly shaped polygon. Most 3D authoring tools will enable you to create polygons with many sides, but they'll later break them down into three-sided polygons for the computer's convenience (see fig. 5.4).

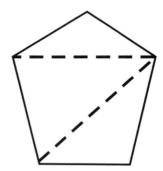

Figure 5.4

A pentagon divided into three triangular polygons.

Polygons, which are really just sets of points, have a *face* or a side. What's rather strange about polygons is that they have only one side. This means that polygons are only visible from one side! While this may seem strange, remember that polygons are mathematical constructions—a one-sided object makes sense mathematically, even though it doesn't make much sense in the real world. It's as if polygons have an "outside" without having an inside.

Now the question is: which side of a polygon is the "outside," that is, the visible side? This is determined by the normal of the polygon. A *normal* is a fancy way of saying a "right angle." The normal of a polygon is a line that passes through the surface of the polygon, at a right angle to it.

The normal can be thought of as a light ray that passes through the polygon's surface on the way to your eye. A polygon has its "outside" on the side of the polygon where the normal points away from the polygon's surface.

As you can see in figure 5.5, a polygon's normal points out from the polygon's surface.

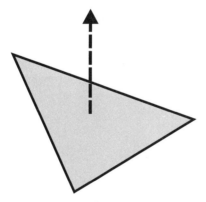

Figure 5.5

A polygon's normal determines its visible side.

Lights

After the computer has taken points in space, connected them to build a frame, and then wrapped that frame in a surface of polygons, the object must be illuminated with a computer-generated light source to create the real-world effects of reflectivity, shininess, and shadow. As in the real world, nothing is visible unless it is lit; 3D applications often provide an "ambient" light source, which provides uniform lighting to an object if no other light source is supplied.

Well-designed lighting can create a mood or effect that makes any scene more realistic. Think about it—if mystery and horror films were brightly lit, they'd be less tense, less brooding. A bright scene makes people feel happy and contented, while a darker scene implies danger and foreboding. Light is mood; the same is true in computer-generated environments.

Lights come in several varieties, as they do in the real world. A bare lamp can illuminate an entire room, whereas a spot light can highlight specific features of the environment. The Sun gives a brilliant illumination, while the Moon casts a pale glow. Each of these have an analog in the world of 3D graphics.

Point Lights

Point lights are light sources that radiate out equally in all directions from a single point. An incandescent light bulb, without a shade, is a good example of a point light (see fig. 5.6). Point lights can be near, like a lamp, or very far away, like the Sun.

Figure 5.6
A point light source.

A *parallel* point light is very much like a point light. All of the light rays that come from a parallel point light are parallel to each other (see fig. 5.7). That means the light behaves as if it were very far away, which is a useful characteristic if you want to re-create sunlight; the Sun is so far away from us that it appears as if all of its rays are parallel to us here on Earth.

Figure 5.7
A parallel point light source.

Directional Lights

It's often quite useful to have track lighting in 3D environments; that is, light sources that can be pointed at particular objects in the computer-generated world. These are called *directional lights*, and they have both a location (given in x, y, and z coordinates) and an orientation (given in yaw, pitch, and roll degrees), which specifies where the light is *and* which direction it points toward (see fig. 5.8). Again, a traffic light is a good example of a directional light.

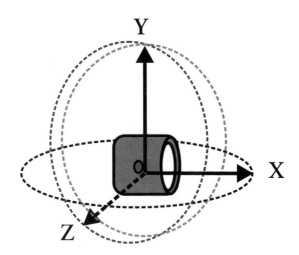

Figure 5.8
A directional light.

Spot Lights

Spot lights are a type of directional light. Along with having a direction toward which their light rays project, they also have a focus, called an *umbra* (see fig. 5.9). The umbra determines the width of the beam of light and how quickly it widens as it passes through space in the computer-generated world. A laser beam is an extreme example of this kind of spot light; it remains perfectly straight as it radiates outward from its point source. Stage lights, used in the theater, are quite often adjustable spot lights.

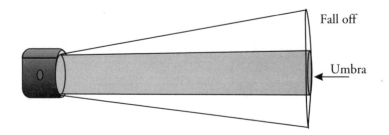

Figure 5.9
A spot light and umbra.

Rendering

We've created our object from points, frames, and surfaces, and illuminated it. Suppose, however, that I just wanted to look at the frame of the object; it would be see-through, and would look much like our Tinker Toy framework. This type of drawing, or rendering, as it's called in computer graphics, is called *wireframe* rendering. The computer connects the dots in the point cloud with lines or wires, and displays on these wires.

The computer can render a wireframe object very quickly, so wireframe rendering is often used on low-power computers to show 3D models without painfully slowing down things.

A sphere shown in wireframe might look like figure 5.10.

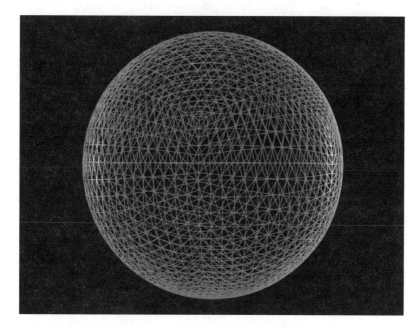

Figure 5.10
A wireframe model of a sphere.

Conversely, if you want to see the surfaces of an object, you would use *solid* rendering. In solid rendering, the polygons are "colored in" (technically known as "polygon filling"). This creates a rendered view of an object that appears solid.

Shading

Solid objects are composed of polygon faces; these faces have normals that determine how light is reflected off these faces. The computer calculates how much light is shining onto any polygon face from any of the light sources in the 3D scene; this is known as *shading*. There are several types of calculations that can be used to determine the shading of an object; some of these are simple and fast, others are complicated and very slow.

We've all seen video games that look cartoonish, and we've seen incredible computer graphics in films that almost appear alive. The biggest difference between DOOM at the low end and *Jurassic Park* at the high end is the shading model used in each. DOOM is fast because it uses an uncomplicated shading model; it creates 3D, but at the expense of realism.

Flat Shading

Flat shading is the simplest type of shading. Using the normal—that is, the light ray that might project outward from the polygon's face—the computer calculates a single value for the angle between the polygon face's normal and the light source, and uses that value to shade the entire polygon face.

To get some understanding of how this might work, consider a light source that is directly in front of a polygon face that is facing it head-on. In this case, the polygon face will be quite bright—it's reflecting light coming directly from the source. If, on the other hand, the polygon face is at some angle so that the light strikes it at an oblique angle—like sunlight on the Earth during winter-time—the polygon face reflects less light, and therefore is less brilliant.

Flat shading, while fast, does make objects look rather artificial. The flat-shaded sphere is shown in figure 5.11.

Figure 5.11

A flat-shaded sphere, head-on light source.

Gouraud Shading

Each progressive level of shading uses more of the computer's mathematical ability to smooth the shading model. The next level after flat shading is called *Gouraud shading*. Gouraud shading uses the normal of the polygon's face and the normal of the faces of all of polygon's neighbors—it averages the shading from one polygon face to the next. There's a lot more math going on—all of the normals and the averaging—so Gouraud shading takes about 10 times more computer processing power than flat shading.

Gouraud shading makes objects look more realistic; take a look at our sphere now (see fig. 5.13).

Figure 5.12

Same sphere, flat shaded, light source at an angle.

Phong Shading

Even with Gouraud shading, complex objects can still show *banding*—that is, lines where the math used to do the shading falls short. While Gouraud shading is very common on computers, it still looks somewhat artificial.

Phong shading was invented to overcome some of the deficiencies of Gouraud shading. Using even more mathematical calculations, the computer uses the normal of the polygon face, and calculates more normals for every corner of the polygon's face (which can be very many if the polygon has an irregular shape), and averages these together with the normals (both center and corners) from all of the adjoining polygons. This again is about 10 times more processing-intensive than Gouraud shading, but it produces results that are pretty spectacular. Our sphere now looks quite nice, as shown in figure 5.14.

Figure 5.13

Same sphere, Gouraud shaded.

Ray Tracing

Ray tracing, used in TV commercials, Hollywood films, and photo-realistic still images, is the most mathematically intensive form of shading. The computer literally calculates the path of every ray of light through the scene—traces the paths—and from this, generates a "realistic" view of the 3D world. Depending on the complexity of the world, this can take anywhere from a few minutes to a few days, even on the most powerful computers in the world.

Figure 5.14
Same sphere, Phong shaded.

Texture Mapping

The real world is rich and detailed. Computers have trouble maintaining that complexity (unless they are very big and very expensive)—so we cheat a lot. One way we cheat is by using something called texture maps. *Texture maps* are a kind of "wallpaper" that is applied to polygon faces. Often, an entire object is "wrapped" with a single texture map.

As an example, consider a model of Earth. We could, if we chose, model every feature of the planet—every mountain range, every sea floor rift, and so forth. It would be a complex model, with billions if not trillions of polygons. It's unlikely we could ever get that onto any computer we have today. But what if, instead, we took our sphere, and then "wrapped" a detailed texture map of the Earth's surface onto it (see fig. 5.15). It would not have depth, but it would have detail. And it would be visible on almost any computer.

Figure 5.15
Same sphere, texture mapped with the surface of the Earth.

Texture maps are a great way to cheat the complex. Using them, you can create scenes that are rich with images—billboards in cyberspace, wood grain on a floor, or wallpaper in a room—without creating a complicated environment.

Conclusion

While those are the basics of three-dimensional graphics, we've left a great deal of ground uncovered. Many of these topics—ray tracing, texture mapping, lighting—take an entire book to cover in detail. You now have a basis for understanding how 3D graphics work, but the best way to learn is by experimentation, and that's what the next chapter guides you through. Using VRML, you'll start from a basic example and work your way up to a realistic model of the solar system; on the way, we'll cover each of these topics in more detail.

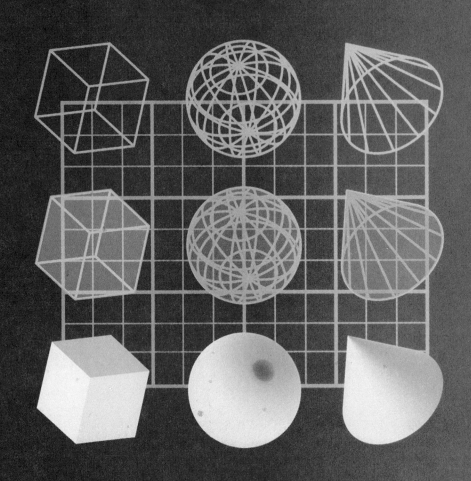

Chapter 6

An Introduction to VRML

First and foremost, VRML is a computer language. While it shares some similarities with other computer languages, such as BASIC or "C," VRML is specifically designed to be an excellent language for computer graphics. VRML has a number of built-in features that make it very easy to create rich models (as you'll see).

The ancestry of VRML is the biggest reason why it's such a strong graphics language. VRML was adapted from a language developed at Silicon Graphics, Inc. This predecessor to VRML, *Open Inventor*, was itself developed as an all-encompassing graphics language. Open Inventor was created by SGI to enable programmers to create realistic 3D environments with only minimal knowledge of graphics programming, but also provides features for the graphics hackers. The developers of Open Inventor gleaned the best parts of all of the graphics languages available and synthesized them, giving Open Inventor a large amount of expressiveness and flexibility, while keeping it easy to learn and understand.

Open Inventor is not completely identical to VRML, however. VRML added some features to make it compatible with the World Wide Web and improved upon some features that existed in Open Inventor, but needed to be made more flexible. Gavin Bell of SGI, one of the developers of Open Inventor, is one of the principle architects of VRML. Gavin brought his experience—and feedback from Open Inventor's thousands of users—into the design of VRML, and modified Open Inventor, removing several features that weren't useful and adding others needed for the Web. This work formed the basic specification for VRML.

One point needs to be made clear at the beginning—VRML is a *scene description* language, and **not** a programming language. Other computer languages, like "C," are compiled in programs (turned into a language the computer understands) and then executed. VRML is *parsed* (turned into a set of objects the computer understands) and is displayed on the screen. Scene description is static—nothing changes once the VRML file is loaded. You can change your point of view, but you can't change the scene itself. (In future versions of VRML, you will be able to manipulate the scene, but today you can't.) What you see in a VRML file is what you get. There are no surprises—such as computer viruses—hidden in a VRML file. Just as HTML creates static Web pages, VRML creates static Web worlds.

About the Primer

Over the course of this chapter, we're going to start from very simple concepts and gradually work toward the more sophisticated features of VRML. One of the great strengths of VRML and of graphic languages in general is that you can see your work right away. The positive feedback of actually building a working VRML world—seeing it working—will keep you moving through the examples. Many computer languages, such as "C++," can take several minutes to turn your program into a computer-executable application; with VRML, however, you'll have results as soon as you finish typing in your program.

The VRML world we're going to build through these examples is a very simple orrey. *Orreys* have been used since ancient times to plot the course of the planets as they travel through their paths in space. We'll begin with what we consider to be the three basic bodies in the Solar system—the Sun, the Earth, and the Moon—and progressively move toward a more realistic representation of these astronomical bodies as we increase our understanding of VRML. By the end of this chapter, we'll have constructed an astronomical clock, using VRML, PERL, and the World Wide Web.

The VRML File Header

The parsers that interpret VRML—that is, translate it from human-readable text to objects a computer can manipulate—have a few requirements. The first requirement is that all of the information in the file be text—characters from the ASCII character set. Beyond that, every VRML document must have a header that identifies it as a valid VRML document. Even if nothing else is in the VRML file, the header must be included. So, the simplest VRML file is the following:

```
#VRML V1.0 ascii
```

A VRML browser will reject any VRML file that does not contain this as its first line.

The pound symbol (#) indicates the presence of a *comment*—information useful to humans, but thrown away by the computer. Whenever a pound occurs in a VRML document, the computer ignores text that follows it, until the end of the line. (The exception to this, of course, is the header line, which the computer looks at, even though it begins with a pound symbol. Go figure.)

Here Comes the Sun—VRML Nodes and Scene Graphs

A VRML document consists of a list of objects, known as *nodes*. These nodes are arranged into a hierarchical structure—this means that one node can be embedded within another node (you'll see exactly what this means a bit later on). The entire list of nodes is known as a *scene graph*. Every VRML document is a scene graph.

Every node has a few basic qualities associated with it. First, there's the node's type, which determines its behavior in the scene graph. Some examples of node types are **Sphere**, **Cube**, **WWWInline**, and **Separator**. You'll see lots of these later.

The node may have one or more fields. *Fields* are places for the node to store information specific to itself. For example, the **Sphere** node has a **radius** field, which supplies a value for the radius of the **Sphere**.

We'll begin our solar system, quite naturally, with the Sun. VRML has a built-in shape—the **Sphere**. The **Sphere** node has one field—the radius. Because this is an uncomplicated world, the example VRML is very short, just six lines of text. Our first file looks like this:

```
#VRML V1.0 ascii
# Example two - Using a VRML built-in shape to create a
➥simple world

# Here comes the Sun
Sphere {
        radius 10             # The Sun is pretty big
}
```

If we take a look at this file in WebSpace, it looks like figure 6.1.

The big whitish ball in the center of the WebSpace window is the **Sphere** we've created. That was pretty easy, wasn't it?

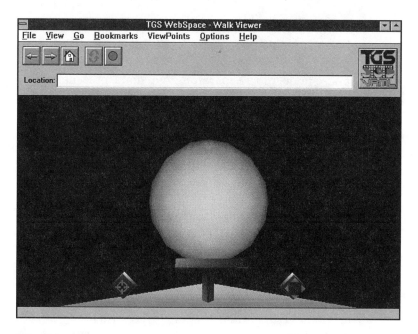

Figure 6.1
WebSpace is used to view the simple VRML world.

Big Yellow Balls and VRML Group Nodes

Some nodes, known as *group nodes*, can have other nodes within them. Group nodes are the VRML equivalent of a box of objects; everything in the box can be treated as a unit, and can be painted, resized, or twisted with the same operation. Group nodes are a very important concept in VRML; they give you the power to manipulate many objects with a single operation.

The most useful group node is the **Separator**. The **Separator** node acts like a generic box; it just gathers everything within it into a single unit. In addition, changes made to the items within the box do not affect items outside of it. For example, the **Material** node in VRML can specify the qualities of a surface: what color it is, if it emits light, if it is reflective, and so forth. By putting a **Sphere** node into a **Separator** group node, preceded by a **Material** node, it's possible to "color" the **Sphere** with the **Material**.

We really would like a big yellow sun—after all, that's the color we're used to. To make it yellow, we'll put the **Sphere** inside of a group node, and put a **Material** node before it.

The **Material** node has several fields inside of it, which you can use (or leave out) to create such visible characteristics as color and shininess. The field in the **Material** node used to set the basic color of an object is called the **diffuseColor**. This field must be specified with three values, numbers between 0 and 1, which correspond to the intensity of the red, green, and blue components of the color desired. We want to create a bright yellow sun; we know from additive color—which we use in VRML—that yellow is created as the product of red and green. We want a bright yellow, so we fully *saturate* the color by setting its value to 1. (A value of zero would mean no saturation, which appears as black.)

Our example now looks like the following:

```
#VRML V1.0 ascii
# Example three - Using the Separator and Material nodes

# Here comes the Sun
# The Separator node groups everything within it together
Separator {

        # The material will affect all subsequent nodes
        # The sun is yellow, isn't it? Additive color means
➥red + green = yellow
        Material {
                diffuseColor 1 1 0          # Color it yellow
```

```
        }

        Sphere {
                radius 10              # Big Sun
        }
}
```

It looks much the same as before, but our big white ball is now a big yellow ball—definitely more solar.

There's something very important to note about this example: in VRML, the scene graph is *ordered*. That means that within a group node, nodes that come first affect nodes that come later. If we reversed the position of the **Sphere** and **Material** nodes in the previous example, the **Sphere** wouldn't have the **Material** qualities.

Great Balls of Fire—More about the Material Node

Our sun should be glowing, like the real one. The **Material** node has a number of fields, which you can choose to include in the node's definition—but if you don't, it makes no difference. If we drop our **diffuseColor** field in favor of **emissiveColor**—that is, a field that defines how much color is emitted from the surface—our sun brightens up immediately. The **emissiveColor** field takes the same red, green, and blue values as **diffuseColor**; all we need to do is change the name of the field. We'll change the **Material** node to the following:

```
#VRML V1.0 ascii
# Example four - Using emissive colors


# Here comes the Sun
# The Separator node groups everything within it together
Separator {

        # The material will affect all subsequent nodes
        # The sun is yellow, isn't it? Additive color means
➥red + green = yellow
```

```
          # We're switching to emissive color because the Sun
➡gives off light.
          Material {
                    emissiveColor 1 1 0          # The Sun emits
➡lots of yellow light
          }

          Sphere {
                    radius 10          # Big Sun
          }
}
```

Changing the Material changes the look quite a bit. See figure 6.2 for how it appears now.

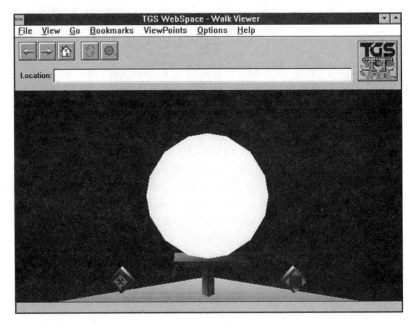

Figure 6.2
A glowing sun created with the Material node.

Other fields of the Material node include **shininess**, **transparency**, **ambientColor**, and **specularColor**. Experiment with this example to see what the various settings can create; it is possible to generate a wide range of effects with the **Material** node. Any of the **Material** node's fields can be used with any other, and each can be used by themselves.

The Little Blue Marble and the Transform Node

Our sun seems to be cooking right along—now it needs a planet to circle it. The Earth circles the Sun, and all of its motion is relative to the Sun. That means that when we create the Earth, we have to do it relative to the Sun. These parent-child relationships are very easy to express in VRML.

That's what the group node is really all about. Any nodes within a group node all adopt the group node's frame of reference. The **Separator** node, at its essence, tells us when and where a frame of reference exists.

Once we have established a frame of reference—inside the **Separator** node that defines the Sun—it is now possible to use that frame and move to another point relative to it. To move to another point in the same frame of reference, VRML defines the **Transform** node. The **Transform** node changes the position, orientation, size, and center of any nodes that follow it in a group. To move the position of subsequent nodes, the **Transform** node uses the **translation** field, which provides for x, y, and z values. Setting any of these values to zero causes no change, so a **translation 0 0 0** would leave everything in the same place. Using a field **translation 1 2 12**, however, would move all subsequent nodes in the group by 1 unit in the x axis, 2 units in the y axis, and 12 units in the z axis. (By convention, units in VRML are equivalent to one meter; that would put our Earth very close to the Sun, but this is just a demonstration, not an astronomically correct observation.)

As always, an example can make things a lot clearer. We need to put the Earth in orbit around the Sun; we do that using the **Transform** node to move away from the Sun, then we use the **Sphere** node to create the Earth. We also use the **Material** node so we don't end up with a yellow Earth—we want it to be blue.

Our example now looks like the following:

```
#VRML V1.0 ascii
# Example five- Using the Transform node, creating the Earth

# Here comes the Sun
# The Separator node groups everything within it together
Separator {

        # The material will affect all subsequent nodes
        # The sun is yellow, isn't it? Additive color means
➥red + green = yellow
        # We're switching to emissive color because the Sun
➥gives off light.
        Material {
                emissiveColor 1 1 0          # The Sun emits
➥lots of yellow light
        }

        Sphere {
                radius 10           # Big Sun
        }

        # We place the Earth within its own Separator
        # To keep everything good and isolated
        Separator {

                # Let's move things out of the way here
                Transform {
                        translation 0 20 20
                }

                # Color the Earth blue, and make it absorb
➥light
                Material {
                        diffuseColor 0 0 1 # Big blue marble
                }

                # Finally, create the earth
```

```
        Sphere {
                radius 2      # Little Earth
        }
    }
}
```

This example creates a VRML world that looks like figure 6.3.

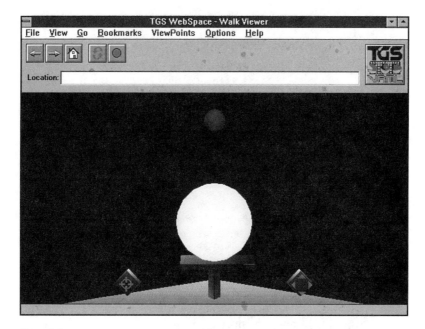

Figure 6.3
The Sun-Earth system.

Oceans are rather shiny—and Earth is covered with oceans. Using the **shininess** field of the Earth's **Material** node, we can change the Earth's surface to reflect this fact, as follows:

```
#VRML V1.0 ascii
# Example six - A shiny Earth

        [..etc..]

        # We place the Earth within its own Separator
```

```
# To keep everything good and isolated
Separator {

        # Let's move things out of the way here
        Transform {
                translation 0 20 20
        }

        # Color the Earth blue, and make it absorb
 ➥light

        # But also make it a reflective, like water
        Material {
                diffuseColor 0 0 1 # Big blue marble
                shininess 0.9 # Water is rather shiny
        }

        # Finally, create the earth
        Sphere {
                radius 2        # Little Earth
        }
}

[..etc..]
```

This change in the Material node gives the Earth a healthy shine.

The Moon-Child and Children of Children

There's no limit to how deep a set of group nodes can go. One group node can contain another, can contain another, and so forth, infinitely. Consider the solar system. The Sun is the center, and the Earth revolves around it. The Moon revolves around the Earth, and perhaps a spaceship revolves around the Moon. These relationships—frames of reference—are represented in group nodes.

To add the Moon to our model, we'll add a group node within the group node that defines the Earth. This means that the Moon will be placed near the Earth, in the Earth's frame of reference. Once again, we'll use the **Transform** node to place the Moon near the Earth, use the **Material** node to color it grayish, and the **Sphere** node to create it.

Our VRML file now looks like the following:

```
#VRML V1.0 ascii
# Example seven - Create the Moon as a child of the Earth

# Here comes the Sun
# The Separator node groups everything within it together
Separator {

        # The material will affect all subsequent nodes
        # The sun is yellow, isn't it? Additive color means
➥red + green = yellow
        # We're switching to emissive color because the Sun
➥gives off light.
        Material {
                emissiveColor 1 1 0          # The Sun emits
➥lots of yellow light
        }

        Sphere {
                radius 10          # Big Sun
        }

        # We place the Earth within its own Separator
        # To keep everything good and isolated
        Separator {

                # Let's move things out of the way here
                Transform {
                        translation 0 20 20
                }
```

```
                              # Color the Earth blue, and make it absorb
➥light

                              # But also make it a reflective, like water
                              Material {
                                      diffuseColor 0 0 1 # Big blue marble
                                      shininess 0.9 # Water is rather shiny
                              }

                              # Finally, create the earth
                              Sphere {
                                      radius 2      # Little Earth
                              }

                              # The Moon gets its own Separator
                              # Because we really do keep everything separate
                              Separator {

                                      # The Moon is just outside the Earth
                                      Transform {
                                              translation 4 4 0
                                      }

                                      # Color the Moon gray, make it absorb
➥light

                                      # It's a little shiny, but not much
                                      Material {
                                              diffuseColor 0.7 0.7 0.7
                                              shininess 0.3
                                      }

                                      # And now, create the Moon
                                      Sphere {
                                              radius 1              # Tiny Moon
                                      }
                              }
                      }
              }
```

Now we have something that's starting to look like home (see fig. 6.4).

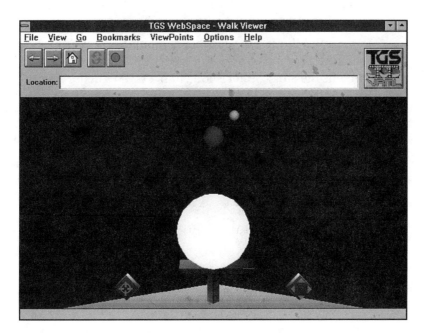

Figure 6.4

The Sun-Earth-Moon system.

A Click on the Sun—Linking VRML into the World Wide Web

We've now created a basic model of the solar system. VRML is well-suited to create scenes such as this. Beyond this, though, VRML can anchor objects—for example, our Sun—into the World Wide Web. There's a node for this, called **WWWAnchor**. **WWWAnchor** is a group node, which means that all of the nodes within the **WWWAnchor** node are anchored to the same *Uniform Resource Locator* (URL) within the Web.

WWWAnchor has a number of fields, the most important of which is the **name** field. It specifies the URL of the anchor, and is always enclosed in quotes. You can create an anchor to anything in the Web—to a Web page, a movie, or even another VRML world.

In order to link our Sun—and just our Sun—into the Web, we'll create a **WWWAnchor** node that contains only the **Sphere** node used to define the Sun. If we turned the **Separator** node that contains the Sun's **Sphere** node into a **WWWAnchor** node, the Earth and Moon groups would also be anchored to the same URL. We don't want that here, however—though you might want that in your own projects.

We'll link our Sun to www.w3.org, which is the home page for the entire World Wide Web. Here's what it looks like now:

```
#VRML V1.0 ascii
# Example eight - Create a link from the Sun to an HTML
document

# Here comes the Sun
# The Separator node groups everything within it together
Separator {

        # The material will affect all subsequent nodes
        # The sun is yellow, isn't it? Additive color means
➥red + green = yellow
        # We're switching to emissive color because the Sun
➥gives off light.
        Material {
                emissiveColor 1 1 0       # The Sun emits lots
➥of yellow light
        }

        # The WWWAnchor node is a group node
        # This means that all objects within it are linked
➥with the anchor's URL
        # We want to link the Sun, so the Sun's Sphere node
➥goes inside of it.
        WWWAnchor {
                name "http://www.w3.org/" # The root URL of the
➥World Wide Web

                # Inside the anchor, because WWWAnchor is a
➥group node
```

```
        Sphere {
                radius 10                    # Big Sun
        }
}

# We place the Earth within its own Separator
# To keep everything good and isolated
Separator {

        # Let's move things out of the way here
        Transform {
                translation 0 20 20
        }

        # Color the Earth blue, and make it absorb
light
        # But also make it a reflective, like water
        Material {
                diffuseColor 0 0 1 # Big blue marble
                shininess 0.9 # Water is rather shiny
        }

        # Finally, create the earth
        Sphere {
                radius 2      # Little Earth
        }

        # The Moon gets its own Separator
        # Because we really do keep everything separate
        Separator {

                # The Moon is just outside the Earth
                Transform {
                        translation 4 4 0
                }

                # Color the Moon gray, make it absorb
light
                # It's a little shiny, but not much
                Material {
```

```
                                    diffuseColor 0.7 0.7 0.7
                                    shininess 0.3
                        }

                        # And now, create the Moon
                        Sphere {
                                    radius 1              # Tiny Moon
                        }
                }
            }
        }
}
```

If you click on the Sun in WebSpace, it will send a message to the HTML browser to go to the page http://www.w3.org/.

Context, Context, Context—The Description Field of the WWWAnchor Node

VRML browsers have many different methods by which they can tell the user if there's a link on a VRML object. In WebSpace, the object turns bright orange while the cursor is over it. (Try this with example eight—you'll see the Sun turn orange!) In WorldView, the cursor simply changes to a hand—as it does in Netscape Navigator or NCSA Mosaic. In both browsers, the *status area*—the area at the bottom of the browser window—displays the URL of the link. This information, while sometimes very useful, can also be rather confusing, especially for people who don't know much about how the Web works.

Rather than showing the URL of the **WWWAnchor** node in the status area, it is possible to display a line of text that you can design. Using the **description** field of the **WWWAnchor** node, you can attach a text string to the anchor. The text must always be surrounded by quotes.

Let's modify the file from the previous example, so that the
WWWAnchor surrounding the Sun reads as follows:

```
#VRML V1.0 ascii
# Example nine - A descriptive link

        [..etc..]

        # The WWWAnchor node is a group node
        # This means that all objects within it are linked
➡with the anchor's URL
        # We want to link the Sun, so the Sun's Sphere node
➡goes inside of it.
        # Using the description field, we provide context for
➡the user
        WWWAnchor {
                name "http://www.w3.org/" # The root URL of the
➡World Wide Web
                description "A link from the Sun to W3.ORG" #
➡Descriptive text

                # Inside the anchor, because WWWAnchor is a
➡group node
                Sphere {
                        radius 10                    # Big Sun
                }
        }

        [..etc..]
```

Now, if we look at that anchor in the VRML browser, we see the
description text in the status area (see fig. 6.5).

The **description** field doesn't change the behavior of the
WWWAnchor. When used judiciously, however, it can provide
badly needed context in a heavily linked environment.

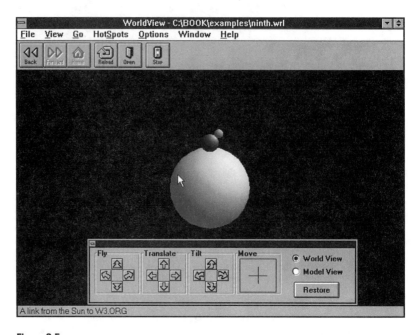

Figure 6.5
WorldView displaying the description field of the Sun's WWWAnchor.

Earth as a Teleportal—Linking VRML Worlds Together

Just as you can link from a VRML world into the Web of HTML pages, it is possible to establish a link between two VRML worlds. This is called a *teleport* because when you travel from one world to another, you unceremoniously dump the old world in favor of the new. One click—and all of a sudden you'll find yourself someplace else.

We'll take our Earth and use it as a teleport to a different VRML world. We do this using the **WWWAnchor** node, as we did with the Sun. This time, however, we attach it to a VRML file. Again, we'll use the **description** field of **WWWAnchor** to provide context for the user. Our example VRML file now looks like this:

```
#VRML V1.0 ascii
# Example ten - Create a portal from the Earth to another
➥VRML world
```

```
# Here comes the Sun
# The Separator node groups everything within it together
Separator {

        # The material will affect all subsequent nodes
        # The sun is yellow, isn't it? Additive color means
➥red + green = yellow
        # We're switching to emissive color because the Sun
➥gives off light.
        Material {
                emissiveColor 1 1 0        # The Sun emits
➥lots of yellow light
        }

        # The WWWAnchor node is a group node
        # This means that all objects within it are linked
➥with the anchor's URL
        # We want to link the Sun, so the Sun's Sphere node
➥goes inside of it.
        # Using the description field, we provide context for
➥the user
        WWWAnchor {
                name "http://www.w3.org/" # The root URL of the
➥World Wide Web
                description "A link from the Sun to W3.ORG" #
➥Descriptive text

                # Inside the anchor, because WWWAnchor is a
➥group node
                Sphere {
                        radius 10                # Big Sun
                }
        }

        # We place the Earth within its own Separator
        # To keep everything good and isolated
        Separator {

                # Let's move things out of the way here
                Transform {
                        translation 0 20 20
```

```
                          }

                          # Color the Earth blue, and make it absorb
➥light

                          # But also make it a reflective, like water
                          Material {
                                  diffuseColor 0 0 1 # Big blue marble
                                  shininess 0.9 # Water is rather shiny
                          }

                          # The WWWAnchor node is a group node
                          # This means that all objects within it are
➥linked with the anchor's URL
                          # We want to link the Earth, so the Earth's
➥Sphere node goes inside of it.
                          # Using the description field, we provide
➥context for the user
                          WWWAnchor {
                                  # Heres the link to another VRML
➥document

                                  name "http://hyperreal.com/~mpesce/book/
➥examples/second.wrl"
                                  description "A link to another world" #
➥Descriptive text

                                  # Finally, create the earth
                                  Sphere {
                                          radius 2              # Little
➥Earth

                                  }
                          }

                          # The Moon gets its own Separator
                          # Because we really do keep everything separate
                          Separator {

                                  # The Moon is just outside the Earth
                                  Transform {
                                          translation 4 4 0
                                  }
```

```
                        # Color the Moon gray, make it absorb
➥light
                        # It's a little shiny, but not much
                        Material {
                                diffuseColor 0.7 0.7 0.7
                                shininess 0.3
                        }

                        # And now, create the Moon
                        Sphere {
                                radius 1              # Tiny Moon
                        }
                    }
                }
            }
```

Click on the Earth and whoosh!—you'll find yourself in front of the simple Sun from example two. In this way, it's easy to link VRML worlds together. You can put a universe inside of your dresser drawer, or just link rooms together through teleport doorways.

Multimedia Moon—Links to Other Web Data Types

In our final example in this introduction to VRML, we'll link the Moon to a sound file located on the Web. The Moon's group node changes to the following:

```
#VRML V1.0 ascii
# Example nine - A descriptive link

        [..etc..]

        # The Moon gets its own Separator
        # Because we really do keep everything separate
        Separator {

                # The Moon is just outside the Earth
                Transform {
                        translation 4 4 0
```

```
                }

                # Color the Moon gray, make it absorb light
                # It's a little shiny, but not much
                Material {
                        diffuseColor 0.7 0.7 0.7
                        shininess 0.3
                }

                # The WWWAnchor node is a group node
                # All objects within it are linked with the
➥anchor's URL
                # We link to the Moon, so the Moon's Sphere
➥node goes inside of it.
                # Using the description field, we provide
➥context for the user
                WWWAnchor {
                        name "http://www.cyborganic.com/People/
➥paul/The_new_dogs/pescewrd.au"
                        description "Sounds from a talk about
➥VRML"

                        # And now, create the Moon
                        Sphere {
                                radius 1              # Tiny Moon
                        }
                }
        }
}

        [..etc..]
```

When the user clicks on the link, the sound file is retrieved—generally by a Web browser (such as Netscape *Navigator*) and not by the VRML browser. If necessary, the Web browser will then launch a helper application to play the sound. Using the same technique, you can anchor a VRML object to any data type in the World Wide Web—movies, images, PostScript files—and thereby bring it into the VRML world.

In this introduction, we've created a basic—but rich—VRML world, and linked it into the World Wide Web. This is it; it doesn't get any harder than this!

In the next two chapters, we'll continue to expand upon this example; we'll make it more realistic, and even turn it into a type of astronomical clock.

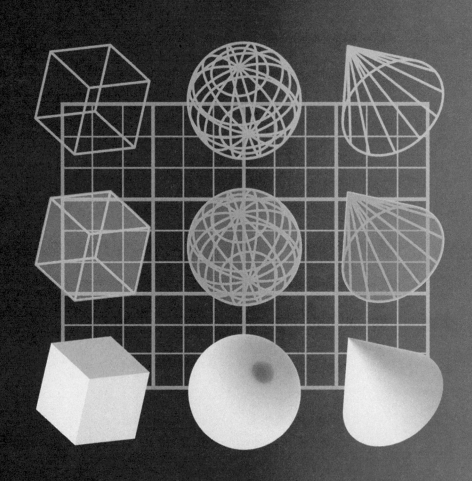

Chapter 7

Intermediate VRML

With the basic features of VRML defined and behind us, it's time to move into the more sophisticated features of VRML—features like naming, lighting, and inlining. By the end of this section, we'll have modified our solar system, constructing a VRML world that's aesthetically pleasing, uses network bandwidth well, and runs successfully on a wide range of platforms.

What's in a Name—DEF Nodes in VRML

VRML nodes have one quality we haven't yet covered—a name, which identifies that node in particular from all other nodes in the VRML scene graph. Giving a node a name is a very simple procedure, but a node can only be given one name. To confuse matters a little bit, it is possible to give several nodes the same name; this isn't advisable in most situations, but might be required from time to time.

Nodes are given names using **DEF**. Placing **DEF**, and then the name of a node, before the node's definition gives the node that name. If we wanted to name a **Separator** node, we do it as follows:

```
DEF ThisIsTheNodeName Separator {
        [ .... ]
}
```

If you want to put spaces in the node name, enclose it in quotes, like this: "This is the node name." Our solar system—which we're still working with—would look like this:

```
#VRML V1.0 ascii
# Example twelve - We're giving our objects DEF names


# Here comes the Sun
# The Separator node groups everything within it together
DEF TheWholeThing Separator {

        # The material will affect all subsequent nodes
        # The sun is yellow, isn't it? Additive color means
➥red + green = yellow
        # We're switching to emissive color because the Sun
➥gives off light.
        DEF SolarStuff Material {
                emissiveColor 1 1 0              # The Sun emits
➥lots of yellow light
        }

        # The WWWAnchor node is a group node
        # This means that all objects within it are linked
➥with the anchor's URL
        # We want to link the Sun, so the Sun's Sphere node
➥goes inside of it.
        # Using the description field, we provide context for
➥the user
        # The DEF node attaches the name "SUN" to the
➥WWWAnchor group
        DEF SUN WWWAnchor {
                name "http://www.w3.org/" # The root URL of the
➥World Wide Web
                description "A link from the Sun to W3.ORG" #
➥Descriptive text

                # Inside the anchor, because WWWAnchor is a
➥group node
```

```
                    DEF SunBall Sphere {
                            radius 10                    # Big Sun
                    }
            }

            # We place the Earth within its own Separator
            # To keep everything good and isolated
            DEF EarthSystem Separator {

                    # Let's move things out of the way here
                    DEF EarthPlacement Transform {
                            translation 0 20 20
                    }

                    # Color the Earth blue, and make it absorb
➡light
                    # But also make it a reflective, like water
                    DEF BlueMarble Material {
                            diffuseColor 0 0 1 # Big blue marble
                            shininess 0.9 # Water is rather shiny
                    }

                    # The WWWAnchor node is a group node
                    # This means that all objects within it are
➡linked with the anchor's URL
                    # We want to link the Earth, so the Earth's
➡Sphere node goes inside of it.
                    # Using the description field, we provide
➡context for the user
                    # The DEF node attaches the name "Earth" to the
➡WWWAnchor node
                    DEF EARTH WWWAnchor {
                            name "http://hyperreal.com/~mpesce/book/
➡examples/second.wrl"
                            description "A link to another world" #
➡Descriptive text

                            # Finally, create the earth
                            DEF EarthBall Sphere {
                                    radius 2        # Little Earth
                            }
                    }
```

```
                          # The Moon gets its own Separator
                          # Because we really do keep everything separate
                          DEF MoonSystem Separator {

                                  # The Moon is just outside the Earth
                                  DEF MoonPlacement Transform {
                                          translation 4 4 0
                                  }

                                  # Color the Moon gray, make it absorb
➥light
                                  # It's a little shiny, but not much
                                  DEF MoonDust Material {
                                          diffuseColor 0.7 0.7 0.7
                                          shininess 0.3
                                  }

                                  # The WWWAnchor node is a group node
                                  # This means all objects within it are
➥linked with the anchor's URL
                                  # We want to link the Moon, so the
➥Moon's Sphere node goes inside of it.
                                  # Using the description field, we
➥provide context for the user
                                  # The DEF node attaches the name "Moon"
➥to the WWWAnchor node
                                  DEF Moon WWWAnchor {
                                          name
"http://www.cyborganic.com/People/paul/The_new_dogs/
➥pescewrd.au"
                                          description "Sounds from a talk
➥about VRML"

                                          # And now, create the Moon
                                          DEF MoonBall Sphere {
                                                  radius 1              #
➥Tiny Moon
                                          }
                                  }
                          }
                  }
          }
```

All of this naming has precisely zero effect on how the world appears in a VRML browser. You're probably wondering why VRML nodes have names at all, but have patience—a little further along, you'll see that scene cameras (which are VRML nodes) can have names as well, and that can be very useful indeed.

Good Day, Sunshine—Lighting VRML Worlds and the PointLight Node

Although our scene looks pretty nice right now, the lighting is all wrong. We've used the **emissiveColor** field of the **Material** node to make it look as if the Sun is giving off light, but it's an illusion— our Sun is dark. Most VRML browsers will install a light within the scene if we haven't defined one, so we're seeing scenes with default illumination, coming from outside the scene. If we install a light into the scene, we'll drop the default illumination, and only use the lights as defined within the VRML world.

VRML defines several nodes for various lighting models. These nodes correspond to the lighting models described in Chapter 5, "3D Graphics Primer." The Sun is a source that radiates equally in all directions, which means it is a point source of light—we'll need to use the VRML **PointLight** node. The **PointLight** node has a few fields that specify if the light is **on**, what **color** it is, and its **intensity**—that is, how bright the light is. The light shows up at the location in the scene graph into which it is placed. If we put it in the midst of our definitions for the Sun, it will place the light source into the Sun.

Something interesting about VRML is revealed here. Even though we specify the Sun as a **Sphere**, which presumably is a solid and not explicitly transparent, the light comes shining through the solid surface of the Sun to illuminate the Earth and Moon. Our file, with sunlight, now looks like the following:

```
#VRML V1.0 ascii

# Example thirteen - We're lighting our Sun. It illuminates
➥the Earth and Moon
# Here comes the Sun
# The Separator node groups everything within it together
DEF SOLAR_SYSTEM Separator {

        # The material will affect all subsequent nodes
        # The sun is yellow, isn't it? Additive color means
➥red + green = yellow
        # We're switching to emissive color because the Sun
➥gives off light.
        Material {
                emissiveColor 1 1 0            # The Sun emits
➥lots of yellow light
        }


        # We'll make the Sun shine here
        # A PointLight shines equally in all directions, like
➥the Sun does.
        DEF SUNLIGHT PointLight {
                intensity 1            # The Sun is way
➥bright
        color 1 1 0.9   # Sunlight is basically white, though
➥the Sun is yellow.
        }


        # The WWWAnchor node is a group node
        # This means that all objects within it are linked
➥with the anchor's URL
        # We want to link the Sun, so the Sun's Sphere node
➥goes inside of it.
        # Using the description field, we provide context for
➥the user
        # The DEF node attaches the name "SUN" to the
➥WWWAnchor group
        DEF SUN WWWAnchor {
                name "http://www.w3.org/" # The root URL of the
➥World Wide Web
                description "A link from the Sun to W3.ORG" #
➥Descriptive text
```

```
            # Inside the anchor, because WWWAnchor is a
↪group node
            Sphere {
                    radius 10                  # Big Sun
            }
      }

            # We place the Earth within its own Separator
            # To keep everything good and isolated
            Separator {

                    # Let's move things out of the way here
                    Transform {
                            translation 0 20 20
                    }

                    # Color the Earth blue, and make it absorb
↪light
                    # But also make it a reflective, like water
                    Material {
                            diffuseColor 0 0 1 # Big blue marble
                            shininess 0.9 # Water is rather shiny
                    }

                    # The WWWAnchor node is a group node
                    # This means that all objects within it are
↪linked with the anchor's URL
                    # We want to link the Earth, so the Earth's
↪Sphere node goes inside of it.
                    # Using the description field, we provide
↪context for the user
                    # The DEF node attaches the name "Earth" to the
↪WWWAnchor node
                    DEF EARTH WWWAnchor {
                            name "http://hyperreal.com/~mpesce/book/
↪examples/second.wrl"
                            description "A link to another world" #
↪Descriptive text

                            # Finally, create the earth
                            Sphere {
```

```
                            radius 2            # Little
➥Earth
                    }
            }

            # The Moon gets its own Separator
            # Because we really do keep everything separate
            Separator {

                    # The Moon is just outside the Earth
                    Transform {
                            translation 4 4 0
                    }

                    # Color the Moon gray, make it absorb
➥light

                    # It's a little shiny, but not much
                    Material {
                            diffuseColor 0.7 0.7 0.7
                            shininess 0.3
                    }

                    # The WWWAnchor node is a group node
                    # This means all objects within it are
➥linked with the anchor's URL
                    # We want to link, so the Moon's Sphere
➥node goes inside of it.
                    # Using the description field, we
➥provide context for the user
                    # The DEF node attaches the name "Moon"
➥to the WWWAnchor node
                    DEF Moon WWWAnchor {
                            name
"http://www.cyborganic.com/People/paul/The_new_dogs/
➥pescewrd.au"
                            description "Sounds from a talk
➥about VRML"

                            # And now, create the Moon
                            Sphere {
```

```
                              radius 1              #
➥Tiny Moon
                              }
                  }
              }
          }
      }
```

Looking at this world in our VRML browser, we now see a crescent Earth and a crescent Moon, in a scene very reminiscent of the opening shots of Stanley Kubrick's film, *2001: A Space Odyssey* (see fig. 7.1). If you rotate the scene so that the Earth and Moon are positioned in front of the Sun, you'll see them partially eclipse the disk of the Sun. Neat, huh?

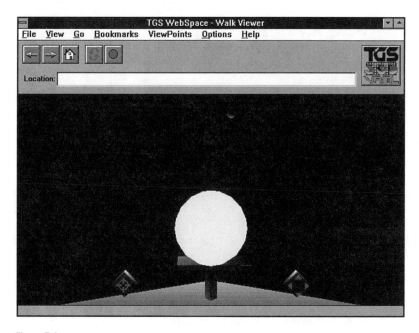

Figure 7.1

A shining Sun creates a crescent Earth and Moon.

The other VRML light nodes, **SpotLight** and **DirectionalLight**, operate in very much the same way that a **PointLight** does. **DirectionalLight** specifies an **orientation** that defines the direction of the most intense portion of the beam, and **SpotLight** provides for that and can also define an *umbra*—the circle of greatest intensity of the light. The **SpotLight** node would be useful to create the impression of track lighting in a VRML world, while a **DirectionalLight** node might be used to create automobile headlights.

Finally, let's make the Earth even shinier. It should be able to reflect all of the glorious sunlight now hitting it. We'll do this by modifying the Earth's **Material** node, adding the **specularColor** field to the node. Our file would look like the following:

```
]#VRML V1.0 ascii
# Example fourteen - The Earth gets a specular coloring to
➥reflect the sunlight

                [ ... ]

                # Color the Earth blue, and make it absorb
➥light
                # But also make it a reflective, like water
                DEF EARTH_MATERIAL Material {
                        diffuseColor 0 0 1 # Big blue marble
                        specularColor 0.9 0.9 0.9 # And a little
➥more shiny
                        shininess 0.9 # Water is rather shiny
                }

                [ ... ]
```

Now our universe looks like figure 7.2.

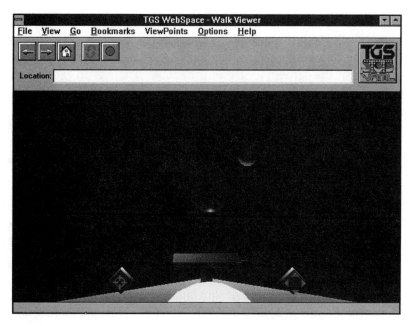

Figure 7.2
A shiny crescent Earth.

Smile for the Camera—Setting Up Viewpoints in VRML Worlds

So far, we've been gambling on using the built-in behaviors of
VRML browsers—which might not be the same from browser to
browser—to show us our worlds. To view a scene in VRML, you
must create a camera, which presents the scene as if the camera
were capturing it to film. If you don't create a camera, one will be
created automatically for you. A camera can be moved once it is
created. That's what happens as you move through a VRML
scene—you're actually moving the camera position. It's very
much like using a video camera to record an event—if part of
the event doesn't make it in front of the camera, it doesn't get
recorded.

When a camera is defined *anywhere* within the VRML scene graph, it becomes the camera for the entire scene. If more than one camera is defined, the first one in the scene graph will become the camera for the entire scene. (There is an exception to this rule, which we'll discuss later.)

There are two VRML nodes that define camera viewpoints—**OrthographicCamera** and **PerspectiveCamera**. The differences between the two cameras are related to perspective and how that perspective is represented with the camera. Since the Renaissance, artists have used the concept of perspective and vanishing point to add the illusion of depth to scenes that are drawn or onto a flat surface, perhaps a painting or a fresco. In a *perspective* projection, figures further in the background appear smaller and all move to the center, converging upon the "vanishing point," which is infinitely far away. As you pull away from a scene represented with perspective, all of the scene's objects move toward the center. In an *orthographic* projection, there is no perspective, and no vanishing point. Objects get smaller as you move away from them, but recede into the background without approaching the vanishing point.

Most often, 3D worlds are represented using perspective; it adds to the sense of depth within the scene and creates a more realistic experience. People using *Computer Aided Design* (CAD), however, generally use orthographic projections; their worlds are usually quite small—say a car or a refrigerator—and benefit more from a flat, orthographic projection than a warped perspective projection. All of the examples given here use the **PerspectiveCamera**. You can always experiment—replace the **PerspectiveCamera** in one of the examples with an **OrthographicCamera**; you'll see that there's a big difference.

We'll now add a **PerspectiveCamera** node to our solar system, and place it outside of the **Separator** node that defines the file. Here's how it looks:

```
#VRML V1.0 ascii
# Example fifteen - Define a camera for the world using the
➥PerspectiveCamera node
```

```
# This camera gives you a point of view reversed from the
➥default
# You see the whole body of the Earth and Moon reflecting
➥sunlight.
DEF StartingCamera PerspectiveCamera {
        position 2 10 73   # x, y, and z values of position
        orientation 0.25 0 0.63 0 # We'll twist the
➥orientation of the camera a bit
        focalDistance 200 # Set it to a nice big value.
}


# Here comes the Sun
# The Separator node groups everything within it together
DEF SOLAR_SYSTEM Separator {

        # The material will affect all subsequent nodes
        # The sun is yellow, isn't it? Additive color means
➥red + green = yellow
        # We're switching to emissive color because the Sun
➥gives off light.
        Material {
                emissiveColor 1 1 0            # The Sun emits
➥lots of yellow light
        }


        # We'll make the Sun shine here
        # A PointLight shines equally in all directions, like
➥the Sun does.
        DEF SUNLIGHT PointLight {
                intensity 1            # The Sun is way
➥bright
                color 1 1 0.9   # Sunlight is basically white,
➥though the Sun is yellow.
        }


        # The WWWAnchor node is a group node
        # This means that all objects within it are linked
➥with the anchor's URL
        # We want to link the Sun, so the Sun's Sphere node
➥goes inside of it.
```

```
        # Using the description field, we provide context for
➥the user
        # The DEF node attaches the name "SUN" to the
➥WWWAnchor group
        DEF SUN WWWAnchor {
                name "http://www.w3.org/" # The root URL of the
➥World Wide Web
                description "A link from the Sun to W3.ORG" #
➥Descriptive text

                # Inside the anchor, because WWWAnchor is a
➥group node
                Sphere {
                        radius 10                      # Big Sun
                }
        }

        # We place the Earth within its own Separator
        # To keep everything good and isolated
        Separator {

                # Let's move things out of the way here
                Transform {
                        translation 0 20 20
                }

                # Color the Earth blue, and make it absorb
➥light
                # But also make it a reflective, like water
                DEF EARTH_MATERIAL Material {
                        diffuseColor 0 0 1 # Big blue marble
                        specularColor 0.9 0.9 0.9 # And a little
➥more shiny

                        shininess 0.9 # Water is rather shiny
                }

                # The WWWAnchor node is a group node
                # This means that all objects within it are
➥linked with the anchor's URL
                # We want to link the Earth, so the Earth's
➥Sphere node goes inside of it.
```

```
                # Using the description field, we provide
➥context for the user
                # The DEF node attaches the name "Earth" to the
➥WWWAnchor node
                DEF EARTH WWWAnchor {
                        name "http://hyperreal.com/~mpesce/book/
➥examples/second.wrl"
                        description "A link to another world" #
➥Descriptive text

                        # Finally, create the earth
                        Sphere {
                                radius 2                # Little
➥Earth
                        }
                }

                # The Moon gets its own Separator
                # Because we really do keep everything separate
                Separator {

                        # The Moon is just outside the Earth
                        Transform {
                                translation 4 4 0
                        }

                        # Color the Moon gray, make it absorb
➥light
                        # It's a little shiny, but not much
                        Material {
                                diffuseColor 0.7 0.7 0.7
                                shininess 0.3
                        }

                        # The WWWAnchor node is a group node
                        # This means all objects within it are
➥linked with the anchor's URL
                        # We want to link so the Moon's Sphere
➥node goes inside of it.
                        # Using the description field, we
➥provide context for the user
```

```
                             # The DEF node attaches the name "Moon"
➥to the WWWAnchor node
                        DEF Moon WWWAnchor {
                                name
"http://www.cyborganic.com/People/paul/The_new_dogs/
➥pescewrd.au"
                                description "Sounds from a talk
➥about VRML"

                                # And now, create the Moon
                                Sphere {
                                        radius 1              # Tiny
➥Moon
                                }
                        }
                }
        }
}
```

And of course, with a new camera position, the scene looks different when first viewed (see fig. 7.3).

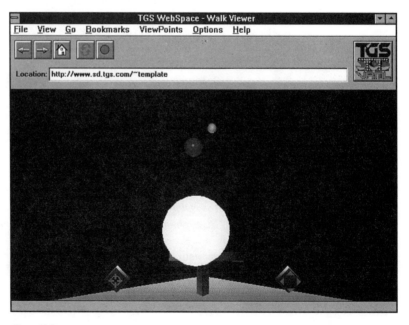

Figure 7.3

Another camera's view of our solar system.

Close-Up Shots—Using PerspectiveCamera Inside a VRML Group Node

In VRML, the group nodes act as insulators—they really do prevent nodes within the scene graph from knowing anything about other nodes in other groups within the scene graph. This can be a very powerful feature—it can insulate one part of a VRML document from other parts—but sometimes it can have strange side effects. If we put our camera into the **Separator** that defines the Earth-Moon system, we won't be able to see the Sun; it's not within the **PerspectiveCamera** group, so that camera doesn't know about it.

We can modify the example, as follows:

```
#VRML V1.0 ascii
# Example sixteen - We'll define a camera inside a group node
# Because it's inside the group node, we only see the Earth
➥and Moon


# Here comes the Sun
# The Separator node groups everything within it together
DEF SOLAR_SYSTEM Separator {

        # The material will affect all subsequent nodes
        # The sun is yellow, isn't it? Additive color means
➥red + green = yellow
        # We're switching to emissive color because the Sun
➥gives off light.
        Material {
                emissiveColor 1 1 0           # The Sun emits
➥lots of yellow light
        }


        # We'll make the Sun shine here
        # A PointLight shines equally in all directions, like
➥the Sun does.
        DEF SUNLIGHT PointLight {
                intensity 1            # The Sun is way
➥bright
```

```
                color 1 1 0.9   # Sunlight is basically white,
➥even though the Sun is yellow.
        }


        # The WWWAnchor node is a group node
        # This means that all objects within it are linked
➥with the anchor's URL
        # We want to link the Sun, so the Sun's Sphere node
➥goes inside of it.
        # Using the description field, we provide context for
➥the user
        # The DEF node attaches the name "SUN" to the
➥WWWAnchor group
        DEF SUN WWWAnchor {
                name "http://www.w3.org/" # The root URL of the
➥World Wide Web
                description "A link from the Sun to W3.ORG" #
➥Descriptive text


                # Inside the anchor, because WWWAnchor is a
➥group node
                Sphere {
                        radius 10                 # Big Sun
                }
        }


        # We place the Earth within its own Separator
        # To keep everything good and isolated
        Separator {


                # Let's move things out of the way here
                Transform {
                        translation 0 20 20
                }


                # From this point of view, all you can see is
➥the Earth and the Moon
                DEF EarthView PerspectiveCamera {
                        position 0 0 13
                        orientation 0 0 1 0
                        focalDistance 200
                }
```

```
                # Color the Earth blue, and make it absorb
➥light
                # But also make it a reflective, like water
                DEF EARTH_MATERIAL Material {
                        diffuseColor 0 0 1 # Big blue marble
                        specularColor 0.9 0.9 0.9 # And a little
➥more shiny
                        shininess 0.9 # Water is rather shiny
                }

                # The WWWAnchor node is a group node
                # This means that all objects within it are
➥linked with the anchor's URL
                # We want to link the Earth, so the Earth's
➥Sphere node goes inside of it.
                # Using the description field, we provide
➥context for the user
                # The DEF node attaches the name "Earth" to the
➥WWWAnchor node
                DEF EARTH WWWAnchor {
                        name "http://hyperreal.com/~mpesce/book/
➥examples/second.wrl"
                        description "A link to another world" #
➥Descriptive text

                        # Finally, create the earth
                        Sphere {
                                radius 2                # Little
➥Earth
                        }
                }

                # The Moon gets its own Separator
                # Because we really do keep everything separate
                Separator {

                # The Moon is just outside the Earth
                        Transform {
                                translation 4 4 0
                        }
```

```
                        # Color the Moon gray, make it absorb
➥light

                        # It's a little shiny, but not much
                        Material {
                                diffuseColor 0.7 0.7 0.7
                                shininess 0.3
                        }


                        # The WWWAnchor node is a group node
                        # This means all objects within it are
➥linked with the anchor's URL
                        # We want to link, the Moon's Sphere node
➥goes inside of it.
                        # Using the description field, we provide
➥context for the user
                        # The DEF node attaches the name "Moon"
➥to the WWWAnchor node
                        DEF Moon WWWAnchor {
                                name
"http://www.cyborganic.com/People/paul/The_new_dogs/
➥pescewrd.au"
                                description "Sounds from a talk
➥about VRML"


                                # And now, create the Moon
                                Sphere {
                                        radius 1               # Tiny
➥Moon
                                }
                        }
                }
        }
}
```

Now our VRML browser shows us just the Earth and the Moon (see fig. 7.4).

Figure 7.4

A camera within a Separator node sees only the Earth and Moon.

You could use this technique to hide portions of a VRML world that might be confusing to the user, or to present several different close-ups of the same data. For example, you might have a model of the human body, with many different parts; you could use this technique to create cameras that produced views of specific organs or groups of organs.

The Guided Tour—Defining Viewpoints in VRML and the Switch Node

There is one technique—developed for use in WebSpace, but rapidly being adopted by other VRML browsers—which enables you to set up a list of viewpoints—several named cameras— which are then made available for the user. This is *not* a VRML standard and may change in the future, but works well and provides a mechanism by which you can create a guided tour of a VRML world.

All of the viewpoints within a VRML world are grouped at the very beginning of the VRML world file. They are inside of a group node given the name "Cameras." This group node is a **Switch** node, which selects one node from an entire group based upon the index value of its one field, **whichChild**. The first node within the **Switch** group is considered to be node zero—programmers like to begin counting from zero rather than one like the rest of us—and the nodes count upward from that. For example, if you give a list of 20 cameras, and **whichChild** is set to 3, you would select the *fourth* camera in the list.

The **Switch** node is used like this:

```
    Switch {                        # Switch is a group node
            whichChild 2                # Third item in the
➡list is selected

            Sphere {
                    radius 10
            }

            Cube {
                    width 3
                    height 3
                    depth 3
            }

            Cone {
                    bottomRadius 5
                    height 3
            }
    }
```

As far as the VRML scene graph is concerned, the **Switch** node is the **Cone** node within it, because **whichChild** has a value of two; this means the third node within the **Switch** node is "picked."

In our solar system, we'll define two cameras—using the one from the previous example, and one a little bit different. The names we give the cameras will be installed in the "ViewPoints" menu of WebSpace—the user can select which camera to use, and can then move back and forth between them at will. By convention, we always define one of the cameras to be the "entry view," and the value of **whichChild** corresponds to the camera node whose definition is the entry view itself.

Our VRML file now looks like the following:

```
#VRML V1.0 ascii

# Example seventeen - Define a list of viewpoints
# We use the convention established by WebSpace
# It uses the Switch node and a bunch of named cameras


# The Switch node creates a group
# Only the node that corresponds to whichChild is visible to
➡VRML
# Entries start from zero and count upward
# WebSpace looks for a Switch node named Cameras
DEF Cameras Switch {
        whichChild 1          # Start with the second node in
➡group

        # This camera gives you a point of view reversed from
➡the default
        # You see the whole body of the Earth and Moon
➡reflecting sunlight.
        # This is group node zero in the Switch node
        DEF EarthCamera PerspectiveCamera {
                position 20 10 73              # x, y, and z
➡values of position
                orientation 0.25 0 0.63 0 # We'll twist the
➡orientation of the camera a bit
                focalDistance 200          # Set it to a nice
➡big value.
        }

        # This is the default
```

```
# It's group node one in the Switch node
# You can only see the Sun from here.
DEF EntryView PerspectiveCamera {
        position 0 0 60
        orientation 0 0 1 0
        focalDistance 200
    }
}

# Here comes the Sun
# The Separator node groups everything within it together
DEF SOLAR_SYSTEM Separator {

    # The material will affect all subsequent nodes
    # The sun is yellow, isn't it? Additive color means
➥red + green = yellow
    # We're switching to emissive color because the Sun
➥gives off light.
    Material {
            emissiveColor 1 1 0               # The Sun
➥emits lots of yellow light
    }

    # We'll make the Sun shine here
    # A PointLight shines equally in all directions, like
➥the Sun does.
    DEF SUNLIGHT PointLight {
            intensity 1          # The Sun is way bright
            color 1 1 0.9        # Sunlight is basically
➥white, even though the Sun is yellow.
    }

    # The WWWAnchor node is a group node
    # This means that all objects within it are linked
➥with the anchor's URL
    # We want to link the Sun, so the Sun's Sphere node
➥goes inside of it.
    # Using the description field, we provide context for
➥the user
    # The DEF node attaches the name "SUN" to the
➥WWWAnchor group
```

```
DEF SUN WWWAnchor {
        name "http://www.w3.org/" # The root URL of the
➥World Wide Web
        description "A link from the Sun to W3.ORG" #
➥Descriptive text

        # Inside the anchor, because WWWAnchor is a
➥group node
        Sphere {
                radius 10                # Big Sun
        }
    }

    # We place the Earth within its own Separator
    # To keep everything good and isolated
    Separator {

        # Let's move things out of the way here
        Transform {
                translation 0 20 20
        }

        # Color the Earth blue, and make it absorb
➥light
        # But also make it a reflective, like water
        DEF EARTH_MATERIAL Material {
                diffuseColor 0 0 1 # Big blue marble
                specularColor 0.9 0.9 0.9 # And a little
➥more shiny
                shininess 0.9 # Water is rather shiny
        }

        # The WWWAnchor node is a group node
        # This means that all objects within it are
➥linked with the anchor's URL
        # We want to link the Earth, so the Earth's
➥Sphere node goes inside of it.
        # Using the description field, we provide
➥context for the user
        # The DEF node attaches the name "Earth" to the
➥WWWAnchor node
```

```
                        DEF EARTH WWWAnchor {
                            name "http://hyperreal.com/~mpesce/book/
➥examples/second.wrl"
                            description "A link to another world" #
➥Descriptive text

                            # Finally, create the earth
                            Sphere {
                                    radius 2              # Little
➥Earth
                            }
                        }

                        # The Moon gets its own Separator
                        # Because we really do keep everything separate
                        Separator {

                            # The Moon is just outside the Earth
                            Transform {
                                    translation 4 4 0
                            }

                            # Color the Moon gray, make it absorb
➥light
                            # It's a little shiny, but not much
                            Material {
                                    diffuseColor 0.7 0.7 0.7
                                    shininess 0.3
                            }

                            # The WWWAnchor node is a group node
                            # This means all objects within it are
➥linked with the anchor's URL
                            # We want to link, so the Moon's Sphere
➥node goes inside of it.
                            # Using the description field, we
➥provide context for the user
                            # The DEF node attaches the name "Moon"
➥to the WWWAnchor node
                            DEF Moon WWWAnchor {
                                    name
➥"http://www.cyborganic.com/People/paul/The_new_dogs/
➥pescewrd.au"
```

```
                              description "Sounds from a talk
➥about VRML"


                              # And now, create the Moon
                              Sphere {
                                     radius 1              #
➥Tiny Moon
                              }
                       }
                }
          }
}
```

When we look at the ViewPoints menu in WebSpace, it looks like figure 7.5.

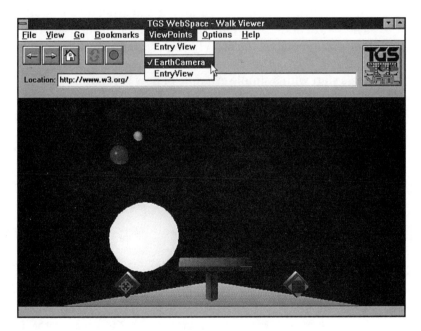

Figure 7.5

The solar system now has two predefined view points.

You can define as many view points as desired within a VRML document and, using the **Switch** node, make any one of them the entry point.

Come and Get It—The WWWInline Node

One of the nicer things about the World Wide Web is inclusion by reference. That means that you don't have to build something explicitly, but can reference parts from all over the world. For example, say a Web page is composed of text and several pictures. In HTML, you can say <img src="http://www.blah.org/image.gif">. When the page is brought into your Web browser, the Web browser goes and gets the image file at the same time it gets the page of text. This is called *image inlining*—the image is included by reference—and we have a similar construct inside of VRML. The VRML node, **WWWInline**, is a group node, and can replace any group node inside of a VRML document.

Let's start with a simple example of how **WWWInline** works. In this example, we replace the **Sphere** node that defines the Sun with a reference to our second VRML example, which also defines a **Sphere** node:

```
#VRML V1.0 ascii
# Example eighteen - We reference the Sun using WWWInline

# Here comes the Sun
# The Separator node groups everything within it together
DEF SOLAR_SYSTEM Separator {

        # The material will affect all subsequent nodes
        # The sun is yellow, isn't it? Additive color means
➡red + green = yellow
        # We're switching to emissive color because the Sun
➡gives off light.
        Material {
                emissiveColor 1 1 0               # The Sun
➡emits lots of yellow light
        }
```

```
        # We'll make the Sun shine here
        # A PointLight shines equally in all directions, like
➡the Sun does.
        DEF SUNLIGHT PointLight {
                intensity 1              # The Sun is way
➡bright
                color 1 1 0.9   # Sunlight is basically white,
➡even though the Sun is yellow.
        }


        # The WWWAnchor node is a group node
        # This means that all objects within it are linked
➡with the anchor's URL
        # We want to link the Sun, so the Sun's Sphere node
➡goes inside of it.
        # Using the description field, we provide context for
➡the user
        # The DEF node attaches the name "SUN" to the
➡WWWAnchor group
        DEF SUN WWWAnchor {
                name "http://www.w3.org/" # The root URL of the
➡World Wide Web
                description "A link from the Sun to W3.ORG" #
➡Descriptive text

                # Inside the anchor, because WWWAnchor is a
➡group node
                # We reference using the WWWInline node
                WWWInline {
                        name "http://hyperreal.com/~mpesce/book/
➡examples/second.wrl"
                        bboxSize 10 10 10  # As big as the Sun
➡is
                        bboxCenter 0 0 0            # From the
➡center of the sun
                }
        }

        [...]
```

The **WWWInline** node has three fields. The URL referenced by the **WWWInline** node is given in the name field, surrounded by quotes. The other two fields are very important. Because of the way the Web works, you don't get everything you ask for all at once. Sometimes you have to wait a very long time to get lengthy files. For this reason, the **WWWInline** node provides all the information needed to create a bounding box that occupies the space that will be occupied by the node(s) when they are retrieved across the Web. A *bounding box* is simply a wireframe cube—a type of three-dimensional placeholder that says, "there will soon be something here, but we don't have it yet...." This helps users work with large VRML environments (which can have many **WWWInline** nodes), before all files have been retrieved. The bounding box is defined in two fields: **bboxSize**, which enables you to set the width, height, and depth of the box; and **bboxCenter**, which enables you to set the x, y, and z coordinates of the center of the bounding box. Used together, these fields can provide a visitor to a VRML world with useful information about that world, before it's fully loaded.

While our example file is loading, it looks like figure 7.6.

We've defined the bounding box to be roughly the same size as our **Sphere** node, so it looks as if the Sun "blips" into the scene once it's been loaded.

Along with **WWWAnchor** and **LOD**, which we'll cover next, **WWWInline** is one of the most powerful features of VRML. With it, you can construct an entire world with objects "on loan" from other VRML sites, all across the Web. You can use objects that are in "repositories"—locations on the Web with storehouses of pre-built VRML objects—and so create your own world from prebuilt parts. Using **WWWInline** is a lot like going to the hardware store—you'll find all of the nails, screws, and wood to make anything you like, but it's your creative spark that turns them into something original.

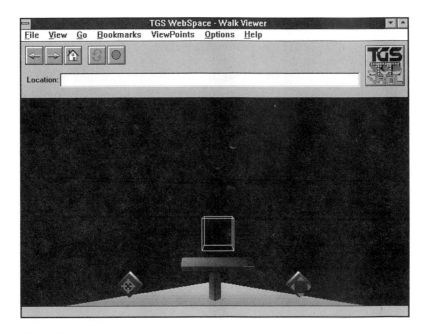

Figure 7.6

The bounding box appears while an inline object is loading.

The Changeling—Understanding Level-of-Detail and the LOD Node

Have you ever lost your car in a big parking lot? Or thought you recognized someone from a great distance and, as they approached, realized it was someone else? Both of these situations—quite common in real life—have something in common with VRML. In these cases, as with VRML, we understand a visible object as we approach it. In the real world, we say that we "resolve" an object from poor detail into fine detail.

In VRML, a special node, called **LOD** (short for *level-of-detail*) gives you that kind of capability. Using it, you can switch between different representations of the same node based upon how far away you are from the node. The **LOD** node has one field, **range**, which is an array of distance values (an *array* in VRML is a list of values separated by commas and enclosed in brackets). The **LOD** node is a group node; within it are a number of other nodes. This number is determined by the number of values in the **range** field—it's always that number of values, *plus one*. If you have the wrong number of nodes in an **LOD** node, you'll probably confuse the VRML browser into crashing.

It's best to illustrate how all of this works with a simple example. In the following, we use **LOD** to change our view of an object as we move toward it or away from it:

```
#VRML V1.0 ascii

# Example nineteen - Using the level-of-detail (LOD) node
# Doesn't really do anything practical, but demonstrates LOD

DEF LOD_EXAMPLE Separator {

        # This is a simple example
        # The LOD node groups everything within it together
        DEF LOD_NODE LOD  {
                range [ 50,100 ]

                # If closer than 50 units, the object is a
➥yellow Sphere
                DEF CloseIn Separator {

                        # The object is yellow, isn't it?
                        Material {
                                emissiveColor 1 1 0
➥# MFColor
                        }
                        Sphere {
                                radius 10
➥# Big Sphere
                        }
                }
```

```
                   # If closer than 100 units, but greater than
➡50, a magenta Cone
                   DEF Medium Separator {

                          # The object is magenta, isn't it?
                          Material {
                                 emissiveColor 1 0 1
➡# MFColor
                          }
                          Cone {
                                 bottomRadius 10               #
➡Conical Object

                                 height 10
                          }
                   }


                   # If further away than 100 units, a white Cube
                   DEF FarAway Separator {

                          # The object is white, isn't it?
                          Material {
                                 emissiveColor 1 1 1
➡# MFColor
                          }
                          Cube {
                                 width 10                 # Cube
➡Object

                                 height 10
                                 depth 10
                          }
                   }
            }
      }
}
```

The LOD node's **range** field has two values within it—50 and 100. (All values are specified in VRML units, which, unless stated otherwise, are a meter per unit.) If we're closer to the object than 50 units, the first node within the **LOD** group is active, and it looks like figure 7.7.

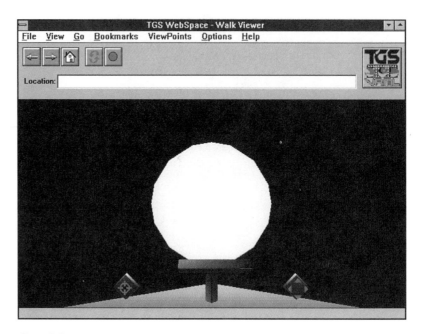

Figure 7.7

At close range, we see a sphere...

If we're between 50 and 100 units away, the second node with the **LOD** group is active, and the object looks like figure 7.8.

Finally, if we're farther away than 100 units—the highest value given in the **range** field of the **LOD** node—the final node in the **LOD** group is active (see fig. 7.9).

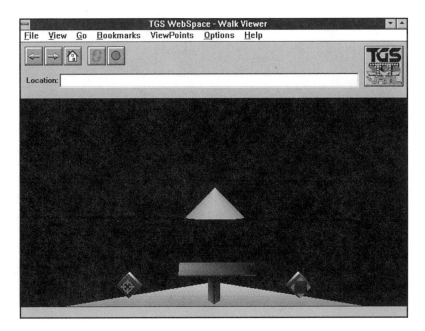

Figure 7.8
Farther away, we see a cone...

While this might seem like a trivial example of the **LOD** node, it doesn't really get much more sophisticated than this. In any world, you might have several representations of a single object—using **WWWInline** makes this very easy. With a well-constructed **LOD** node, you can switch between them.

LOD can also be used by the VRML browser to provide "hints" on how to improve the performance of a browser while examining a rich VRML world. There's a lot more about that subject in Chapter 10, "VRML Optimization and Publishing Issues."

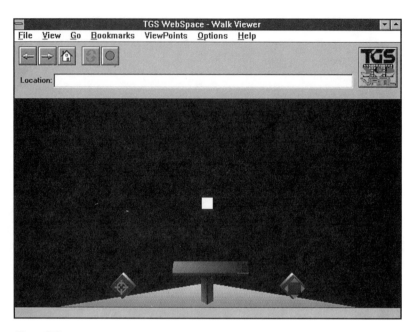

Figure 7.9
Far away, we see a cube.

This concludes our intermediate lesson. You've passed through apprentice and journeyman stages, and are now ready to move on into VRML mastery.

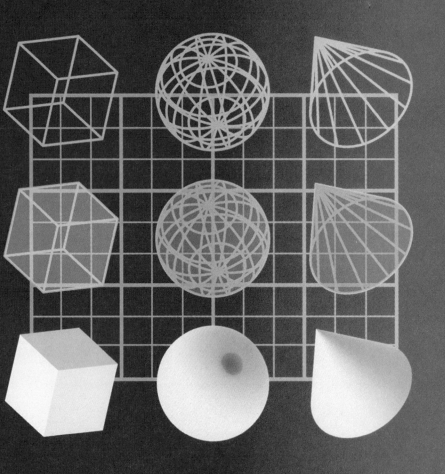

Chapter 8

Advanced VRML and Server Scripts

We've come to our last section of the primer, where you'll learn the advanced features of VRML—ones you may need to make a simple environment appear rich and appealing. Many of these advanced features are implemented within VRML modeling tools, but it's useful to have a thorough understanding of how these features work. You never know when you'll want to hand-edit a VRML file to give it a unique quality.

In this section, we'll discuss texture mapping—both how to create your own texture maps by hand and how to use graphic images as maps. Moving on from there, we'll detail how to create complex shapes, everything from floor lamps to sculptures in cyberspace. We'll also show how to employ one of the special features of VRML to create multiple copies of a single object. Finally, tying all our lessons together, we'll construct a real *orrey*—a heliocentric clock that uses server-side scripts to provide a 3D snapshot of the solar system, as it is, right now.

All of the advanced material we'll cover here is developed directly from the solar system example we've been working on in the two previous chapters; if you've skipped ahead to this point, you may want to take a peek back and review the example as we've built it up.

The Dark Side of the Moon and the Texture2 Node

Texture maps are images applied to the surfaces of polygons. It's analogous to wallpapering a wall in that the texture map is "wrapped" onto the polygons and warps to the surfaces upon which it's placed. Texture maps have many different uses—from creating cyberspace billboards to detailing the surfaces of buildings in a city model to placing human facial features on an *avatar*, a representation of yourself in cyberspace.

Our solar system looks good, but it lacks character. The Sun, Earth, and Moon are all a single color. They have none of the uniqueness that marks them as our heavenly bodies. Using texture maps, we can set out to change that. VRML defines the **Texture2** node to provide a mechanism by which texture maps can be applied to any visible VRML object.

A texture map is an image, a picture. The **Texture2** node has an **image** field that defines the picture associated with the texture map. This field is specified in *SFImage* format. The SFImage format defines an image or picture to be used in a VRML world. This format is a little bit complicated, as VRML formats go—most of them are absolutely straightforward—but that's because SFImage uses text to describe the contents of a picture. A text description of the color values of a picture doesn't give you a good mental image of the picture, so a little imagination is required as we discuss how the **image** field works.

The SFImage definition enables you to create a two-dimensional image. This image has a width and a height, defines itself as black and white or color, then explicitly provides the value at every point within the image. The first values in the SFImage definition are the width and height of the image, specified as integers.

Following that, SFImage must define the type of image—that is, black and white, black and white with transparency, color, or color with transparency. These types are defined by specifying the number of bytes of data associated with each pixel. Black and white data is one byte per pixel, where 0 is black and 255 is white; black and white with transparency is two bytes per pixel, where 0 is opaque and 255 is transparent. Color texture maps use three bytes per pixel—one byte each for red, green, and blue—where 255 is a fully saturated color and 0 is completely unsaturated. Finally, color with transparency is four bytes per pixel—three specifying the RGB intensity and one byte specifying transparency—and as with black and white, 0 is opaque and 255 is transparent.

Some examples will help. Here's the definition of a **Texture2** node that has a 2-pixel wide by 3-pixel high black and white image, without transparency:

```
Texture2 {
     image 2 3 1     # 2 pixels wide, 3 pixels high,
➥black & white
        [ ...etc... ]
     }
```

Here's an example of a color image, 300×200 pixels, without transparency:

```
Texture2 {
     image 300 200 3    # 300 pixels wide, 200 pixels
➥high, RGB color
        [ ...etc... ]
     }
```

And, finally, here's a 144-pixel wide by 36-pixel high black and white image, with transparency:

```
Texture2 {
     image 144 36 2    # 144 pixels wide, 36 pixels
➥high, b/w with transparency
        [ ...etc... ]
     }
```

Immediately following the image definition are the values for each pixel in the image. These values are given from the lower left hand corner of the image through the upper right hand corner of the image, one row at a time. This means that the lowest row is specified first, then the row above it, and the row above it, etc., until the top row is specified. If we complete the first example, it will look like this:

```
Texture2 {
       image 2 3 1     # 2 pixels wide, 3 pixels high,
➥black & white
            255 128        # Bottom row, 2 pixels wide
            128 0          # Middle row, 2 pixels wide
            0 128          # Top row, 2 pixels wide
    }
```

A 2×3 image contains six pixels, and the values for each of these black and white pixels are specified within the image field, immediately following the image definition. Color texture maps work along very much the same lines, but the SFImage field requires that the 3-byte values for color texture maps be concatenated into a single number. This is best done with *hexadecimal* notation—used quite a bit by computer programmers and by almost no one else—which takes all of the bytes and crams them together into a single number. If the preceding example was converted to a full color image, it might look like this:

```
Texture2 {
       image 2 3 3     # 2 pixels wide, 3 pixels high, RGB
➥color
       0xffffff 0x808080          # Bottom row, 2 pixels
➥wide
       0x808080 0x000000          # Middle row, 2 pixels
➥wide
       0x000000 0x808080          # Top row, 2 pixels wide
    }
```

Despite the change in the definition, it looks exactly the same as the preceding example.

To give our Moon a mottled gray, black, and white surface—like the real Moon—we'd specify a simple texture map. We'll use a color texture map, a rather small one, to keep the example simple:

```
#VRML V1.0 ascii
# Example twenty - We texture map the Moon manually

# Here comes the Sun
# The Separator node groups everything within it together
DEF SOLAR_SYSTEM Separator {

    # The material will affect all subsequent nodes
    # The sun is yellow, isn't it?  Additive color means red
➥+ green = yellow
    # We're switching to emissive color because the Sun
➥gives off light.
    Material {
        emissiveColor 1 1 0        # The Sun emits lots of
➥yellow light
    }

    # We'll make the Sun shine here
    # A PointLight shines equally in all directions, like
➥the Sun does.
    DEF SUNLIGHT PointLight {
        intensity 1        # The Sun is way bright
        color 1 1 0.9   # Sunlight is basically white, even
➥though the Sun is yellow.
    }

    # The WWWAnchor node is a group node
    # This means that all objects within it are linked with
➥the anchor's URL
    # We want to link the Sun, so the Sun's Sphere node goes
➥inside of it.
    # Using the description field, we provide context for
➥the user
    # The DEF node attaches the name "SUN" to the WWWAnchor
➥group
    DEF SUN WWWAnchor {
```

```
            name "http://www.w3.org/" # The root URL of the
➥World Wide Web
            description "A link from the Sun to W3.ORG" #
➥Descriptive text

            Sphere {
                radius 10
            }
        }

        # We place the Earth within its own Separator
        # To keep everything good and isolated
        Separator {

            # Let's move things out of the way here
            Transform {
                translation 0 20 20
            }

            # Color the Earth blue, and make it absorb light
            # But also make it a reflective, like water
            DEF EARTH_MATERIAL Material {
                diffuseColor 0 0 1 # Big blue marble
                specularColor 0.9 0.9 0.9 # And a little more
➥shiny

                shininess 0.9 # Water is rather shiny
            }

            # The WWWAnchor node is a group node
            # This means that all objects within it are linked
➥with the anchor's URL
            # We want to link the Earth, so the Earth's Sphere
➥node goes inside of it.
            # Using the description field, we provide context
➥for the user
            # The DEF node attaches the name "Earth" to the
➥WWWAnchor node
            DEF EARTH WWWAnchor {
                name "http://hyperreal.com/~mpesce/book/
➥examples/second.wrl"
```

```
            description "A link to another world" #
➥Descriptive text

            # Finally, create the Earth
            Sphere {
                radius 2      # Little Earth
            }
        }

        # The Moon gets its own Separator
        # Because we really do keep everything separate
        Separator {

            # The Moon is just outside the Earth
            Transform {
                translation 4 4 0
            }

            # Color the Moon gray, make it absorb light
            # It's a little shiny, but not much
            Material {
                diffuseColor 0.7 0.7 0.7
                shininess 0.3
            }

            # This is a sample texture map
            # Just to show how it all works.
            # Using it, you'll get a 2 x 4 image
            # It's in black/gray/white to make it look
➥like a faux lunar surface
            Texture2 {
                # Define a 4 x 4 pixel texture map using
➥RGB values

                image 4 4 3

                # Here's the map, from lower left to
➥upper right
                0xC0C0C0 0x808080 0xFFFFFF 0x404040 #
➥Bottom row
                0x808080 0x202020 0x808080 0xC0C0C0 #
➥Lower Middle Row
```

```
                          0x202020 0x808080 0xFFFFFF 0x808080 #
➥Upper Middle Row
                          0x808080 0xC0C0C0 0x808080 0x202020 #
➥Upper Row
                  }

                  # The WWWAnchor node is a group node
                  # This means that all objects within it are
➥linked with the anchor's URL
                  # We want to link the Moon, so the Moon's
➥Sphere node goes inside of it.
                  # Using the description field, we provide
➥context for the user
                  # The DEF node attaches the name "Moon" to the
➥WWWAnchor node
                  DEF Moon WWWAnchor {
                          name "http://www.cyborganic.com/People/
➥paul/The_new_dogs/pescewrd.au"
                          description "Sounds from a talk about
➥VRML"

                  # And now, create the Moon
                  Sphere {
                          radius 1      # Tiny Moon
                  }
              }
          }
      }
}
```

If we pop this VRML document into a browser and take a close-up look at the Moon, we'll see that it has acquired a rather mottled appearance, like the real Moon (see fig. 8.1).

You can modify the **image** field within the Moon's **Texture2** node to give it any surface you like.

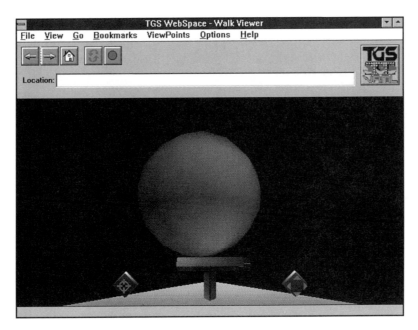

Figure 8.1
The lunar surface is a texture map.

Giving the Earth a Surface

Hand-crafting texture maps is a difficult process, unless the images are quite simple. A more complex representation is well beyond the ability of most people to compose—unless you happen to excel in creating mosaics! The **Texture2** node has another field, **filename**, which can be used to specify the name of an image file to be read in and used as the texture map. If the **filename** field is used within a **Texture2** node, the **image** field should not be used; otherwise, the browser would have to determine which texture map—the one given by the **filename** or the one specified in the **image**—should be used. The browser probably won't make the right decision.

We've got a texture map of the Earth's surface in a CD-ROM file named WORLDMAP.RGB. To wrap that texture map onto our Earth, our VRML file will look like this:

```
#VRML V1.0 ascii
# Example twenty-one - We texture map the Earth with its
➥surface

# Here comes the Sun
# The Separator node groups everything within it together
DEF SOLAR_SYSTEM Separator {

        # The material will affect all subsequent nodes
        # The sun is yellow, isn't it?  Additive color means red
➥+ green = yellow
        # We're switching to emissive color because the Sun
➥gives off light.
        Material {
                emissiveColor 1 1 0    # The Sun emits lots of
➥yellow light
        }

        # We'll make the Sun shine here
        # A PointLight shines equally in all directions, like
➥the Sun does.
        DEF SUNLIGHT PointLight {
                intensity 1        # The Sun is way bright
                color 1 1 0.9   # Sunlight is basically white, even
➥though the Sun is yellow.
        }

        # The WWWAnchor node is a group node
        # This means that all objects within it are linked with
➥the anchor's URL
        # We want to link the Sun, so the Sun's Sphere node goes
➥inside of it.
        # Using the description field, we provide context for
➥the user
        # The DEF node attaches the name "SUN" to the WWWAnchor
➥group
        DEF SUN WWWAnchor {
```

```
        name "http://www.w3.org/" # The root URL of the
➥World Wide Web
        description "A link from the Sun to W3.ORG" #
➥Descriptive text

        Sphere {
            radius 10
        }
    }

    # We place the Earth within its own Separator
    # To keep everything good and isolated
    Separator {

        # Let's move things out of the way here
        Transform {
            translation 0 20 20
        }

        # Color the Earth blue, and make it absorb light
        # But also make it a reflective, like water
        DEF EARTH_MATERIAL Material {
            diffuseColor 0 0 1 # Big blue marble
            specularColor 0.9 0.9 0.9 # And a little more
➥shiny

            shininess 0.9 # Water is rather shiny
        }

        # Here's the definition for the Earth's texture map
        # As you can see, the definition is very straight-
➥forward
        # Just a file name given in the filename field
        Texture2 {
            filename "WORLDMAP.RGB"     # There it is.
        }

        # The WWWAnchor node is a group node
        # This means that all objects within it are linked
➥with the anchor's URL
        # We want to link the Earth, so the Earth's Sphere
➥node goes inside of it.
```

```
          # Using the description field, we provide context
➥for the user
          # The DEF node attaches the name "Earth" to the
➥WWWAnchor node
          DEF EARTH WWWAnchor {
              name "http://hyperreal.com/~mpesce/book/
➥examples/second.wrl"
              description "A link to another world" #
➥Descriptive text

              # Finally, create the Earth
              Sphere {
                  radius 2     # Little Earth
              }
          }

          # The Moon gets its own Separator
          # Because we really do keep everything separate
          Separator {

              # The Moon is just outside the Earth
              Transform {
                  translation 4 4 0
              }

              # Color the Moon gray, make it absorb light
              # It's a little shiny, but not much
              Material {
                  diffuseColor 0.7 0.7 0.7
                  shininess 0.3
              }

              # This is a sample texture map
              # Just to show how it all works.
              # Using it, you'll get a 2 x 4 image
              # It's in black/gray/white to make it look
➥like a faux lunar surface
              Texture2 {
                  # Define a 4 x 4 pixel texture map using
➥RGB values
```

```
                              image 4 4 3

                              # Here's the map, from lower left to
➥upper right
                              0xC0C0C0 0x808080 0xFFFFFF 0x404040 #
➥Bottom row
                              0x808080 0x202020 0x808080 0xC0C0C0 #
➥Lower Middle Row
                              0x202020 0x808080 0xFFFFFF 0x808080 #
➥Upper Middle Row
                              0x808080 0xC0C0C0 0x808080 0x202020 #
➥Upper Row
                  }

                  # The WWWAnchor node is a group node
                  # This means that all objects within it are
➥linked with the anchor's URL
                  # We want to link the Moon, so the Moon's
➥Sphere node goes inside of it.
                  # Using the description field, we provide
➥context for the user
                  # The DEF node attaches the name "Moon" to the
➥WWWAnchor node
                  DEF Moon WWWAnchor {
                          name "http://www.cyborganic.com/People/
➥paul/The_new_dogs/pescewrd.au"
                          description "Sounds from a talk about
➥VRML"

                          # And now, create the Moon
                          Sphere {
                              radius 1     # Tiny Moon
                          }
                      }
                  }
              }
      }
```

If we take a look at Earth inside our VRML browser, we'll find we've got something much closer to the real thing (see fig. 8.2).

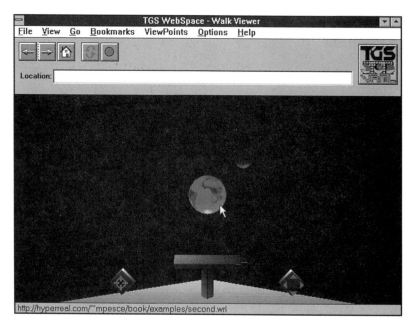

Figure 8.2

The Earth looks quite real with its texture map.

Our example has a problem—it only works if WORLDMAP.RGB is in the same directory as the example file, on a local machine. That's not Web friendly; no one else will be able to share this view of the Earth with you. Fortunately, the **filename** field can also take a URL, so you can reference a texture map image anywhere inside the Web. If we modify our example just a little bit, we see the following:

```
#VRML V1.0 ascii
# Example twenty-two - We texture map the Earth with its
surface, using a URL

        [ ...etc... ]

    # We place the Earth within its own Separator
```

```
# To keep everything good and isolated
Separator {

    # Let's move things out of the way here
    Transform {
        translation 0 20 20
    }

    # Color the Earth blue, and make it absorb light
    # But also make it a reflective, like water
    DEF EARTH_MATERIAL Material {
        diffuseColor 0 0 1 # Big blue marble
        specularColor 0.9 0.9 0.9 # And a little more
➡shiny
        shininess 0.9 # Water is rather shiny
    }

    # Here's where we specify the texture map
    # Instead of a local RGB file, we access one across
➡the Web
    Texture2 {
        filename "http://hyperreal.com/~mpesce/
➡WORLDMAP.RGB"
    }

    # The WWWAnchor node is a group node
    # This means that all objects within it are linked
➡with the anchor's URL
    # We want to link the Earth, so the Earth's Sphere
➡node goes inside of it.
    # Using the description field, we provide context
➡for the user
    # The DEF node attaches the name "Earth" to the
➡WWWAnchor node
    DEF EARTH WWWAnchor {
        name "http://hyperreal.com/~mpesce/book/
➡examples/second.wrl"
        description "A link to another world" #
➡Descriptive text

        # Finally, create the Earth
        Sphere {
```

```
                           radius 2      # Little Earth
                    }
               }
          [ ...etc... ]
```

This texture map is accessible to anyone across the Web and will produce exactly the same results as the previous example, which used a local file name.

Before we move on to a discussion of complex shapes in VRML, it's important to note one of the holes in the VRML specification, large enough to drive a truck through. There is *no* standard texture map image file format. The WORLDMAP.RGB file is in Silicon Graphics' *RGB* format—a proprietary format inherited from Open Inventor. An RGB format texture map will be read in and wrapped properly in WebSpace, but it won't work in WorldView or QMosaic. WorldView will read in GIF and JPEG images for texture maps, but won't read in RGB format. And so forth.

Although the VRML community will settle on a basic set of image formats that must be supported within a VRML browser (part of the VRML 1.*x* specification process), you might find the texture maps that work well in one VRML browser don't work at all in another. The solution? When in doubt, use the **image** field of the **Texture2** node, rather than the filename field.

Connect the Dots—Shapes Using Coordinate3 and IndexedFaceSet Nodes

So far, we've been using VRML nodes that provide predefined shapes. There are three predefined shape nodes in VRML: **Sphere**, **Cone**, and **Cube**. While a great many interesting scenes can be created with various combinations and placements of these nodes, the real world is constructed from an infinite variety of forms. These basic solids aren't enough to create a compelling cyberspace.

VRML has the capacity to define arbitrary shapes, and it defines several nodes that must be used in concert to create these shapes. All shapes in VRML are composed of polygons—most often, triangular polygons—and any arbitrary shape can be specified as a set of polygons. These polygons are themselves specified as sets of points in space, grouped together to create a surface. To specify a set of points, VRML provides the **Coordinate3** node, which can define an arbitrary array of points, sometimes called a *point cloud.*

Once a set of points has been defined, the **IndexedFaceSet** node is used to create polygons from these points. These two nodes are always used together: the **Coordinate3** node gives a list (called an *array*) of points, and the **IndexedFaceSet** node "connects the dots" between the points to create polygons from them.

The array of points is specified within the point field of the **Coordinate3** node. Each point is given by specifying the x, y, and z position of the point, followed by a comma, then the value for the next point, and so on, until all the points have been specified. **IndexedFaceSet** references this array of points—where the first point is defined as array entry zero—as it specifies the connection between these points to create polygons.

This will become clearer if we illustrate with an example, as follows:

```
#VRML V1.0 ascii
# Example twenty-three - A cube defined with Coordinate3 and
IndexedFaceSet

    # Just like the name says, a green cube.
    DEF Cube_Green Separator {

        # It's a nice bright green cube
        Material {
            diffuseColor 0.000000 1.000000 0.000000
            ambientColor 0.000000 0.100000 0.000000
        }
```

```
# The Coordinate3 node gives a list of points.
# A cube has eight points.
# Here they are.
Coordinate3 {
    point [
            1.0 -1.0  1.0, # Point Zero
            1.0 -1.0 -1.0, # Point One
           -1.0 -1.0 -1.0, # Point Two
           -1.0 -1.0  1.0, # Point Three
            1.0  1.0 -1.0, # Point Four
           -1.0  1.0 -1.0, # Point Five
           -1.0  1.0  1.0, # Point Six
            1.0  1.0  1.0. # Point Seven
    ]
}


# Each line defines a triangular polygon,
# By referencing points in the Coordinate3 node.
# A cube has six faces.
# But each face has two triangular polygons
# So here's twelve polygons that define the cube.
# The definition of each polygon ends with -1.
IndexedFaceSet {
    coordIndex [
            2, 1, 0, -1, # Polygon composed of Point
➥2, Point 1, Point 0
            2, 0, 3, -1, # Polygon composed of Point
➥2, Point 0, Point 3
            4, 1, 2, -1, # Polygon composed of Point
➥4, Point 1, Point 2
            4, 2, 5, -1, # etc.
            5, 2, 3, -1,
            5, 3, 6, -1,
            6, 3, 0, -1,
            6, 0, 7, -1,
            4, 5, 6, -1,
            4, 6, 7, -1,
            1, 4, 7, -1,
            1, 7, 0, -1
    ]
  }
}
```

Starting with a cube—a very simple shape, admittedly—we can see how a shape is composed of points defined in a **Coordinate3** node and connected together using **IndexedFaceSet**. The VRML world looks like a cube, just as you'd suspect (see fig. 8.3).

Figure 8.3

A cube composed from Coordinate3 and IndexedFaceSet nodes.

Although a cube has only six sides, twelve polygon faces are defined in the **IndexedFaceSet** node. That's because polygons are most often composed of triangles—these being the easiest shapes for a computer to render quickly—and each side of the cube, which is a square polygon, is broken down into two triangular polygons. So actually, the cube looks like figure 8.4.

Nonetheless, the eight points of the cube are used, whether it's composed of square polygons or triangular polygons. The **Coordinate3** and **IndexedFaceSet** nodes together define something known as a *polygon mesh* or *polymesh*; that is, the surface of a complex object. The **Sphere**, **Cube**, and **Cone** nodes are all converted to polymeshes by the VRML browser before they are rendered to the display—they're just a shorthand for specifying certain types of polymeshes.

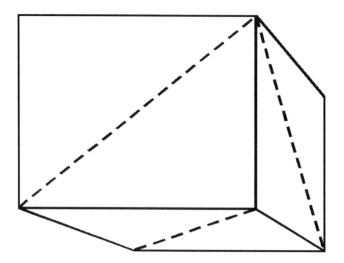

Figure 8.4

A cube with faces broken into triangular polygons.

The following is a more complex polymesh, which is what a **Sphere** node really looks like, under the hood:

```
#VRML V1.0 ascii
# Example twenty-four - A complex shape using Coordinate3 and
➥IndexedFaceSet nodes

# I cheated and used the WCVT2POV.EXE tool to produce the
➥VRML file.
# This started off as a DXF model of a sphere.

# Being good little VRML do-bees, we give the sphere a name.
DEF Sphere_White Separator {

        # We give it a simple material to make it visible
        Material {
```

```
            diffuseColor 1.000000 1.000000 1.000000
            ambientColor 0.100000 0.100000 0.100000
       }

       # The Coordinate3 node defines a set of points in
➡space
       # Which are used later in the IndexedFaceSet node
       # Each row specifies the X Y Z position of a point.
       Coordinate3 {
            point [      # Begins the list of points
                -0.382683  0.000000  0.923880, # Point
➡Zero
                -0.353553  0.146447  0.923880, # Point
➡One
                 0.000000  0.000000  1.000000, # Point
➡Two
                -0.270598  0.270598  0.923880, # etc...
                -0.146447  0.353553  0.923880,
                 0.000000  0.382683  0.923880,
                 0.146447  0.353553  0.923880,
                 0.270598  0.270598  0.923880,
                 0.353553  0.146447  0.923880,
                 0.382683  0.000000  0.923880,
                 0.353553 -0.146447  0.923880,
                 0.270598 -0.270598  0.923880,
                 0.146447 -0.353553  0.923880,
                 0.000000 -0.382683  0.923880,
                -0.146447 -0.353553  0.923880,
                -0.270598 -0.270598  0.923880,
                -0.353553 -0.146447  0.923880,
                -0.653282  0.270598  0.707107,
                -0.707107  0.000000  0.707107,
                -0.500000  0.500000  0.707107,
                -0.270598  0.653282  0.707107,
                 0.000000  0.707107  0.707107,
                 0.270598  0.653282  0.707107,
                 0.500000  0.500000  0.707107,
                 0.653282  0.270598  0.707107,
                 0.707107  0.000000  0.707107,
                 0.653282 -0.270598  0.707107,
```

```
 0.500000 -0.500000  0.707107,
 0.270598 -0.653282  0.707107,
 0.000000 -0.707107  0.707107,
-0.270598 -0.653282  0.707107,
-0.500000 -0.500000  0.707107,
-0.653282 -0.270598  0.707107,
-0.853553  0.353553  0.382683,
-0.923880  0.000000  0.382683,
-0.653282  0.653282  0.382683,
-0.353553  0.853553  0.382683,
 0.000000  0.923880  0.382683,
 0.353553  0.853553  0.382683,
 0.653282  0.653282  0.382683,
 0.853553  0.353553  0.382683,
 0.923880  0.000000  0.382683,
 0.853553 -0.353553  0.382683,
 0.653282 -0.653282  0.382683,
 0.353553 -0.853553  0.382683,
 0.000000 -0.923880  0.382683,
-0.353553 -0.853553  0.382683,
-0.653282 -0.653282  0.382683,
-0.853553 -0.353553  0.382683,
-0.923880  0.382683  0.000000,
-1.000000  0.000000  0.000000,
-0.707107  0.707107  0.000000,
-0.382683  0.923880  0.000000,
 0.000000  1.000000  0.000000,
 0.382683  0.923880  0.000000,
 0.707107  0.707107  0.000000,
 0.923880  0.382683  0.000000,
 1.000000  0.000000  0.000000,
 0.923880 -0.382683  0.000000,
 0.707107 -0.707107  0.000000,
 0.382683 -0.923880  0.000000,
 0.000000 -1.000000  0.000000,
-0.382683 -0.923880  0.000000,
-0.707107 -0.707107  0.000000,
-0.923880 -0.382683  0.000000,
-0.853553  0.353553 -0.382683,
-0.923880  0.000000 -0.382683,
-0.653282  0.653282 -0.382683,
```

```
-0.353553   0.853553  -0.382683,
 0.000000   0.923880  -0.382683,
 0.353553   0.853553  -0.382683,
 0.653282   0.653282  -0.382683,
 0.853553   0.353553  -0.382683,
 0.923880   0.000000  -0.382683,
 0.853553  -0.353553  -0.382683,
 0.653282  -0.653282  -0.382683,
 0.353553  -0.853553  -0.382683,
 0.000000  -0.923880  -0.382683,
-0.353553  -0.853553  -0.382683,
-0.653282  -0.653282  -0.382683,
-0.853553  -0.353553  -0.382683,
-0.653281   0.270598  -0.707107,
-0.707107   0.000000  -0.707107,
-0.500000   0.500000  -0.707107,
-0.270598   0.653281  -0.707107,
 0.000000   0.707107  -0.707107,
 0.270598   0.653281  -0.707107,
 0.500000   0.500000  -0.707107,
 0.653281   0.270598  -0.707107,
 0.707107   0.000000  -0.707107,
 0.653281  -0.270598  -0.707107,
 0.500000  -0.500000  -0.707107,
 0.270598  -0.653281  -0.707107,
 0.000000  -0.707107  -0.707107,
-0.270598  -0.653281  -0.707107,
-0.500000  -0.500000  -0.707107,
-0.653281  -0.270598  -0.707107,
-0.353553   0.146447  -0.923880,
-0.382683   0.000000  -0.923880,
-0.270598   0.270598  -0.923880,
-0.146447   0.353553  -0.923880,
 0.000000   0.382683  -0.923880,
 0.146447   0.353553  -0.923880,
 0.270598   0.270598  -0.923880,
 0.353553   0.146447  -0.923880,
 0.382683   0.000000  -0.923880,
 0.353553  -0.146447  -0.923880,
 0.270598  -0.270598  -0.923880,
 0.146447  -0.353553  -0.923880,
```

```
                     0.000000 -0.382683 -0.923880,
                    -0.146447 -0.353553 -0.923880,
                    -0.270598 -0.270598 -0.923880,
                    -0.353553 -0.146447 -0.923880,
                     0.000000  0.000000 -1.000000
                ]
        }


        # The IndexedFaceSet node takes the array of points
➥defined
        # In the Coordinate3 node, and forms triangular
➥polygon faces
        # Each polygon ends with a -1
        IndexedFaceSet {
                coordIndex [ # Begins the list of polygon
➥faces
                     2,   1,   0,   -1,
                     2,   3,   1,   -1,
                     2,   4,   3,   -1,
                     2,   5,   4,   -1,
                     2,   6,   5,   -1,
                     2,   7,   6,   -1,
                     2,   8 ,  7,   -1,
                     2,   9,   8,   -1,
                     2,   10,  9,   -1,
                     2,   11,  10,  -1,
                     2,   12,  11,  -1,
                     2,   13,  12,  -1,
                     2,   14,  13,  -1,
                     2,   15,  14,  -1,
                     2,   16,  15,  -1,
                     2,   0,   16,  -1,
                     0,   1,   17,  -1,
                     0,   17,  18,  -1,
                     1,   3,   19,  -1,
                     1,   19,  17,  -1,
                     3,   4,   20,  -1,
                     3,   20,  19,  -1,
                     4,   5,   21,  -1,
                     4,   21,  20,  -1,
```

```
5,    6,    22,   -1,
5,    22,   21,   -1,
6,    7,    23,   -1,
6,    23,   22,   -1,
7,    8,    24,   -1,
7,    24,   23,   -1,
8,    9,    25,   -1,
8,    25,   24,   -1,
9,    10,   26,   -1,
9,    26,   25,   -1,
10,   11,   27,   -1,
10,   27,   26,   -1,
11,   12,   28,   -1,
11,   28,   27,   -1,
12,   13,   29,   -1,
12,   29,   28,   -1,
13,   14,   30,   -1,
13,   30,   29,   -1,
14,   15,   31,   -1,
14,   31,   30,   -1,
15,   16,   32,   -1,
15,   32,   31,   -1,
16,   0,    18,   -1,
16,   18,   32,   -1,
18,   17,   33,   -1,
18,   33,   34,   -1,
17,   19,   35,   -1,
17,   35,   33,   -1,
19,   20,   36,   -1,
19,   36,   35,   -1,
20,   21,   37,   -1,
20,   37,   36,   -1,
21,   22,   38,   -1,
21,   38,   37,   -1,
22,   23,   39,   -1,
22,   39,   38,   -1,
23,   24,   40,   -1,
23,   40,   39,   -1,
24,   25,   41,   -1,
24,   41,   40,   -1,
25,   26,   42,   -1,
```

```
25,  42,  41,  -1,
26,  27,  43,  -1,
26,  43,  42,  -1,
27,  28,  44,  -1,
27,  44,  43,  -1,
28,  29,  45,  -1,
28,  45,  44,  -1,
29,  30,  46,  -1,
29,  46,  45,  -1,
30,  31,  47,  -1,
30,  47,  46,  -1,
31,  32,  48,  -1,
31,  48,  47,  -1,
32,  18,  34,  -1,
32,  34,  48,  -1,
34,  33,  49,  -1,
34,  49,  50,  -1,
33,  35,  51,  -1,
33,  51,  49,  -1,
35,  36,  52,  -1,
35,  52,  51,  -1,
36,  37,  53,  -1,
36,  53,  52,  -1,
37,  38,  54,  -1,
37,  54,  53,  -1,
38,  39,  55,  -1,
38,  55,  54,  -1,
39,  40,  56,  -1,
39,  56,  55,  -1,
40,  41,  57,  -1,
40,  57,  56,  -1,
41,  42,  58,  -1,
41,  58,  57,  -1,
42,  43,  59,  -1,
42,  59,  58,  -1,
43,  44,  60,  -1,
43,  60,  59,  -1,
44,  45,  61,  -1,
44,  61,  60,  -1,
45,  46,  62,  -1,
45,  62,  61,  -1,
```

```
46,    47,    63,    -1,
46,    63,    62,    -1,
47,    48,    64,    -1,
47,    64,    63,    -1,
48,    34,    50,    -1,
48,    50,    64,    -1,
50,    49,    65,    -1,
50,    65,    66,    -1,
49,    51,    67,    -1,
49,    67,    65,    -1,
51,    52,    68,    -1,
51,    68,    67,    -1,
52,    53,    69,    -1,
52,    69,    68,    -1,
53,    54,    70,    -1,
53,    70,    69,    -1,
54,    55,    71,    -1,
54,    71,    70,    -1,
55,    56,    72,    -1,
55,    72,    71,    -1,
56,    57,    73,    -1,
56,    73,    72,    -1,
57,    58,    74,    -1,
57,    74,    73,    -1,
58,    59,    75,    -1,
58,    75,    74,    -1,
59,    60,    76,    -1,
59,    76,    75,    -1,
60,    61,    77,    -1,
60,    77,    76,    -1,
61,    62,    78,    -1,
61,    78,    77,    -1,
62,    63,    79,    -1,
62,    79,    78,    -1,
63,    64,    80,    -1,
63,    80,    79,    -1,
64,    50,    66,    -1,
64,    66,    80,    -1,
66,    65,    81,    -1,
66,    81,    82,    -1,
65,    67,    83,    -1,
```

```
65,  83,  81,   -1,
67,  68,  84,   -1,
67,  84,  83,   -1,
68,  69,  85,   -1,
68,  85,  84,   -1,
69,  70,  86,   -1,
69,  86,  85,   -1,
70,  71,  87,   -1,
70,  87,  86,   -1,
71,  72,  88,   -1,
71,  88,  87,   -1,
72,  73,  89,   -1,
72,  89,  88,   -1,
73,  74,  90,   -1,
73,  90,  89,   -1,
74,  75,  91,   -1,
74,  91,  90,   -1,
75,  76,  92,   -1,
75,  92,  91,   -1,
76,  77,  93,   -1,
76,  93,  92,   -1,
77,  78,  94,   -1,
77,  94,  93,   -1,
78,  79,  95,   -1,
78,  95,  94,   -1,
79,  80,  96,   -1,
79,  96,  95,   -1,
80,  66,  82,   -1,
80,  82,  96,   -1,
82,  81,  97,   -1,
82,  97,  98,   -1,
81,  83,  99,   -1,
81,  99,  97,   -1,
83,  84,  100,  -1,
83,  100, 99,   -1,
84,  85,  101,  -1,
84,  101, 100,  -1,
85,  86,  102,  -1,
85,  102, 101,  -1,
86,  87,  103,  -1,
```

```
                    86,   103,  102,  -1,
                    87,   88,   104,  -1,
                    87,   104,  103,  -1,
                    88,   89,   105,  -1,
                    88,   105,  104,  -1,
                    89,   90,   106,  -1,
                    89,   106,  105,  -1,
                    90,   91,   107,  -1,
                    90,   107,  106,  -1,
                    91,   92,   108,  -1,
                    91,   108,  107,  -1,
                    92,   93,   109,  -1,
                    92,   109,  108,  -1,
                    93,   94,   110,  -1,
                    93,   110,  109,  -1,
                    94,   95,   111,  -1,
                    94,   111,  110,  -1,
                    95,   96,   112,  -1,
                    95,   112,  111,  -1,
                    96,   82,   98,   -1,
                    96,   98,   112,  -1,
                    98,   97,   113,  -1,
                    97,   99,   113,  -1,
                    99,   100,  113,  -1,
                    100,  101,  113,  -1,
                    101,  102,  113,  -1,
                    102,  103,  113,  -1,
                    103,  104,  113,  -1,
                    104,  105,  113,  -1,
                    105,  106,  113,  -1,
                    106,  107,  113,  -1,
                    107,  108,  113,  -1,
                    108,  109,  113,  -1,
                    109,  110,  113,  -1,
                    110,  111,  113,  -1,
                    111,  112,  113,  -1,
                    112,  98,   113,  -1
                ]
            }
        }
```

This file creates something that looks remarkably similar to our second example, shown in figure 8.5.

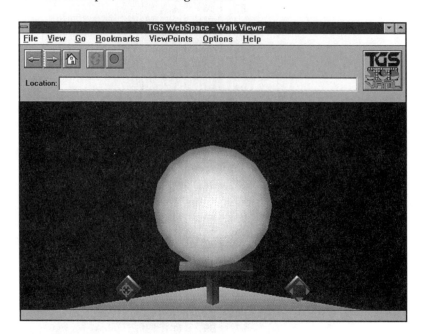

Figure 8.5

A sphere constructed from Coordinate3 and IndexedFaceSet nodes.

Although this might look more complicated than our previous example, it really isn't. There are more polygons in a sphere than a cube, so there are more points in the **Coordinate3** node and more faces defined in the **IndexedFaceSet** node. Using these two nodes together, a shape of any complexity can be defined in VRML.

Go Forth and Multiply—Using USE

When we're creating complex shapes in VRML files, their definitions take up lots of room—and lots of download time. Wouldn't it be great if we could treat a complex object defined with **Coordinate3** and **IndexedFaceSet** as a "rubber stamp," which we could put down wherever we liked? In VRML, you can do exactly that.

The **USE** feature of VRML enables you to create multiple *instances* (or copies) of a node or a group. **USE** isn't really a node, but it tells the VRML browser to use a previously defined node, without having to specify the content of that node again.

USE relies upon the naming ability provided with the **DEF** construct. **DEF** gives a node (which might be a group of nodes) a name. This name can then be supplied to **USE**, and then—poof!—another instance of the node is created. This new instance of the node has exactly the same characteristics as the **DEF** instance of the node—it's like a carbon copy.

This might not seem useful in itself—if you have an object in a world, why use it again? Cyberspace, like the real world, is made up of a common set of objects that might be used many times in a single world—a bookshelf of books, perhaps. It's possible to define a basic book shape using **DEF**—which defines a node containing that shape—and then **USE** that node to define a bookshelf full of books. **USE**-instanced nodes can be grouped with other nodes, so it's possible to take a shape and give it material or texture qualities unique to that instance of the object. They don't all have to look the same, even though they're cut from the same cookie-cutter.

In the following example, we'll take the sphere we defined using **Coordinate3** and **IndexedFaceSet**, and with **USE**, create two other instances of the same sphere. We'll use the **Translation** node to space them apart, however, and the last **USE** instance is within a **WWWAnchor** node—it's linked to my home page.

The file looks like this:

```
#VRML V1.0 ascii
# Example twenty-five - The complex shape gets USEd and
➥abused.

# I cheated and used the WCVT2POV.EXE tool to produce the
➥VRML file.
# This started off as a DXF model of a sphere.
```

```
# Being good little VRML do-bees, we give the sphere a name.
DEF Sphere_White Separator {

        # We give it a simple material to make it visible
        Material {
              diffuseColor 1.000000 1.000000 1.000000
              ambientColor 0.100000 0.100000 0.100000
        }

        # The Coordinate3 node defines a set of points in
➡space
        # Which are used later in the IndexedFaceSet node
        # Each row specifies the X Y Z position of a point.
        Coordinate3 {
              point [      # Begins the list of points
                    -0.382683   0.000000   0.923880,   # Point
➡Zero
                    -0.353553   0.146447   0.923880,   # Point
➡One
                     0.000000   0.000000   1.000000,   # Point
➡Two
                    -0.270598   0.270598   0.923880,   # etc...
                    [ ...etc ... ]
                    -0.353553  -0.146447  -0.923880,
                     0.000000   0.000000  -1.000000
              ]
        }

        # The IndexedFaceSet node takes the array of points
➡defined
        # In the Coordinate3 node, and forms triangular
➡polygon faces
        # Each polygon ends with a -1
        IndexedFaceSet {
              coordIndex [ # Begins the list of polygon
➡faces
                    2, 1, 0, -1,
                    2, 3, 1, -1,
                    [ ...etc... ]
                    111, 112, 113, -1,
                    112, 98, 113, -1
```

```
                ]
            }
        }

# We'll use the Sphere_White again, so we'll move from where
➥we are
Translation {
    translation 2 3 4
}

# And plant another Sphere
# The USE construct creates another instance of the sphere
USE Sphere_White

# And move yet again
# Because we're going to plant another Sphere_White
Translation {
    translation 4 3 2
}

# In this case, we put it inside a WWWAnchor node
# So we'll have a linked Sphere.
# USE nodes can be placed inside of group nodes like this
# And given their own attributes.
WWWAnchor {

    name "http://hyperreal.com/~mpesce/"
    description "USEing a home page well"

    USE Sphere_White
}
```

It produces a world of three white spheres, as you might suspect. The last sphere is anchored to my home page (see fig. 8.6).

The wise application of **USE** when designing a VRML environment can lead to very compact VRML files that are still quite rich and expressive.

These are the basic features of VRML as a language. There are some areas we haven't covered—texture map clamping, for example—that are features only useful to the guru users of VRML. These features are documented in Appendix A, "VRML: The Virtual Reality Modeling Language Version 1.0 Specification," along with all of the details on the node we've covered in this primer.

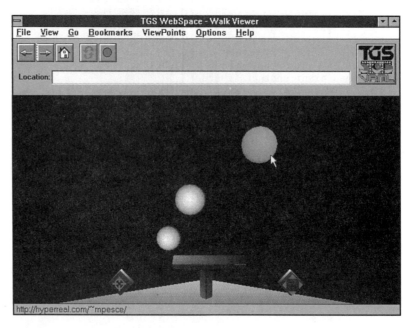

Figure 8.6

White spheres: one explicitly created and two created with USE.

Server Scripting in PERL

One of the most powerful features of the Web is its capability to create documents on demand, through a technology known as *server-side scripting*. A *script* is a program that executes on a Web server, in reply to a request from a Web client. The script creates a document that the server sends back to the client, just as if the server were replying to a request by sending a static document. Unlike static documents, server scripts generate data on-the-fly, and so can be reflective of when and where they are created.

Clay Graham, VRML evangelist at Silicon Graphics, has created an interesting demonstration of a server-side script. When a client VRML browser triggers the script—accessing a URL on SGI's server—the script examines the company's current stock price, its daily and 30-day trends, and creates a "room" where the floor is indicative of the stock price and the trend charts are texture-mapped onto the far walls. The dynamic nature of stock data makes this a very practical example of what you can do with scripting.

Figure 8.7
SGI's VRML Stock Ticker.

Although any computer language can be used to write a server script, most Web administrators and designers use the *Practical Expression and Report Language* (PERL) because it is both quite flexible and very easy to use. Larry Wall, the inventor of PERL, created a language with everything including the kitchen sink; the best features of BASIC, "C," and sed and awk are thrown together, and they create a powerful tool for creating dynamic Web documents. Free versions of PERL are available for almost every computer platform in existence, including Unix, MS-DOS, Windows NT, and Macintosh. For these reasons, we'll create our scripts in PERL.

A server script that creates a VRML document must inform the requesting client that a VRML document has been generated and is on its way back. This means that the first message received by the client application must be a declaration of the "content type" of the document. The script generates this by putting a line at the start of its output that identifies the MIME type of the data as VRML. Then the script can begin creating a valid VRML document, which always begins with the VRML header.

A simple PERL script that demonstrates these essentials looks like this:

```
#!/usr/bin/perl
# The top line gives the Unix shell a hint about how to
➥execute this script
#
# The basic VRML server-side PERL script
# Any PERL script which spits out VRML must have these
➥features
#
# First, we send the client the MIME type of the document
# VRML's MIME type is x-world/x-vmrl
# This is required so that the browser will understand it's
➥getting VRML
#
print "Content-type: x-world/x-vrml\n\n";  # Follow with 2
➥carriage returns
#
# And then our trusty header to identify it to the browser as
➥legitimate VRML
#
print "#VRML V1.0 ascii\n";
#
# That's all that's required!
#
```

This PERL script sends along just enough information for a VRML browser to accept the document as legitimate VRML. Of course, the document contains no VRML nodes, so there's nothing to display.

For our final example in this primer, we'll construct an orrey. An *orrey* (pronounced ow-ry) is a type of celestial timepiece, rather like using a planetarium as a clock. It shows the position of the heavenly bodies—Earth included—in a heliocentric solar system. We've been building the orrey all throughout the primer; all we need to do is add a few features to make it fully dynamic.

Our orrey will tell the time, but on a planetary scale. When the ORREY.PL script executes, it figures out how far the Earth has traveled around the Sun and how far the Moon has traveled around the Earth, and it displays them in their correct configurations. (These celestial objects are much farther apart than is indicated by their distance in the VRML world, but it's the relationships that are important, not accuracy.) Although the math that accompanies such calculations might seem rather formidable, we're blessed by a celestial "zero point" of some significance. New Year's Day, 1995, was a New Moon. That means the Earth and Moon were both in well-known positions at one point in the past, so it's easy to calculate their positions in the future.

PERL calculates time in seconds past the Epoch, which is 1 January 1970. I've taken the liberty of calculating the number of seconds between that time and 1 January 1995. Calculating the difference between these two gives us a figure that can be used to set our clock at our zero point. We know it takes 365.25 days for the Earth to circle the Sun (that's why we have a leap year every four years), and that it takes a little more than 29 days for the Moon to circle the Earth. We've also precomputed these values in seconds—having all our values in the same units (seconds) makes these calculations very straightforward.

As ORREY.PL begins, it gets the current time (in seconds), subtracts 1 January 1995 (again, in seconds) from it, and then calculates how many revolutions of the Earth have occurred since that time. It then multiplies this number by 2Π to convert this value to radians. Taking the sine of this value gives the x ratio of the position; the cosine of this value gives the y ratio of the position. (One thing you'll find about 3D graphics is that it'll make you want to relearn your high-school trigonometry!) We'll use our figure of 20 units as a multiplier for each of these figures; the **Translation** node, which places the Earth into orbit around the Sun, outputs these figures. We do something very similar for the Moon, but we use the lunar month as our basis for calculation and setup the values for its **Translation** node appropriately. In all other respects, this is very much the same example we've been developing throughout the primer.

Although we've been very careful to create VRML files where there's a single node per line, we've done this only for the purposes of readability. We can cram as many nodes onto a single line of a VRML document as we would like—there's no limit. In order to save space in our script—which is really quite small—we'll put several nodes on a single line.

The PERL script is as follows:

```
#!/usr/bin/perl
#
# Sample Orrey VRML server-side script written in PERL
# Written by Mark Pesce, June 1995
# No rights reserved.
#
# Let's do some time math.
#
# Get seconds since start of 1995.
# First get seconds as of 1 Jan 1995
# We cheated and precalculated this number.
# We cheated and got the number of seconds in a year, as
➥well.
# Oh, alright, we did it for the seconds in a lunar month,
➥too!
#
$yearZero = 788918400;
```

```
$secInYear = 31557600;
$secInLuMonth = 2514360;
$rightNow = time();
$sinceZero = $rightNow - $yearZero;
#
# Calculate how far along we are in Earth's orbit around the
➥Sun.
#
$theSpin = ($sinceZero / $secInYear) * (3.1416 * 2);
#
# So now calculate x SIN and y COS values for Earth's
➥position around the Sun
# The value of 20 is preserved from the original Translation
➥node
#
$xVal = 20 * sin($theSpin);
$zVal = 20 * cos($theSpin);
#
# Do precisely the same thing for the Moon's orbit around the
➥Earth
#
$laLune = ($sinceZero / $secInLuMonth) * (3.1416 * 2);
$xMoon = 4 * sin($laLune);
$yMoon = 4 * cos($laLune);
#
# Begin the script's output.
# Always send the content type before everything else
#
print "Content-type: x-world/x-vrml\n\n";
#
# Then send the file header
#
print "#VRML V1.0 ascii\n";
#
# First, define the Sun.
#
print "Separator { Material { emissiveColor 1 1 0 }
➥PointLight { intensity 1 color 1 1 0.9 } \n";
print "Sphere { radius 10 }\n";
#
# Next, the Earth.
#
```

```
print "Separator {\n";
print "Transform { translation ";
printf "%g %g 0 }\n", $xVal, $zVal;
print "Material { diffuseColor 0 0 1 specularColor 0.9 0.9
➥0.9 shininess 0.9 }\n";
print "Texture2 { filename \"http://hyperreal.com/~mpesce/
➥WORLDMAP.RGB\"  } Sphere { radius 2 }\n";
#
# Finally, the Moon.
#
print "Separator {\n";
print "Transform { translation ";
printf "%g %g 0 }\n", $xMoon, $yMoon;
print "Material { diffuseColor 0.7 0.7 0.7 shininess 0.3 }
Texture2 { image 4 4 3\n";
print "0xC0C0C0 0x808080 0xFFFFFF 0x404040 0x808080 0x202020
➥0x808080 0xC0C0C0\n";
print "0x202020 0x808080 0xFFFFFF 0x808080 0x808080 0xC0C0C0
➥0x808080 0x202020 }\n";
print "Sphere { radius 1 } } } }\n";
#
#  All done.
#
```

When executed, ORREY.PL creates the following output (which gets sent back to the client VRML browser):

```
Content-type: x-world/x-vrml

#VRML V1.0 ascii
Separator { Material { emissiveColor 1 1 0 } PointLight {
➥intensity 1 color 1 1 0.9 }
Sphere { radius 10 }
Separator {
Transform { translation 0.669656 -19.9888 0 }
Material { diffuseColor 0 0 1 specularColor 0.9 0.9 0.9
➥shininess 0.9 }
Texture2 { filename "http://hyperreal.com/~mpesce/
➥WORLDMAP.RGB"  } Sphere { radius 2 }
Separator {
Transform { translation 3.86529 1.02934 0 }
```

```
Material { diffuseColor 0.7 0.7 0.7 shininess 0.3 } Texture2
➡{ image 4 4 3
0xC0C0C0 0x808080 0xFFFFFF 0x404040 0x808080 0x202020
➡0x808080 0xC0C0C0
0x202020 0x808080 0xFFFFFF 0x808080 0x808080 0xC0C0C0
➡0x808080 0x202020 }
Sphere { radius 1 } } } }
```

This results in a VRML world that looks like figure 8.8.

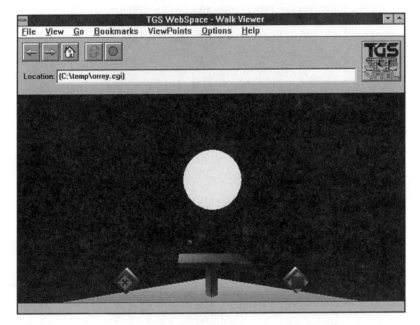

Figure 8.8
ORREY.PL output on 7/14/95.

This is roughly how the solar system looks from space when viewed from above. Our orey is a functioning clock, using Earth as a celestial hour hand and the Moon as the second hand! With some practice, you'll be able to "read" this orey to within a day's accuracy. It's the way the ancients charted the flow of time, but we've brought it forward into cyberspace.

Although it demonstrates all the key features of VRML scripting in PERL, our orrey is only a basic example of how a VMRL script works. I'll leave it to you to add other features and create your own examples with these cyberspace Tinker toys.

For those of you who might want some hints on directions to take this project—and learn VRML at the same time—the following are some suggestions:

1. Rotate the Earth to indicate the time of day.

2. Take the *live* planetary weather map at Michigan State University and texture map it onto Earth. The GIF image of the Earth's surface is at *http://rs560.cl.msu.edu/weather/worldir.gif.*

3. Get an image of the lunar surface from NASA and use it as a texture map. *http://www.nasa.gov/*

4. Rotate the Moon to indicate the time of the lunar month.

5. Use the **map POINT** field of the **WWWAnchor** node on the Earth, and write a script that gives you the weather at whatever point you click on the Earth.

If you take this project in unexpected directions, drop me a note at *mpesce@hyperreal.com,* and let me know what you've done. VRML is a success story built on sharing work with others—let your light shine and let your work show!

Part III

Project 188

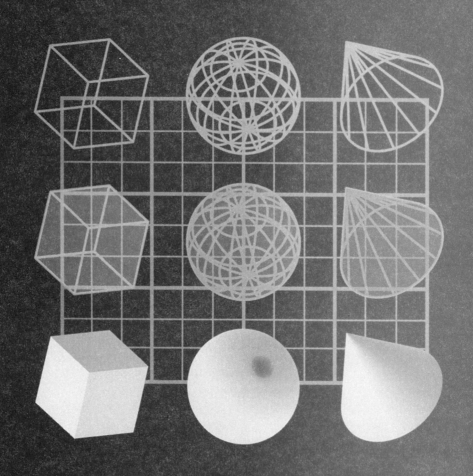

Chapter 9

Homesteading Cyberspace

In July of 1994, the Association for Computing Machinery had their annual conference for the Special Interest Group in Graphics. SIGGRAPH '94 was the first time VRML received widespread public exposure. Working with Scott Young and the Webmasters at the United States Holocaust Memorial Museum, Tony Parisi and I re-created "Daniel's Story," the children's tour through the museum (see fig. 9.1). This VRML world was then linked into museum resources and documentation—available in HTML—to create a virtual tour through a museum almost a thousand miles away. The exhibit was prepared for SIGKIDS, a SIGGRAPH playground where kids could play with the intersection of graphics technologies and educational context. The kids loved it; many of them were already familiar with the Web, and adding a 3D interface to it seemed quite natural to their Nintendo-trained minds.

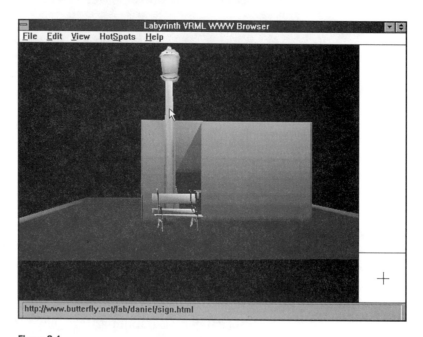

Figure 9.1

"Daniel's Story," created for SIGKIDS '94.

On the last day of the show, I got a visit from Zane Vella, who, together with Coco Conn, runs the CITYSPACE project. CITYSPACE is a work-in-progress that has kids from all across the world building a city in cyberspace—together. CITYSPACE software has multiparticipant capabilities, so the kids can visit with each other and communicate as they build their ideal world. CITYSPACE looks like a cross between Las Vegas and the Matrix— very flashy but very cyber. Zane graced me with the official CITYSPACE tour jacket; it's a white cotton pullover with an image of a CITYSPACE scene on the back. A caption underneath the image reads, "BUILD IT YOURSELF."

That's the theme of this chapter.

Object Builders versus Space Builders

When the Web burst upon the scene in late 1993, you needed to have knowledge of HTML to construct a home page—it's the textual language of the Web, and at that time, there were no editing tools that assisted in the creation of HTML documents. People broke out their old text editors, *vi* and *emacs*. Fortunately, HTML is pretty easy to learn, and with a little practice, even the most sophisticated HTML layouts are possible.

VRML is also easy to learn and use, but the complexity of VRML worlds—objects with thousands of polygons—makes them almost impossible to create by hand. You can create pieces by hand and sew them together in a VRML superstructure, but it's unlikely that you'll produce Rodin's *The Thinker* by defining a cloud of points. HTML done by hand makes sense—after all, text is used to create a textual document. But VRML done by hand— that is, typing—makes no sense at all, except as a lesson. It's an abstract mapping from numbers to shapes, two very different senses. One of our final examples in the Primer takes up pages and pages, and that's to describe just one object—imagine a whole scene of objects that complex!

It took almost two years from the beginning of the Web to the arrival of competent HTML authoring tools like Silicon Graphics' WEBFORCE, Microsoft's Internet Assistant, and Quarterdeck's WebAuthor. VRML has great authoring tools available from the start—in part because many 3D design packages already available needed only small modifications to support VRML. The VRML community has been working hard to make sure the "tools gap" that happened with HTML doesn't reoccur; you'll be able to author in VRML without ever having to learn it.

There are two basic types of VRML world creation tools. The first is an object creation tool, like Caligari *trueSpace*, that provides a "sculpture studio" where arbitrary objects can be designed. The second is a space creation tool, like Virtus *Walkthrough Pro*, that specializes in the construction and layout of VRML spaces and has features for VRML linkage, inlines, and levels-of-detail. These two types of tools are completely complementary; often it's appropriate to create an object, then move it into another program to place it within a space.

The space-building tools—which we'll focus on here—differ in their interfaces and capabilities. The two we'll cover in this chapter, Paragraph's Home Space Builder and Virtus' Walkthrough Pro, are designed for novices and professionals, respectively. Both share the capability to create sensually rich spaces, and both can place items within that space that link to various VRML resources. Home Space Builder is limited in the types of items that can be placed into its environment; however, its friendly drag-and-drop interface for world building makes it accessible to children and the computer-phobic. Virtus Walkthrough Pro can re-create any space in the real world or can become the lathe of the imagination—the price for this freedom is sophistication; it takes longer to learn Walkthrough Pro, but the results also are more professional.

What is to be Done—and How to Do It?

The heart of this chapter is "Project 188," which takes a house in Cambridge, Massachusetts, and re-creates it in cyberspace. This was a medium-sized project by VRML standards. Greg Jacobson, an artist and one of the residents of 188, completed the whole project—including learning how to use 3D modeling software—in about two weeks of part-time efforts. We focused on process— how the project took shape—and from this analysis have developed a project plan that can serve as a set of guidelines for any VRML project, real or imaginary.

Seven Steps to Effective VRML

A VRML project of any size breaks down into several stages: conception, planning, design, sampling, construction, testing, and publishing. While you can launch Home Space Builder and have a nice room up in minutes, that approach won't work well with Walkthrough Pro; professional tools require forethought, planning, and resources. These same points are covered, with a different emphasis, in Chapter 12, "The Cyberspace Style Guide."

Conception

In a perfect world, the conception is easy. If you're building your own house, re-creating your living room in cyberspace, the ground of imagination is guided by reality. But, if the construction is fictional, if fantasy or aesthetic ideal is the guide, conception may be the longest part of the process.

Architecture and sculpture can be useful guides, but freed of the constraints of physics, the imagination can perform feats impossible in the real world. This means that the creative process of conception is always coupled with a tension between what is possible, what is reasonable, and what is sensible. Too often you'll find gorgeous worlds that are easy to get lost in, or worlds that are too faithful to the real, avoiding the features that come naturally to cyberspace.

Conception is the first meeting of artistic evocation with reality; if you don't cover this ground thoroughly, your project may look more like a collision than a collusion between science and art.

Planning

Once a concept has been decided upon, issues of scope and tools begin to resolve. At this point, the creation of a project plan is vital. A plan keeps the overall project in focus and on track. The other elements of the project, as defined in the following, must be considered at this time, scheduled, budgeted, and executed. If the project is quite simple, a tool like Home Space Builder may well be adequate. For an intense VRML project, a plan might include acquisition and training on applications such as Walkthrough Pro, trueSpace, and Autodesk's 3D Studio, as well as other Web-based technologies such as Netscape's NetSite Web server, imaging technologies such as Adobe's PhotoShop, and various sampling technologies.

A well-thought-out planning stage will ensure that appropriate resources are available at every stage of a project and that the work flow will never reach a crisis point because of a misapprehension of requirements.

Design

Design is a touchy issue; here the aesthetic meets the public. The conception of the project should serve as the guide to design. Is this art? Is it public space (which should then conform to the prosaic, accessible nature of public places)? Is this architecture? Is it abstract data reaching for a concrete representation?

Here training becomes a pre-eminent concern. Michael Gough, an architect with many years of experience, was able to re-create Los Angeles' Variety Arts Center from blueprints in just a few days because his professional background gave him fluency in a concrete medium, while his computer training (he used the Macintosh application *FormZ* to construct the models) enabled him to translate that fluency into an electronic form.

Sampling

Through the design stage of a project, the requirements for certain real-world or virtual objects will be defined. The real-world objects must be translated into electronic form through the process of sampling. This can be as simple as an artist creating electronic version drawings—which then can be used as texture maps—or as sophisticated as a 3D scan of a real-world object, so that its wireframe geometry can be imported into the VRML environment.

Construction

If the preceding steps have been articulated carefully, the construction phase should proceed easily and without unforeseen difficulty. The emphasis at this time is upon tools; a well-developed tools strategy must be in place at this point. One of the problems in computer-based design is the persistent lack of interoperability of the various tools. It's a wise person who ensures that all the tools fit together well before he or she actually uses them in a production capacity.

To determine the suitability of tools used in the construction phase, take a simple model and bring it through all of the tools you'll be using. Take care to note any conversion difficulties encountered in the process. Ideally, the tools process will be seamless—objects will pass from tool to tool with no perceptible changes. In reality, however, this is almost never the case. Furthermore, if any tools are used for specific features that are vital to the project, make sure that these features are supported in VRML, and supported by all other tools used in the project.

There are no "perfect" VRML tools at this time—and they're probably some time away. Any complex VRML project will require some degree of "opening the hood" to tinker with the VRML files themselves. In any situation where the direct manipulation of VRML files takes place, *maintain backup copies before these files are manipulated.* If the unspeakable happens—and you damage a VRML file beyond your capacity to repair it—you'll be able to fall back to your pristine originals. Test your files often as you manipulate them; incremental changes can have profound effects.

Testing

As obvious as this may seem, testing your VRML files in every possible environment is an insurance against disaster, or worse, angry visitors to your spaces. While VRML 1.0 is a standard, there are a few holes in it big enough to drive tractor trailers through—in areas such as texture maps and camera definitions—so a file that works with one VRML browser on one platform may not work at all on another. Furthermore, anchors that work well in one VRML browser might elsewhere be handed off to an HTML browser for retrieval—and this might not work as well as planned. Every system, every browser, and every network is a little bit different. When testing, first work locally and then across the Web. You'll find significant differences—in both behavior and performance—between the environments.

Publishing

The creation of an alluring VRML environment is only partially in the hands of the designer. The publisher, in most cases a Web server administrator, must ensure that the VRML documents that create the world and their associated linkages, are valid when placed upon a Web server. Furthermore, only when a world has been "published" do issues like low-speed access enter the realm of testability. If you've created a world with a very simple design but a megabyte of texture maps, it's quite likely that the experience of a visitor using a low-speed link will be unsatisfactory, and even users of high-speed connections may find the environment objectionable.

The five final steps in this methodology must be thought of as a continuous loop. Design, sampling, construction, testing, and publishing each have an effect upon one another, and are process rather than product oriented. Changing any of these elements changes all the others.

Using Paragraph's Home Space Builder

Paragraph International's *Home Space Builder* (HSB) is an excellent example of a well-designed and easy-to-use entry level VRML authoring tool. Its fluid interface makes world creation a click-and-drag process. Rich worlds with colorful surfaces, texture maps, pictures, and links all are no more than a few clicks away.

Home Space Builder's Interface

The HSB uses a museum metaphor—it's excellent at creating spaces within which you can "hang" images. This metaphor is maintained throughout the product. The standard interface on HSB has five windows: the Plane Walker/Builder window, the Chooser window, the Walker toolbar, the Builder toolbar, and the Plane Builder window (see fig. 9.2). Each of these has its own unique relationship to the model under construction. For almost any feature, you can get a bit of explanatory text by holding the mouse over that feature; the text pops up in the status area (which is at the bottom of either the Viewer or the Walker window).

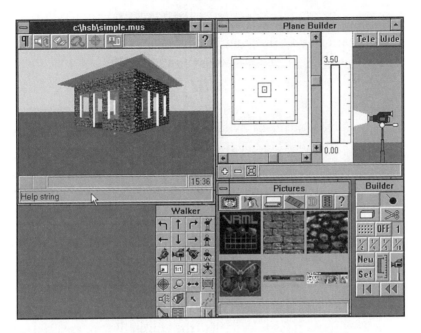

Figure 9.2
The Home Space Builder interface.

The Walk View Window

Of greatest interest to the VRML world builder is the Walk View window. Here you'll see a representation of the world you're creating or manipulating, rendered in real time—very much the way it will look within the VRML browser. Across the top of the window are six buttons; the first button drops the application's only menu—Paragraph doesn't really believe in menus. Standard menu items include "Open Museum," "Save Museum," and "Exit." The "Settings" menu item opens a dialog box with various preference settings, and "Guest Mode" hides the three authoring windows (Plane Builder, Chooser, and Builder toolbar) and replaces them with the Plane Walker window and an abbreviated version of the Walker toolbox.

The last three buttons in the toolbar are significant for VRML. The leftmost of these three, a magnifying glass, is used to examine a picture closely and to edit the image. The second, crosshairs, changes the view so that a picture is viewed head-on. The last button invokes the picture editor—that's important to remember because URLs can be attached to pictures only through the picture editor.

To change the view in the Walk window, either the Walker toolbox or the Plane Builder/Plane Walker window can be used.

The Walker Toolbar

You can move through the model using the Walker toolbar. It has a variety of options, each identified with a particular icon. If you use the arrows for movement, you'll find that Home Space Builder has a feature VRML doesn't (not yet, anyway)—it won't let you stride through walls, but will gently guide you along the wall until you get to a doorway, at which point you'll walk into the room.

The icons on the lower half of the Walker toolbar are used for manipulation of items found in the Chooser window, such as pictures, wallpapers, and so forth. You can resize or delete pictures, undo your last operation, or look at a picture close-up, among other options, using these tools.

The Builder Toolbar

When creating a space, the Builder toolbar contains the items you'll be using. The toolbar has three primary modes. In one, you direct "Pinocchio" around—by his nose!—to change your view of the world. In another, you can build the walls of your creation, and in the third, you can gouge away at walls to create interior spaces, windows, and doors. The toolbar also has facilities for turning the snap-to-grid feature on or off (snap-to-grid keeps all objects that you draw in the Builder window aligned with respect to each other and to a grid), and has buttons that toggle certain features within the Plane Builder window.

The Chooser Window

While worlds are built of walls, it's the decoration on those walls that makes the space visually appealing. HSB defines several different types of surfaces that can be placed on walls, ceilings, or floors—pictures, paint, wallpaper, and movies. (Movies aren't yet VRML-compatible, so we won't discuss them much here.) The Chooser window is an image gallery used to select an image to be dragged onto a surface in the world. The Chooser understands almost every image format there is, but you may need to set it to point to the correct directory for the images you'll be using as pictures or wallpapers. The Select Directory button, second to last in the toolbox at the top of the Chooser window, brings up a file dialog box that enables you to select an entire directory of images. When selected, all images will be present—in thumbnail— in the Chooser.

The Plane Builder Window

The Plane Builder window is the action area—the place where empty cyberspace acquires walls and forms. It has three main components. First, the top view, which shows the top view of objects under construction, displays your location in the world— using Pinocchio as your cyberspace alter-ego. This also is the area where tools selected in the Builder toolbar are used to create or remove spaces. Next, the middle area sets the *extrusion zone*; that is, the height of objects you create when you build or remove walls. Finally, the third area contains the viewing camera, which looks and works much like a real camera. You can raise and lower your point of view by grabbing the circle where the camera meets the tripod, tilt it by grabbing the handle behind the camera, or select a zoom or telephoto shot by pressing on the "Tele" and "Wide" buttons on the toolbox above the window.

Building a Simple Living Room in Cyberspace

To build a simple VRML space with a few links into the Web, we need to launch the Home Space Builder and specify "New Museum" in the "Open Museum File" dialog box. This creates a blank portion of cyberspace, all set up for your creations.

The Builder toolbar has three modes. The first is used to move the user—the Pinocchio icon used to represent the user here and within the Plane Builder window. Pinocchio's nose actually indicates what direction he's looking in. You can grab Pinocchio with your mouse, either at his head—the black dot—or at the tip of his nose. If you grab him by his head, you can't change the direction he looks in, but if you pull him around by his nose, you can twist and turn his point of view as desired.

The second mode creates 3D boxes—and boxes only—within the Plane Builder window. If you select this tool, then create a box within the Plane Builder window—by clicking once, drawing a box of the desired size, and clicking again to release the tool and create the box—you'll probably get something that looks like figure 9.3.

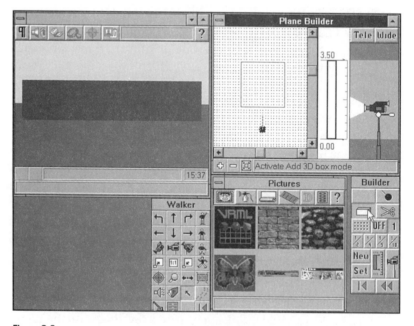

Figure 9.3
Creating exterior walls using the Build tool.

If Pinocchio is stationed in front of the box, you'll see the box in the Walk window as well. Click on the move user icon in the Builder toolbar, and move yourself around all the sides of the box you've just created. Move into the center of the box (see fig. 9.4). What's this? You can't see the walls when you're inside of them!

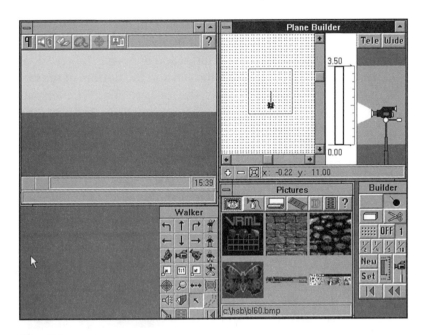

Figure 9.4

Where are the walls we just built?

While this may seem quite nonsensical, this is the way most 3D graphics programs work. Walls only have one side, their visible side, which in this case, is the outside. Looking from inside out, you can't see them. If you move Pinocchio back outside the box, you'll see the walls once again.

In order to see the inside of our box, we need to extrude the area within it. This is rather similar to scooping ice cream out of a carton, but we have a better tool than an ice cream scoop. The box removal tool—represented by a pair of scissors—can create an empty space within the box. This removal of space will create walls that face into the extruded space. That means it will create a visible space within the box.

Before we do this, though, we need to adjust the extrusion controls in the middle pane of the Plane Builder window. If we don't change the extrusion size, we'll extrude an area that will be as tall as the area we've just created with the Add Wall tool, which will leave us no room for a floor or ceiling! We only need to move the values by a little bit—ceilings and floors can be very thin in cyberspace. The values for the top and the bottom of the extrusion are in meters. Generally, the top is set for 3.5 meters (about 11 feet), and the bottom is set for ground level, 0 meters. Adjust the top value—you can click on it and drag it down—to 3.45 meters, and the bottom value to 0.05 meters. That means there's 5 cm of virtual space each for our floor and our ceiling.

Now select the Remove Wall tool and draw a box that is *completely* within the box you created with the Add Box tool. If it isn't completely within the box—or if the walls line up exactly—you'll eat away the wall you've created, which we don't want to do until we're busy making doors and windows. The operation should look like figure 9.5.

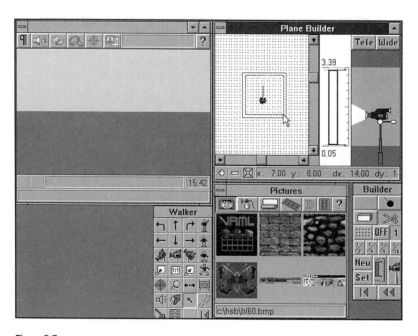

Figure 9.5

The interior is removed; note the settings on the extrusion tool.

Select the Mover tool and move Pinocchio into the center of the box. You can see it now! You've create a hollowed-out space within your box (see fig. 9.6).

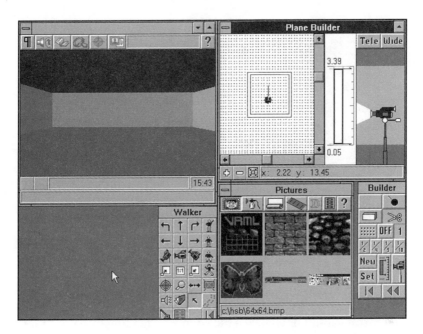

Figure 9.6
Now we have an outside and an inside!

Now we need to make a nice door into our space. Using the mover, place yourself outside of and in front of your box. You create doors by using the Remove Box tool. We don't want to cut away the entire surface, however, so we need to set the extrusion height to be 0.09 meters at the bottom and 2.5 meters at the top. This will give us a small threshold and a door that will be tall enough for almost everybody. Now, with the Remove Box tool selected, remove a narrow box from the front of the building you're creating (see fig. 9.7).

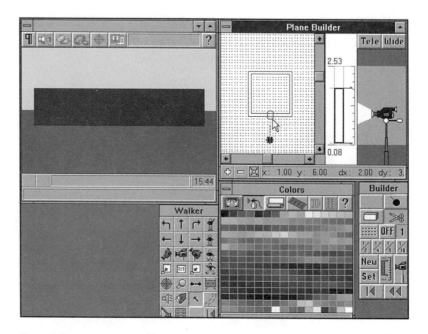

Figure 9.7

Creating a doorway; note the extrusion settings.

You should now have a nice doorway leading into your room in cyberspace (see fig. 9.8).

Windows are made in much the same way, but windows don't go all the way to the floor. Let's set the bottom extrusion height to 1 meter, while raising the top extrusion height to 3 meters. This will give us windows at 3 feet off the ground, going up to 6 feet, but not quite to the ceiling. Using the Remove Wall tool, we'll cut out two areas from the back wall of the building, opposite our door. Moving into the room, we can see the windows (see fig. 9.9).

Congratulations! You've just created a room in cyberspace!

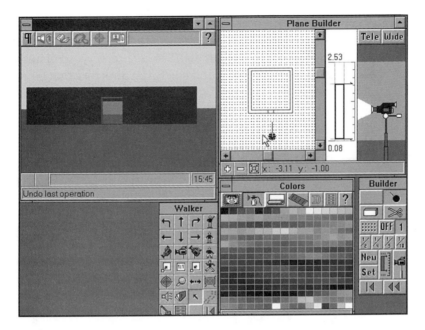

Figure 9.8

A view through the doorway.

Now that we've created a room, we need to decorate it. First
things first, let's color the outside walls of our creation. It's very
easy to do this with HSB. Select the Chooser window, then select
the spray paint icon in the toolbox. The Chooser will display the
palette of colors available to you. Select one of them—I prefer
pink houses myself—and drag it onto the front wall of your
building (in the Walk window). The color of the wall changes as
soon as you release the mouse button. You can color all the walls
in your room in this manner.

Next, let's add a wooden floor to the inside of the room. We'll
need to use a wood wallpaper to do this. Select the wallpaper icon

in the Chooser window. You should see a display of many types of wallpapers, such as bricks, stones, wood, and marble. If you don't, you'll need to click on the "Select Directory" icon in the Chooser window's toolbar and locate the directory that contains these images. (HSB supports many different file formats; you'll be able to use almost any image you have.) You also can use your own images as wallpapers in the same way. Find a wood pattern that appeals to you, then drag-and-drop it onto the floor of your room. (You'll need to be inside the building to do this.) You now have a floor that's a large, repeating texture map of wood (see fig. 9.10).

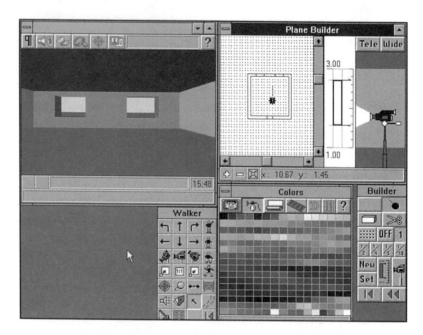

Figure 9.9

Two windows created in the rear wall.

Finally, to complete our model, let's put a picture on one of the walls. Select the picture icon in the Chooser window; if you don't see any pictures, you'll need to "Select Directory" and locate them. Again, you can drag-and-drop one of the pictures onto any of the walls. If we drag one—say the VRML logo—onto the wall space between our windows, it'll look like figure 9.11.

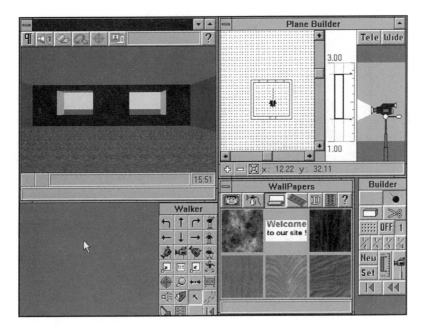

Figure 9.10

A "wood" texture map floor.

That's a little small, isn't it? Select the "Move/Resize" picture tool in the Walker toolbar and grab the picture from its upper right hand corner. You can stretch the picture to whatever size you like. After you've stretched it a bit—notice it preserves its proportions as you stretch it, "snapping back" a bit if you stretch it disproportionately—it will look like figure 9.12.

Now, for the pièce de résistance, we'll make a link from this picture to an URL. To do this, we need to bring up the picture editor. Click on the picture and then select the "Picture Attachments Editor" icon in the Walk View window. You'll see a dialog entitled "Picture Attach Editor." Within the "Function" drop-down menu, select "Link to Universal Resource Locator." Once you've selected it, you'll immediately get another dialog box that requests the URL to link to. Let's link to the San Diego Computer Center VRML Repository. Type **http://sdsc.edu/vrml/** into that box, then press OK. The dialog box should now look like figure 9.13.

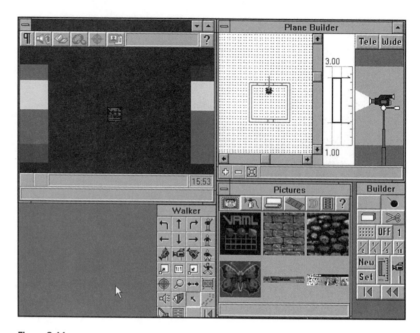

Figure 9.11

Hanging a picture on the wall.

That's it! Hit "OK" and the link is made.

Finally, we have to create a VRML file from this world. HSB will
write out VRML files, but it won't read them in; it only understands its native .mus "museum" format. This means you'll
probably want to save your creation in *both* formats—VRML so
that it's viewable within the Web, and .mus so that you can edit it
or add to it at a later date. From the menu—the first button in the
Walk View toolbar brings it down—select "Save 3D Space." First,
save the worlds as a "3D Space" file, then save it as a "Virtual
Reality Modeling Language" file. In both cases, the correct
extension will be applied to the file name.

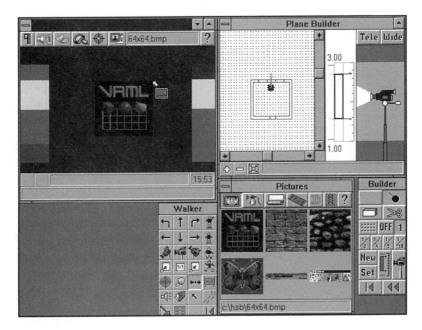

Figure 9.12

Our picture, enlarged with the Move/Resize tool.

If everything has gone well, you can take your .wrl file—whatever
you've named it—and open it within a VRML browser such as
Web space. It should look the same, as shown in figure 9.14.

That's it. It's really no more difficult than that. HSB enables you
to create complex spaces with lots of Add/Remove box activity,
but it doesn't really allow you to create cyberspace sculptures, or
furniture, or other features you might want in your world. But to
create a picture gallery, a museum, or an exhibition, it might just
be the tool for the job. It's very easy to use—as you can now see—
and enables users at any level, including kids, to build
cyberspaces that look rich and authentic.

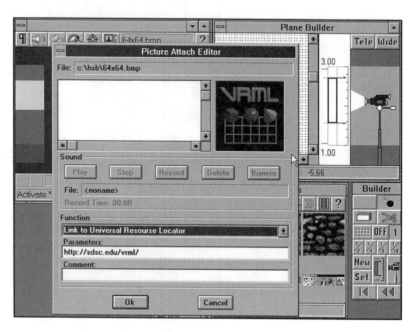

Figure 9.13

The Picture Editor is used to link the picture to an URL.

Publishing Caveats with Home Space Builder

You've created a VRML world site, and have several ways to publish it on the Web. If you have a Web site on your own computer or on a LAN, you typically copy your files to a subdirectory on this site. Otherwise, you can use FTP to accomplish this. In any case, you need to know both the URL of the world file and the URL of all texture files. When you are saving your 3D Space as a VRML file, HSB requests the URL of this file. By default, all texture maps are copied into the Save directory with the .wrl file; because of this, they differ only by file names. You leave all options to browse texture URLs and change some of them, however. This makes the texture map accessible through the Web.

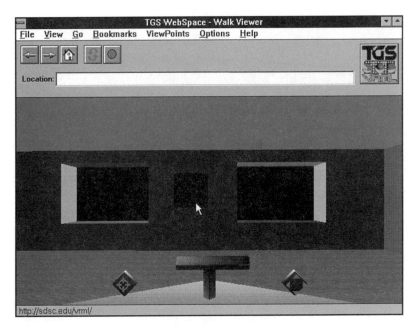

Figure 9.14
Our creation, viewed in WebSpace.

If you're going to "open the hood" on a VRML document, you'll
need to know something about the format of these documents.
The VRML Primer is a good place to start. Texture maps are
covered in some detail in Chapter 8, "Advanced VRML and Server
Scripts."

Project 188

Putting a real house into cyberspace is a reasonably big job, but
the end product—a house that can be visited by anyone with a
VRML browser—makes it more than worth the effort. Project 188
takes a house located in Cambridge, Massachusetts, and brings it

into the Web. The house itself is famous in the community of artists in the Boston-Cambridge area. Four years ago, when the four artists who occupy 188 moved in, the duplex was a dump—peeling wallpaper, decaying ceilings, and so forth. They set out to make the necessary repairs, while coddling the favors of a businessman who owned a wallpaper store in nearby Waltham.

The proprietor gave these artists access to his significant collection of remnant wallpaper—items that had gone out of style or that had been pretty atrocious to begin with. Seizing this opportunity, the industrious four completely wallpapered their domicile in an incredible mixture of 60's psychedelia, 70's flocked chic, and neo-Victorian patterns. Always believing that too much was never enough, they continued on, sewing a cloth ceiling for one room out of panels of remnant silks, creating a furry green ceiling for their foyer, and collecting, arranging, and displaying an incredible collection of knickknacks—some obscure, some bizarre, others just plain funny. The end result is overwhelming, but in a positive sense; it's a riot of visual imagery, sensual surfaces, and lighting that creates a unique environment, unlike any most people have ever seen. It's become such an attraction that friends of friends bring their friends by to see the house, and someone is always dropping off some piece of found art because they "know you'll have a place for it." 188 is approaching a semantic singularity—someday it will all become too dense and vanish in a flash of X-rays and Kool and the Gang 45's.

We approached this project with more than a little trepidation; after all, how could we possibly get all of this into the computer? What follows are the design steps explicated previously, as they applied to the body of Project 188.

Conception

In one sense, the conceptualization of Project 188 was very straightforward. The first floor of 188 was to be developed as a VRML model. That part makes sense. But the detail level of the articulation of a real-world site becomes an important issue, especially when dealing with a space as semantically dense and meaningful as 188. This became a constant theme in our work—how much is enough? We were constrained by time—because, after all, this book had to be published—and by effort. Modeling every piece of art, every lamp, and every knickknack would have been a prohibitively lengthy process. Yet, the beauty of 188 springs partly from this density.

In the end, we made a decision to present the spaces as accurately as possible, although they are much less dense in the VRML models than in real life. Nonetheless, the spaces themselves convey the feeling of 188. Using this as a start, 188 has a foundation that can be incrementally improved in the future.

Planning

The scale of the product necessitated the selection of the appropriate tools and methodologies. We quickly settled upon Virtus Walkthrough Pro as the modeling tool, as it is well-suited to medium-scale space design and excels at object placement. We used a 486/100 PC, with 24 MB of RAM and running Windows for Workgroups 3.11. This was a good environment for developing the models. Texture mapping slows rendering engines down significantly—the fast processor speed gave us a responsive environment while the models were in creation.

Design

Our experimentation showed that if the house had been created exactly to scale, it would seem much smaller than it felt in real life. Because of this, the entire environment was scaled up by a factor of 1.5:1; this gives the rooms more spaciousness. On a computer monitor, where feature density is limited by monitor resolution—which is significantly worse than the resolution of the human eye—the scene density must often be reduced to compensate for pixelation.

In addition, the decision was made to capture only selected objects within the rooms themselves. These objects would be captured as photographs; in no case was an object—other than the space itself—captured in 3D for input to the computer. We made a decision to use texture maps to represent the environment, rather than a large set of 3D objects. We did this for two distinct reasons: first, because the creation of that many 3D objects would have made the project prohibitively labor intensive; second, because a VRML file with that much 3D geometry would have been prohibitively large, both in polygon count—which should in most cases be kept below 10,000 polygons per world—and in file size.

The final design decision was "Which objects do we present within the environment?" We selected objects that would be the most expressive of the overall feel of 188, without requiring the explicit representation of all objects in 188.

These design constraints led directly to the sampling methodology.

Sampling

We knew that we would not model the objects within 188. However, certain features—kitchen appliances, basic furniture, and so forth—had to be placed into the space; without it, the space felt less like a home and more like an abstract gallery. Furniture grounded the space in the concrete and provided a bridge between the fanciful construction of the space and the reality that people lived within it. Virtus Walkthrough Pro comes with an excellent library of stock 3D objects. Many of these approximately matched objects with 188; items like couches, overstuffed chairs, floor lamps, and so forth were brought in from Virtus' libraries and placed into the space.

The overall density of 188 made it impossible to sample the entire space. Instead, we settled on 35 mm photography—with professional lighting and a high-quality camera—and spent a six-hour period photographing. The photography process had three main focal points—first, the rooms themselves, photographed as a whole piece; next, objects specific to each of the rooms that had been identified during the design phase as representative of the feel of a space; finally, very clear samples of wallpaper on each surface.

Although the typical process is to shoot 35 mm slides and then scan the slides into the computer, we decided to take advantage of a newer but tried technology to remove this step from the process. We had a Kodak PhotoCD made from the film—a process that is quite inexpensive and delivers consistently high-quality images. The PhotoCD contained all 128 images shot at 188, data that would have been difficult to transport or manipulate if it hadn't been on a CD-ROM. With the PhotoCD, it was very easy to create texture maps or pictures from the photographs. Going directly to PhotoCD saved us many hours of boring work scanning and manipulating images, and is highly recommended for any VRML project that will be using photographic materials in the design.

Using an ultrasonic rangefinder—these cost about 25 dollars in hardware stores—we took accurate readings for the dimensions of each of the rooms to be modeled. This became the basis for the construction of the space, using Virtus Walkthrough Pro. Because of this, it is necessary to discuss the construction of Project 188 in the context of Virtus Walkthrough Pro.

Virtus Walkthrough Pro

Virtus' Walkthrough product has been on the market for four years, beginning life as a tool used by director James Cameron when he began to design sets for his film, *The Abyss*. It provided Cameron with the ability to see sets before they'd been constructed. He saved time—and plenty of money—by using

Walkthrough to storyboard his film in 3D. Walkthrough Pro, the successor to Walkthrough, was released two years ago on Windows and Macintosh platforms. It includes the capability to create texture-mapped scenes and can be used to create QuickTime movies and Windows AVI movies.

Walkthrough Pro's interface—similar in many respects to Home Space Builder—is much too rich to be discussed fully in this text. We'll cover features that are relevant to Project 188: how to create the spaces themselves, how to place furniture and textures within these spaces, and finally, how to save these files as VRML documents.

The basic Walkthrough Pro environment looks like figure 9.15.

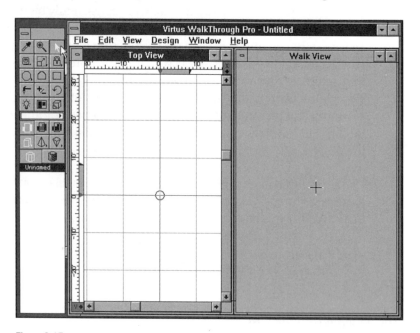

Figure 9.15

Virtus Walkthrough Pro's interface.

There are two basic views of the world. As with Home Space Builder, there's a self, represented by a dot—but this time it's hollow. It sits in the middle of the "Top View" window, which is the world in 2D representation—an architectural projection—as viewed from above. The second window, the "Walk View" window, is the view from the observer's eyepoint, looking outward. The eyepoint is signified by a smaller Pinocchio-type nose pointing out from the self-dot.

Views

The "Views" menu enables you to change to another view, or to add another view to the list of views. The top view shows you the tops of things and enables you to select them from the top. The bottom view, as might seem reasonable, does the same but from underneath. There are views for all six of the projections: left, right, front, back, top, and bottom. Each of them may be used from one time to another, depending on what you are manipulating. Often, to select an object in the world, you have to open a view of the object where it's in front of—or on top of or on the correct side of—other objects.

The Walk View

As is the case with Home Space Builder, the Walk View displays the 3D projection of the world. It updates its content in response to changes in one of the other views. Unlike Home Space Builder, no editing, dragging-and-dropping, or coloring is done in this window—it's just for movement. The crosshairs in the center of the Walk View window serve as a steering wheel for movement. If you click on the crosshairs and move your mouse upward, you'll see the self-dot in the top view move forward. If you move sideways, you'll see the self-dot begin to curve.

Experiment with movement in the Walk View window until you become comfortable with navigation in Walkthrough Pro. Using the shift and control keys in conjunction with the mouse button will produce changes in the pitch and roll of the observer's point of view. If you get disoriented, you can use the "Level Observer" item in the "View" menu to correct your mistakes. If you want to get back to the point where you started, select "Home Observer" from the "View" menu, and you'll find yourself back at the origin again.

The Toolbox

Each Walkthrough window has a set of tool features associated with it. These tools are installed in a toolbar that *floats* alongside the window (it remains in front of all other windows); the toolbox changes its content to reflect the active window. If the active window is one of the 2D views, the Design tools are visible. If the toolbox is the Walk View window, the Walk tools are visible.

Creating a Simple Room with Furniture and Textures

Creating a simple room in Walkthrough Pro is very easy. Select the Top View window—one of the two views that should be created when the program is launched. From the Design toolbox, select the square "space builder" tool. Click on the mouse at a point within the Top View window and drag it, making sure to enclose the self-dot in the area. When you release the mouse button, you'll see your point of view is now enclosed in a gray-colored room, as shown in figure 9.16.

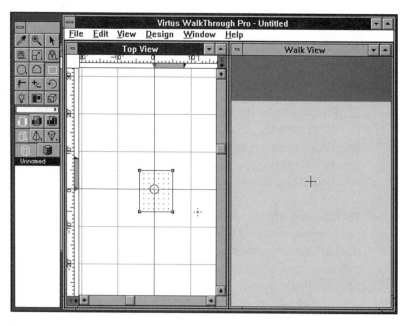

Figure 9.16

Creating a room around your point of view.

If you spin yourself around in the Walk View, you'll see the sides of the room.

Coloring the Walls

In the middle of the Design toolbox is a pane that runs lengthwise across the toolbox. Clicking the mouse on this pane will display a palette with which objects can be colored. If you select one of the colors—once again, I prefer pink buildings, myself—as soon as the selection is made, the walls of the room you've created immediately change to the selected color (see fig. 9.17).

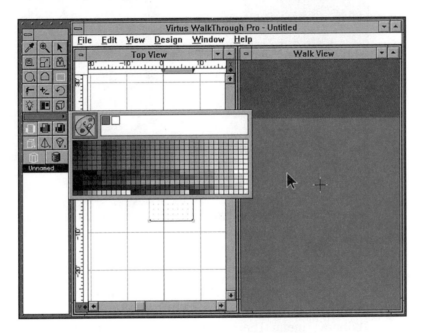

Figure 9.17

The object color selection palette; coloring the walls.

The Surface Editor and Texture Maps

Much of the work done on walls in Walkthrough Pro is done using the Surface Editor. To edit a surface, select the Surface Editor tool (which looks like a doorway and a window), and then click on the surface (in the 2D view) that you want to edit. The Surface Editor will open a window that displays the surface to be edited. To create a surface edit of the front wall of the room we've created, select "Front View" from the "Change View" item of the "Views" menu, and then click on the view with the Surface Edit tool. Walkthrough should now look like figure 9.18.

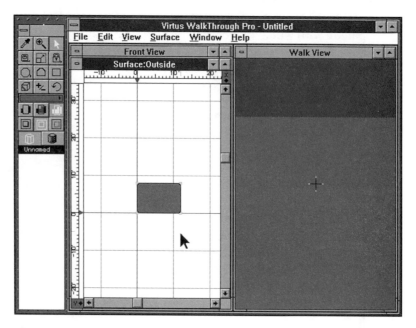

Figure 9.18
Walkthrough's surface editor.

At this point, it's possible to apply a texture map to the surface. To do this, we need to open up the Textures window from the "Window" menu. There are no textures installed when Virtus starts up. The arrow on the top right corner of the window drops a menu from which you can add textures, by selecting the "Add Texture" option. You can choose any of the several hundred textures included with the program or choose any texture you have scanned in, drawn in a paint package, or brought in from clip art. Virtus Walkthrough Pro supports .bmp files for Windows or PICT files and QuickTime movies as textures for Macintosh.

Double click on the texture's entry in the texture window and the surface being edited will be "wallpapered" with the texture map. You can place texture maps on each of the four walls by selecting the appropriate views. You can also make frames using the surface editor and apply textures to only part of the surface. You may want to experiment with editing the tiling and shading of textures in the texture editor. You can place texture maps on each of the four walls by selecting the appropriate views (see fig. 9.19).

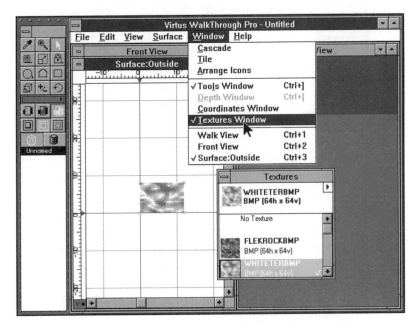

Figure 9.19

Texture mapping from the surface editor.

Adding Furniture

Walkthrough Pro has an extensive library of furniture; to decorate our room, we'll bring in some of it and arrange it within the space. To open the furniture library, select "Library" from the "File" menu and locate the libraries provided with Walkthrough Pro. We want to add a sofa, so select the file SOFASBED.WLB. The library will open, as shown in figure 9.20.

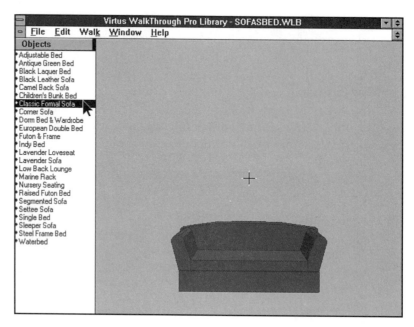

Figure 9.20

A sofa in a Virtus furniture library.

The Walk View in the library works just as it does in the Walk View for your drawing—it's possible to examine each piece of furniture. Select the "Classic Formal Sofa" from the list. To place the sofa into the space, copy it using the "Copy" item from the "Edit" menu, then return to your Walkthrough Pro space, select the "Top View" window, and then select "Paste" from the "Edit" menu. The couch will appear—selected—in the Top view. You can drag it to wherever you like in the scene (see fig. 9.21).

Using this same method, you can create a fully appointed space (see fig. 9.22).

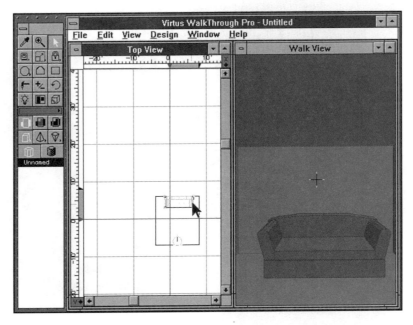

Figure 9.21
Adding furniture to a scene.

Putting a Link from Furniture to an URL

It's very easy to add an URL to an object in a Virtus world. First, select the object that will have the anchor attached to it. (This is done with the selection tool, which looks like a cursor.) Next, select the "VRML Anchor" item from the "Design" menu, as shown in figure 9.23. When the dialog box appears, type in the anchor URL, and press OK.

Saving the File as VRML

To save a file as a VRML world, just select "Export VRML" from the "File" menu. You will be prompted to select a name to save the VRML file under. As with Home Space Builder, Virtus can write but not read VRML files; make sure to save your creations as Walkthrough Pro files as well, so that you can continue to modify and build these files.

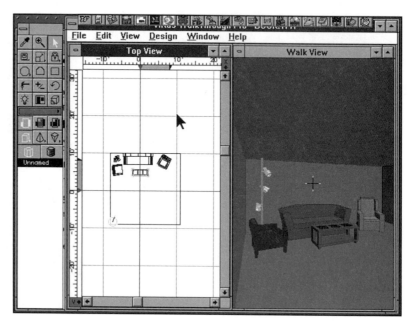

Figure 9.22

More furniture creates a realistic space.

Construction of 188 Using Walkthrough Pro

We began with accurate measurements of each of the rooms and 128 images captured to PhotoCD. These images were brought into CorelDRAW! for retouching (very little was needed) and were then saved as Walkthrough-compatible .bmp images for use as texture maps.

The spaces were created as individual rooms and then "joined" (Walkthrough Pro has a facility for this) after the spaces had been fully articulated. Each phase of room creation had four steps:

1. Creation of the basic room, with all walls, doors, and windows (see fig. 9.24).

Our project consisted of just the first floor of 188; the kitchen, the parlor, and the front room, plus a front foyer. Using the ultrasonic rangefinder, we sampled the wall surfaces and generated accurate readings. Using the Virtus building tools, we created the space for each of the rooms individually. (We later scaled all rooms up by 50 percent because they seemed too cramped at scale.)

All of the surface features, such as doors, windows, and visible moldings (in the kitchen) were added at this time. Virtus provides tools to "cut" polygons; this enabled us to create the surfaces with holes, such as windows and doors. Basic surface colors then were applied for ceilings, floors, and walls that had no texture mapped surfaces.

Finally, the four rooms (kitchen, parlor, front room, and foyer) were "joined" together using the Virtus "join" tool. (This tool looks like a hammer and nail; click on both surfaces to be joined, and the join is made.) This joining created the 188 space.

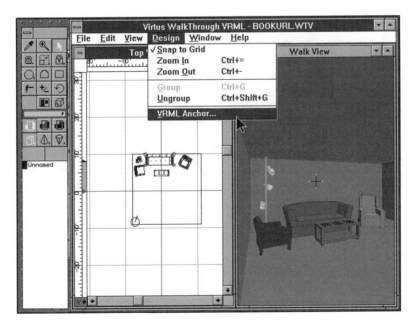

Figure 9.23
Adding an URL to an object in the scene.

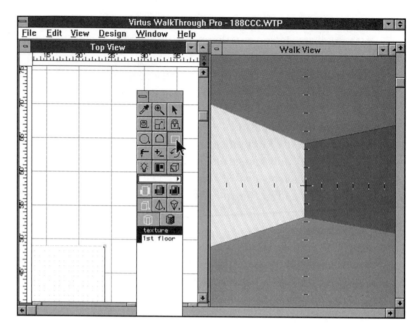

Figure 9.24

The construction of the space of 188.

2. Texture mapping the wallpaper onto the walls, ceilings, and floors (see fig. 9.25).

We examined the images from the PhotoCD and selected areas (using CorelDRAW and Adobe *Photoshop*) that provided a representative texture map. Wallpapers are identical to repeating texture maps; it was important to get a wallpaper sample that was well-lit, and which could be cropped without producing a seam when it was tiled onto a surface. (The texture maps must be brought into Virtus in Microsoft Windows .bmp format.) The texture maps of wallpapers in the kitchen, front room, and foyer are excellent examples of this kind of work; each of the texture maps is quite small, but they've been tiled to cover a very large area.

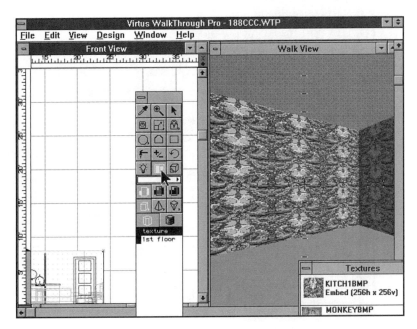

Figure 9.25

Addition of texture maps.

The floor in the front room (also known as the "black room") has a pattern of stars painted onto its surface. This pattern was re-created in Corel *Paint* and then used as a texture map on the floor.

As can be seen in figure 9.25, the addition of the wallpaper texture maps immediately created a much more realistic environment.

3. Placement of "pictures"—individual texture maps displaying specific features of the environment (see fig. 9.26).

The aesthetic quality of 188 is derived primarily from the density of objects within the space. While it would have been impractical to represent every single object within the space, we did decide to sample key objects (photographically) and bring them into our VRML representation.

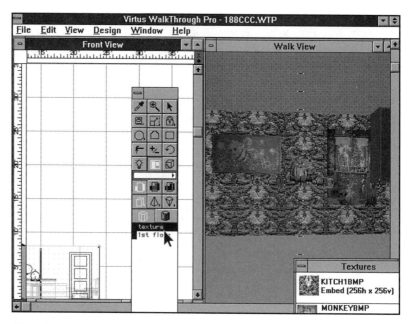

Figure 9.26

Next, individual elements were added.

Of the over 100 photographs taken of 188 during our sampling phase, many were photographs of individual objects. These images were manipulated in CorelDRAW and cropped to remove extraneous details. Then, these images were converted to .bmp format, imported to Virtus as texture maps, and then applied (through the Virtus surface editor) to their respective surfaces.

The kitchen wall in figure 9.26 shows how a basic surface can be layered; the single texture mapped images (which are applied as untiled texture maps) are laid upon the tiled, wallpapered surface.

4. Selection and layout of furniture imported from the Walkthrough Pro furniture library (see fig. 9.27).

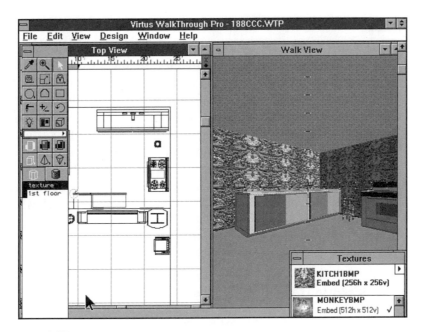

Figure 9.27
Finally, furniture is added to the scenes.

Finally, to give the spaces a realistic feel, the Virtus furniture libraries offered some realistic substitutions for furniture at 188. In some circumstances, the scale of the furniture was altered to fit the room; for example, the sofa in the parlor was stretched to span the entire length of the wall, as it does in 188.

While time-consuming, this process was quite straightforward. We were careful to save the model before and after every major change, and carefully tested the model as it was being built, to make sure that our additions had no unplanned side effects. In the last step, the scene was saved as a VRML .wrl file, from the "Export" item of Virtus' "File" menu.

The end result, while much less dense than the real 188, gives a very accurate flavor for the space.

Testing

There's an oft-heard phrase about cutting one's self on the bleeding edge of technology. In our case, this was true in several dimensions. VRML 1.0 hadn't completely settled out when we began the project—slight fluctuations in the specification caused tools designed to interoperate to fail miserably. We were using versions of Virtus Walkthrough Pro that didn't display texture maps when run under Windows NT—the only environment WebSpace worked within—so we had to continually move back and forth between Windows for Workgroups and Windows NT as the models were developed. We didn't have any other VRML browsers for a large portion of this project—they were still in development! Finally, we had to ship our Walkthrough Pro models to Virtus in North Carolina so they could convert them. Our models were being used to help debug the VRML-compliant version of Walkthrough Pro!

For these reasons, the testing that should be a normal part of a VRML project was almost an afterthought, or more precisely, reversed. We were using the project to test all the tools, a most unlikely situation. As our tools arrived, however, we did check our models against them—on SGIs and PCs—to make sure that they maintained consistency across the platforms and across VRML implementations.

Publishing

One of the major trade-offs made in the creation of 188 was the decision to use texture maps rather than explicit 3D models of all the objects in each of the rooms. While this made the effort significantly easier, the VRML world references approximately 1 MB of texture map data—which takes about 20 minutes to download over a 14.4 Kbps modem. We knew that any attempt to model the density of 188 in 3D would produce a similarly-sized file, and have the additional side effect of introducing so many polygons into the model that the computer running the VRML browser would effectively grind to a halt, or perhaps even crash.

Using this many texture maps in a model means one of two things. Either the texture maps are declared using an **image** field within a **Texture2** node and are spelled out explicitly—this is tedious and wastes space, but is a standard methodology—or they are declared using the **filename** field of the **Texture2** node, which then references an exterior file. In the latter case, you must make sure the texture map images are placed into a Web-accessible directory and that the VRML files are updated to reflect this fact. The VRML Primer describes the Texture2 node; Chapter 8, "Advanced VRML and Server Scripts," provides a great deal of information about texture maps and the Web.

Build It Yourself—Converting to VRML

You've seen two tools at work: one for novices and one for professionals. Don't be scared by Walkthrough Pro's feature set or put-off by Home Space Builder's easy-to-use interface. Both of them, creatively applied, can create compelling cyberspace. One excels at layout, the other at textures; both have their place, and both speak a common language—VRML. These are just the first generation of VRML tools. Others will follow, some more sophisticated, some designed to take advantage of VRML's level-of-detail and inlining features, and some designed to make Web publishing of VRML worlds a breeze.

Before there are a multitude of useful VRML tools, you may be very well served by converting your existing 3D models into VRML. If you're going to do this, you can take advantage of a tool provided in the CD-ROM. WCVT2POV.EXE, a Microsoft Windows-based 3D file converter, will take in several of the more popular 3D file formats (including 3D Studio, Wavefront, and Autodesk's DXF) and convert them to VRML 1.0. If you already have a menagerie of basic objects, you can bring them into cyberspace by converting them and including them in your VRML projects.

If you don't have a Windows-based computer, you can use a publicly available DXF to VRML file converter that runs over the Web. The instructions on how to use this converter are at *http://www.organic.com/vrml/*.

Unfortunately, none of these converters is perfect; often you'll see that the beautifully constructed model you've built in one program is completely ruined when translated and imported into VRML. Beware texture map conversions—although it's not difficult to do, there isn't a tool that does it well. Converting models often means that they lose the artistic qualities that make them interesting.

This early generation of VRML tools will require their share of hand-holding; it's easy to understand why—cyberspace is as new to the programmer as it is to you as the builder. Be patient, and don't be afraid to take a peek "under the hood" at VRML documents. They're quite easy to read and work with—the more you know, the more you'll be able to express.

Use whichever of these meets your needs, but get out there and build something. *Build it yourself!*

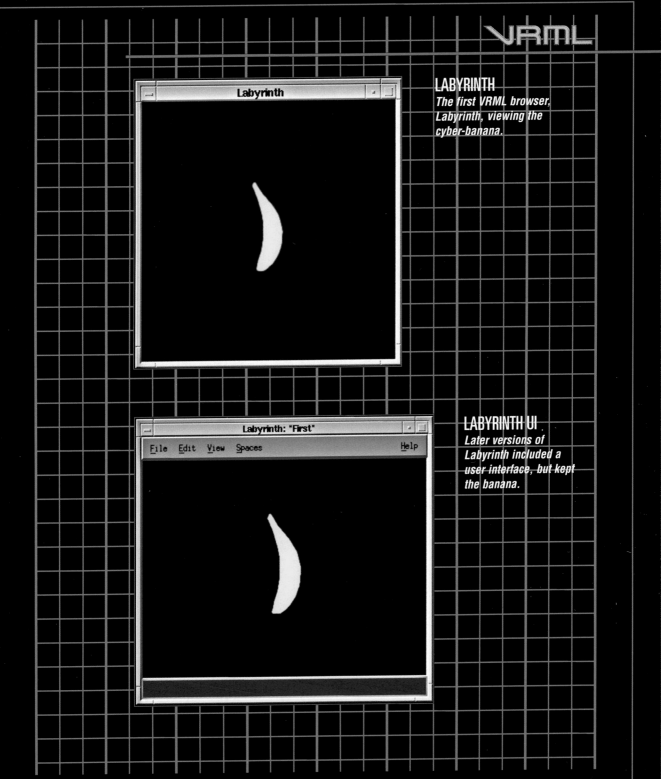

VRML

LABYRINTH
The first VRML browser, Labyrinth, viewing the cyber-banana.

LABYRINTH UI
Later versions of Labyrinth included a user interface, but kept the banana.

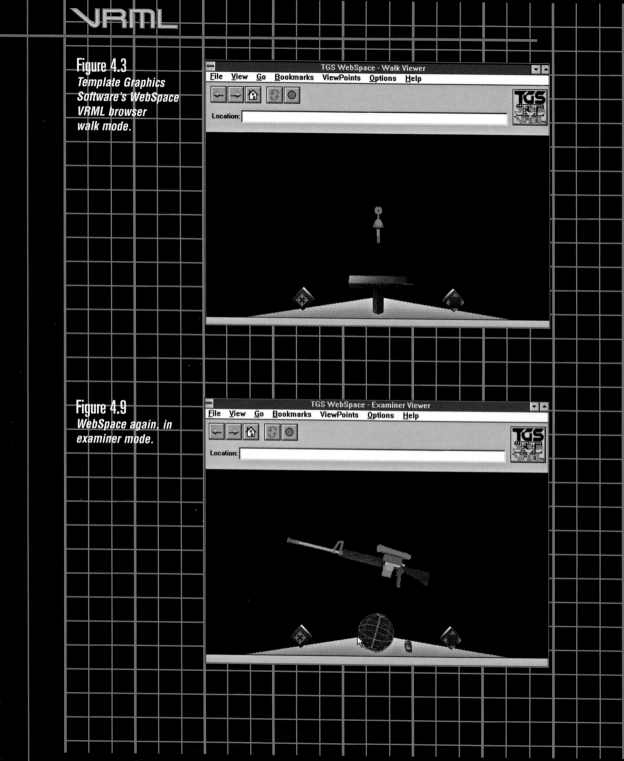

VRML

Figure 4.3
*Template Graphics
Software's WebSpace
VRML browser
walk mode.*

Figure 4.9
*WebSpace again, in
examiner mode.*

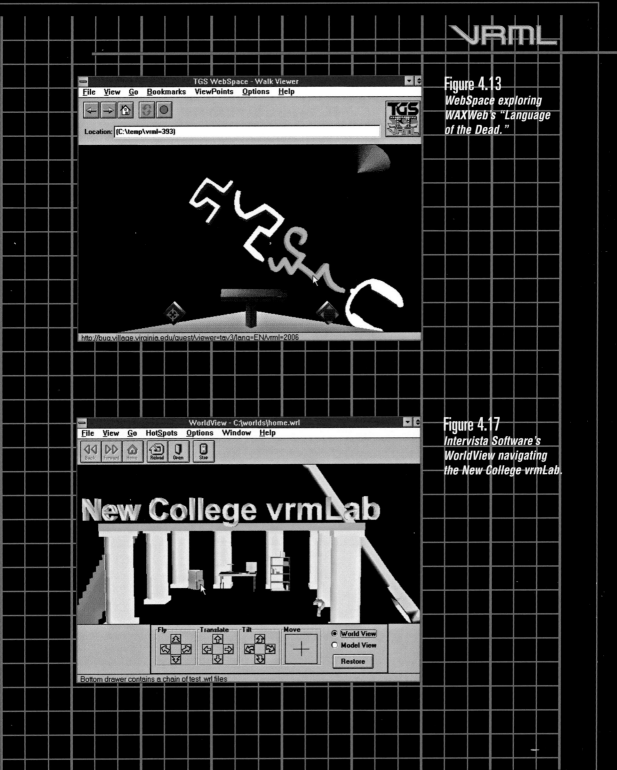

VRML

Figure 4.13
WebSpace exploring WAXWeb's "Language of the Dead."

Figure 4.17
Intervista Software's WorldView navigating the New College vrmLab.

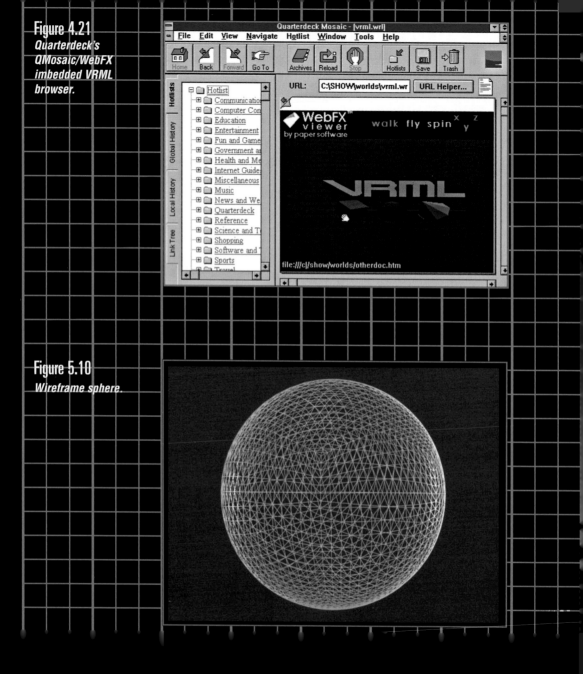

Figure 4.21
Quarterdeck's QMosaic/WebFX imbedded VRML browser.

Figure 5.10
Wireframe sphere.

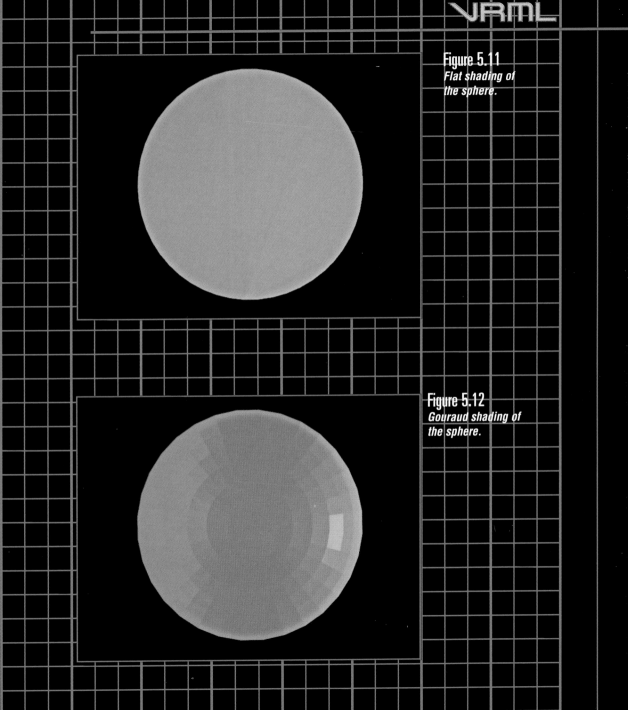

VRML

Figure 5.11
*Flat shading of
the sphere.*

Figure 5.12
*Gouraud shading of
the sphere.*

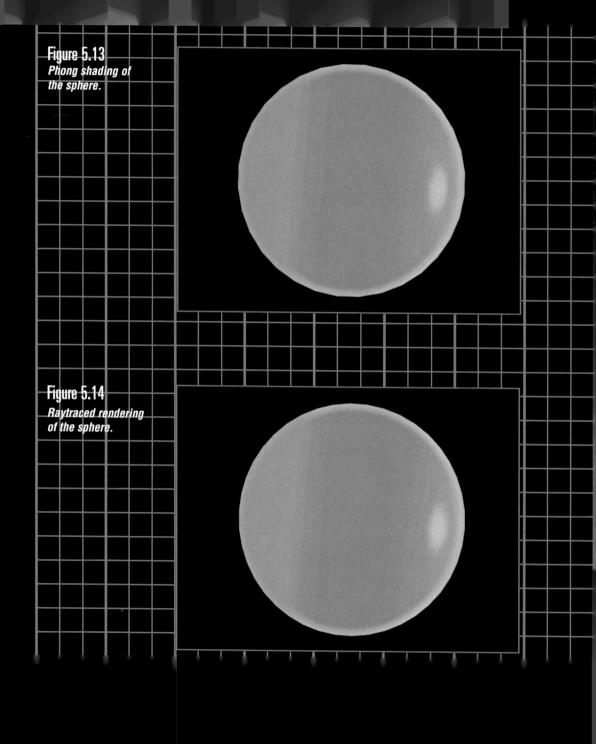

Figure 5.13
Phong shading of the sphere.

Figure 5.14
Raytraced rendering of the sphere.

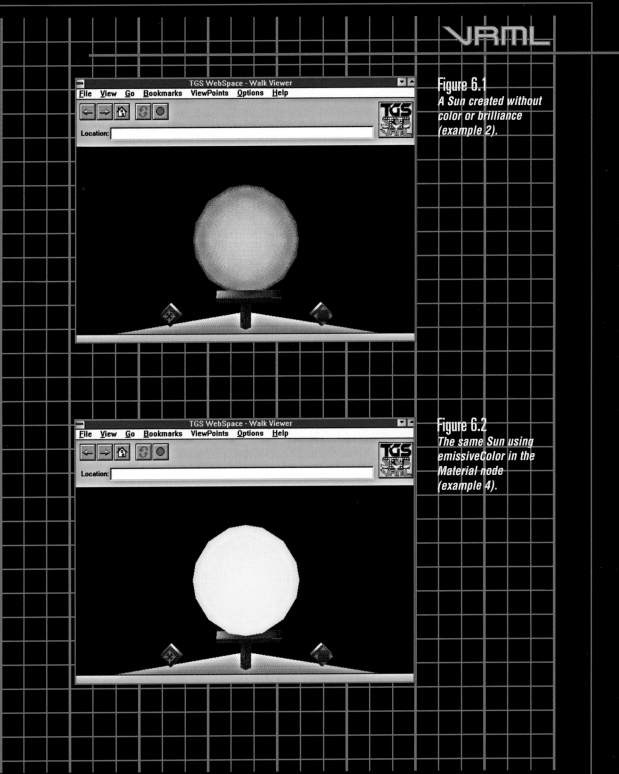

Figure 6.1
A Sun created without color or brilliance (example 2).

Figure 6.2
The same Sun using emissiveColor in the Material node (example 4).

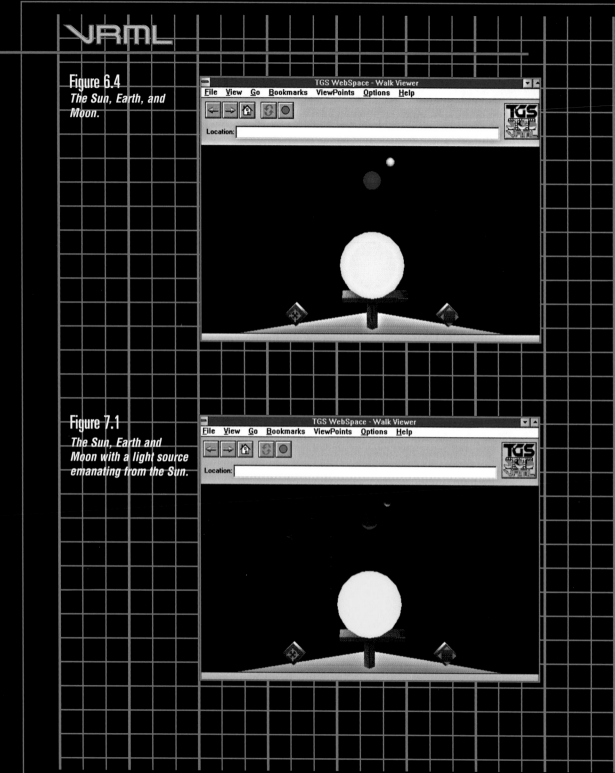

Figure 6.4
The Sun, Earth, and Moon.

Figure 7.1
The Sun, Earth and Moon with a light source emanating from the Sun.

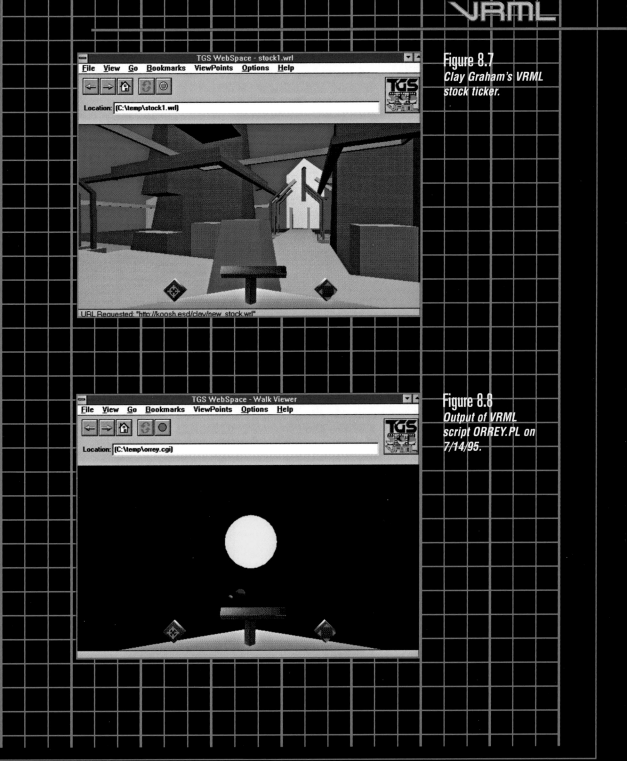

Figure 8.7
Clay Graham's VRML stock ticker.

Figure 8.8
Output of VRML script ORREY.PL on 7/14/95.

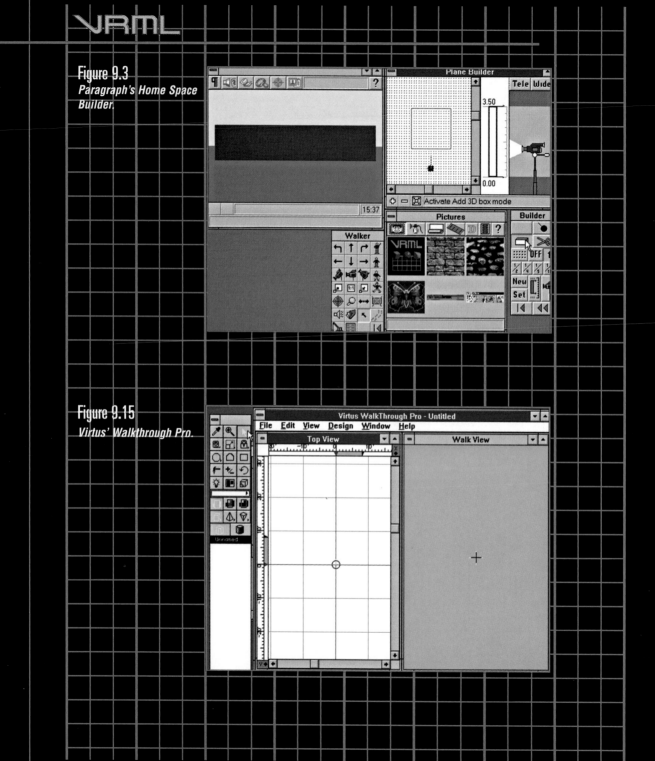

VRML

Figure 9.3
Paragraph's Home Space Builder.

Figure 9.15
Virtus' Walkthrough Pro.

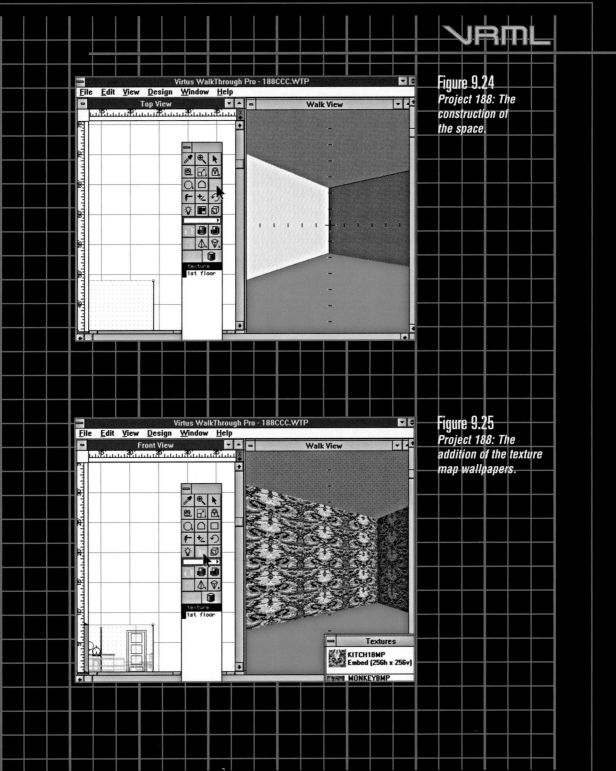

Figure 9.24
Project 188: The construction of the space.

Figure 9.25
Project 188: The addition of the texture map wallpapers.

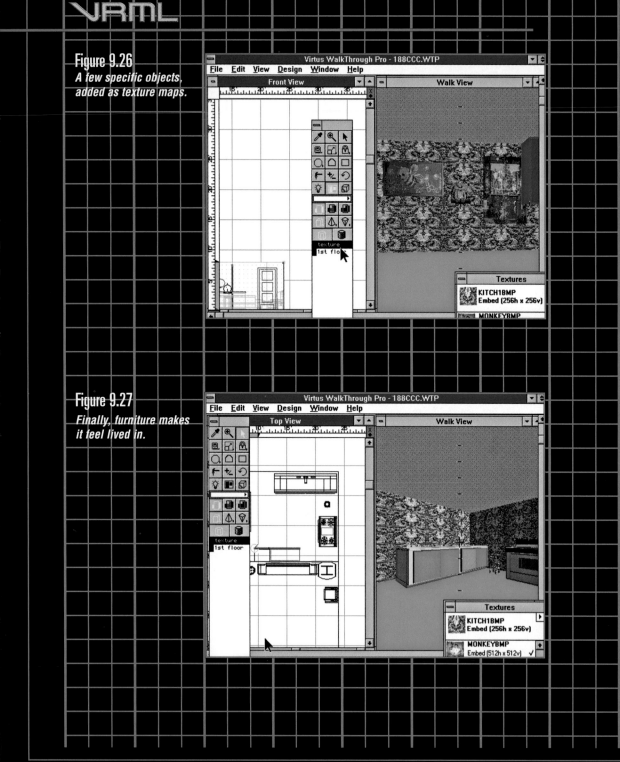

Figure 9.26
A few specific objects, added as texture maps.

Figure 9.27
Finally, furniture makes it feel lived in.

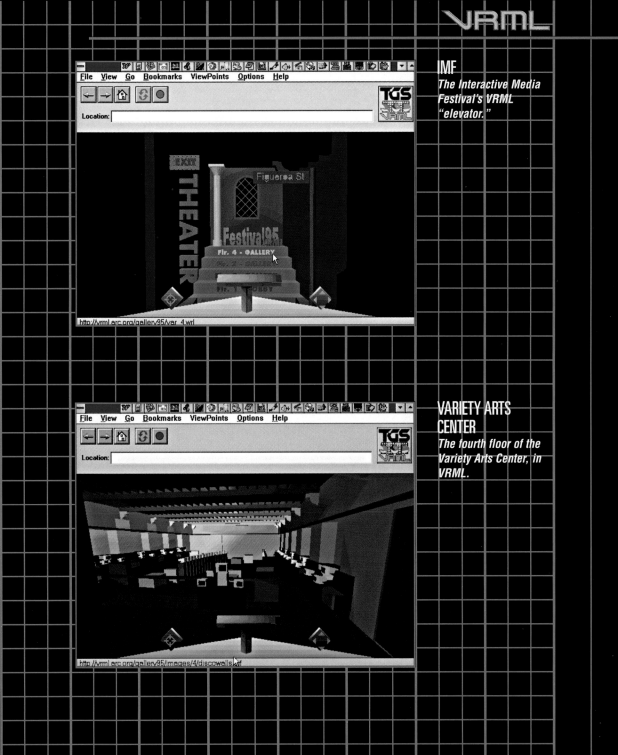

VRML

IMF
The Interactive Media Festival's VRML "elevator."

http://vrml.arc.org/gallery95/var_4.wrl

VARIETY ARTS CENTER
The fourth floor of the Variety Arts Center, in VRML.

http://vrml.arc.org/gallery95/images/4/discowalls.wrl

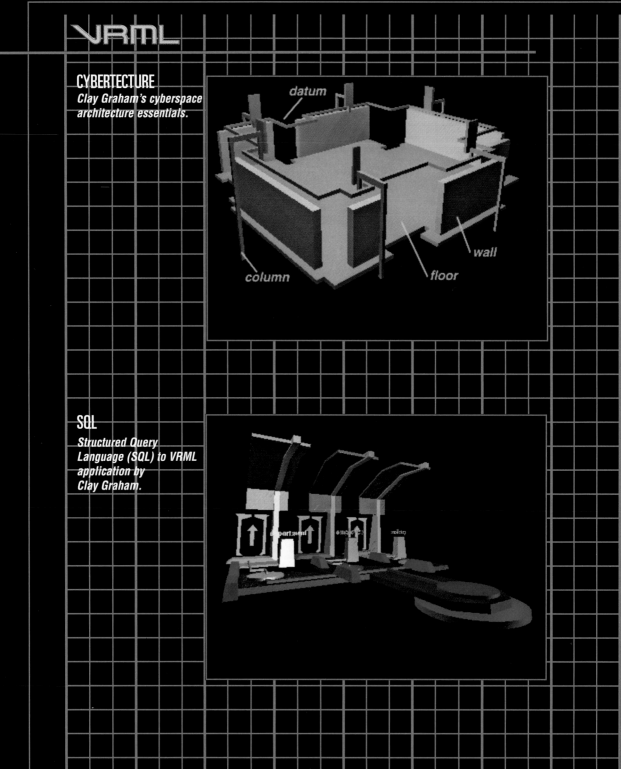

VRML

CYBERTECTURE
Clay Graham's cyberspace architecture essentials.

datum

wall

column

floor

SQL
Structured Query Language (SQL) to VRML application by Clay Graham.

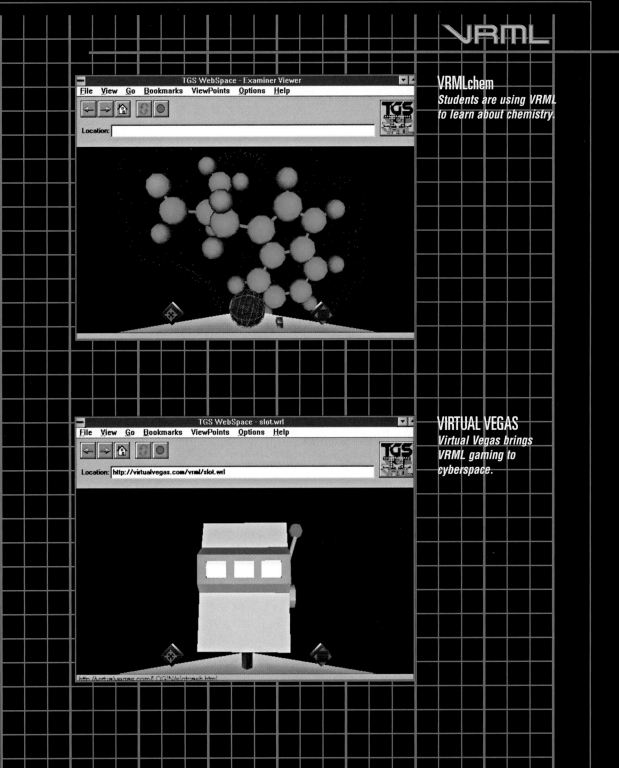

VRML

VRMLchem
Students are using VRML to learn about chemistry.

TGS WebSpace - Examiner Viewer

File   View   Go   Bookmarks   ViewPoints   Options   Help

Location:

TGS

VIRTUAL VEGAS
Virtual Vegas brings VRML gaming to cyberspace.

TGS WebSpace - slot.wrl

File   View   Go   Bookmarks   ViewPoints   Options   Help

Location: http://virtualvegas.com/vrml/slot.wrl

TGS

http://virtualvegas.com/LOGIN/slotcrash.html

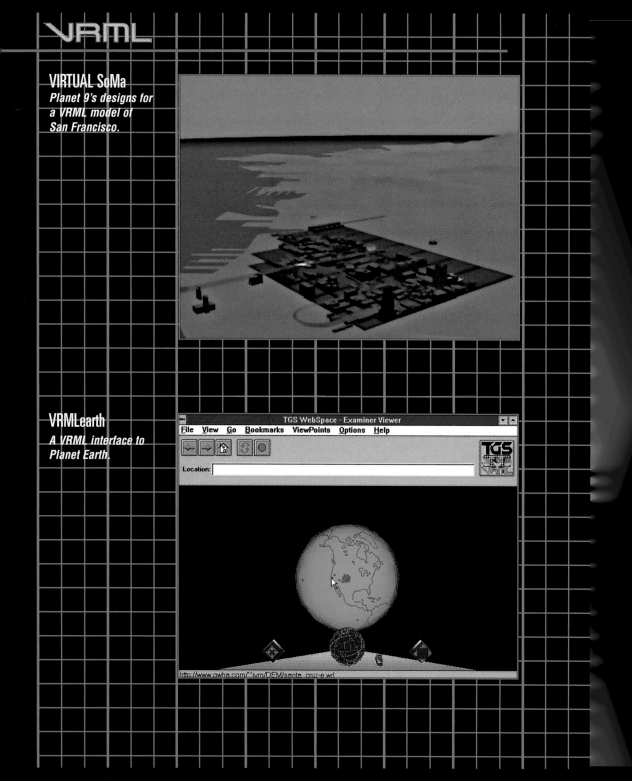

VRML

VIRTUAL SoMa
Planet 9's designs for a VRML model of San Francisco.

VRMLearth
A VRML interface to Planet Earth.

TGS WebSpace - Examiner Viewer

File   View   Go   Bookmarks   ViewPoints   Options   Help

Location:

http://www.awha.com/~tvm/DEM/santa_cruz-e.wrl

Part IV

The Road to Know Where

BROWSING AND BUILDING CYBERSPACE

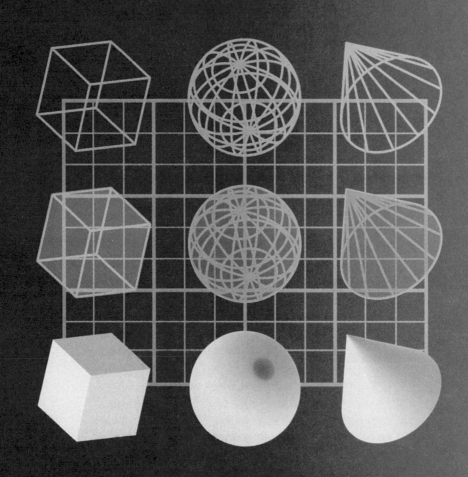

Chapter 10

VRML Optimization and Publishing Issues

A large-scale VRML project will require careful planning in the design stages. Thought must be given to the quality of service (high-speed versus low-speed connections), the capability of the computer and VRML browser (from a 486/SX with 8 MB to an SGI Reality Engine with 128 MB of texture map memory), and the capability of the Web server(s) that handle the requests for VRML documents.

Two nodes in VRML, the level-of-detail node, **LOD**, and the Web inline node, **WWWInline**, should be used as the foundation for creating VRML worlds that execute well in a wide array of situations. Used together, these nodes can create files that are comfortably small, while remaining adequately expressive.

The specific behavior of the **LOD** node is to progressively provide higher levels of scene detail as the user's camera moves toward the portion of the scene within the **LOD** node. In other words, as you approach an object, it *resolves*, and moves to a more explicit self-representation. The browser can also use it as a "hint" to keep the performance of the browser regular and smooth, however, falling back to lower levels of detail (which render more quickly) if browser performance degrades.

The general syntax of the **LOD** node is as follows:

```
LOD {
        range [ closest, closer, further, ..., far
➥of all ]
        center x_center y_center z_center

        # LOD is a group node, so here are the children of the
➥node
        # The Separator nodes aren't strictly necessary...
        Separator {
                how the object looks close up
➥resolution
        }
        Separator {
                how the object looks a bit further/medium
➥resolution
        }
        Separator {
                how it looks a bit further still/medium
➥resolution
        }
        ...
        Separator {
                how it looks at its lowest level of detail
        }
}
```

In this prototypical example, any number of levels of detail can be specified, so long as there is a group node for each specified level. If there is a mismatch between the number of specified ranges and the number of nodes within the group, the results are undefined—meaning you'll probably crash the VRML browser.

The **LOD** node and the **WWWInline** node are meant to work well together, facilitating a technique known as *lazy loading*. This technique, also called *on-demand loading*, allows the VRML browser to make its own decisions about the level-of-detail of any object it loads, and when those objects are loaded. The browser makes this decision based upon *heuristics*—a model that the browser builds of the requirements of the VRML scene and the capabilities of the computer it's running on—to generate the most effective selection at any point in time.

The browser can load the lowest level-of-detail of a scene very quickly, generally because it doesn't have very much information, and can then load successive levels of detail based upon the camera position in the scene—that is, where the user is looking. The browser will then load higher levels of detail in the background—just like Netscape Navigator does with images—to have them ready when they are needed.

A properly constructed **LOD** node would look much like the following example; the lowest level-of-detail—a sphere—can be represented very concisely; using a built-in type for an object's definition is among the most efficient ways of describing it.

```
LOD {
        # Example using LOD with WWWInline
        # Low-resolution is explicit, others by reference

        range [ closest, close, further away, ..., far
➥of all ]
        center x_center y_center z_center

    # how it looks at its greatest level of detail
        WWWInline {
                name "http://www.foo.org/example/hirez.wrl"
                bboxSize x_size y_size z_size
                bboxcenter x_center y_center z_center
        }

        # how the object looks a bit closer still/medium
➥resolution
        WWWInline {
                name "http://www.foo.org/example/medrez.wrl"
                bboxSize x_size y_size z_size
                bboxcenter x_center y_center z_center
        }
```

```
        ...etc...etc...etc...

    # how the object looks a bit closer/medium-low
➥resolution
        WWWInline {
                name "http://www.foo.org/example/lowmedrez.wrl"
                bboxSize x_size y_size z_size
                bboxcenter x_center y_center z_center
        }

        # explicit definition of the object at low resolution
        Sphere {
                radius sphere_size
        }
}
```

The subsequent levels of detail are all given by reference, through **WWWInline** nodes. Thus, a VRML world can be loaded very quickly—in this example, the lowest levels of details are expressed succinctly—and the browser will "fill in" the scene to the appropriate level of detail as more time passes.

VRML browsers can calculate the bandwidth between them and a VRML file server by calculating how long it takes for a given VRML document (of a known size) to arrive. This can serve as a basis for making level-of-detail decisions, independent of the recommendations given in the **range** field of the **LOD** node. The browser makes a determination of which node of an **LOD** group to load based upon this information.

Now we come to the question of the appropriate structure of **LOD** group content. This is where the rubber meets the road—or rather, where the renderer meets the computer. While SGI's Onyx might be the appropriate rendering solution for large-scale VRML environments, very few individuals have access to the hundreds of thousands of dollars of hardware that make mincemeat of even the most complicated environments.

WebSpace (Beta 2 or better) maintains a heuristic of the render-

WebSpace (Beta 2 or better) maintains a heuristic of the rendering complexity of a scene. The *complexity* is calculated from the number of frames per second that the renderer generates as the user navigates through the VRML world. When the number of frames per second falls below two or three, the user begins to experience frustration; clearly the browser should seek to avoid this.

A few browsers do implement this functionality. WebSpace does so by "sensing" the frame rate of the renderer and adjusting the scene complexity appropriately. This could mean losing texture mapping while in motion, only to have it restored when the user stops moving for a moment. It could also mean going all the way to a wireframe model—the fastest of all rendering technologies—in order to preserve the fluidity of navigation on a relatively underpowered computer.

VRML browsers such as WebSpace can change the visible content of the scene one of two ways—either by making their own decisions to scale back on scene details, or by using the **LOD** node as a hint that guides them in the selective replacement of scene elements with lower-resolution, easier-to-render, components.

Here are some basic guidelines that can help you design **LOD** nodes that are meaningful both in terms of transmission time (over slow links) and rendering time (on slow computers):

➤ Large objects (or small objects nearby) take more time to render than smaller (or far away) objects. This is something you have very little control over in many cases, but is something to keep in mind when designing a world. If there is a large object in the background, filling the entire scene, it will be re-rendered in every single frame. Smaller objects enable the renderer to practice culling—that is, the removal of objects from the renderer's list of objects to be rendered—because they're no longer within the user's view of the scene.

➤ Complex objects take more time to render than simple objects. Don't confuse VRML built-in objects, like **Sphere**, with simple objects. A **Sphere** can have several hundred polygons, whereas a simple object like a tetrahedron—the simplest case—has only four. Clearly it takes the computer much less time to manipulate an object with 1/50th as many polygon faces.

➤ Texture-mapped objects take more time to render than simple, colored objects. While a texture map is in view, every frame of movement introduces a transformation over the entire visible length of the texture map. This means that the entire map has to be re-calculated, on a pixel-by-pixel basis.

➤ Texture-mapped objects have two components—their geometry (shape) and their texture map (surface). The geometry may often be quite concise—perhaps a **Sphere** or **Cube** node. The texture map is often a long string of characters that explicitly spell out the value of every pixel in the texture map. This can be a very bandwidth-consuming mechanism for specifying a VRML object. Using URLs that specify texture maps as GIFs or JPEGs (not yet a VRML standard, but implemented in many VRML browsers) take less transmission time, and should be used in most situations. Tiling a repetitive texture map will also save space— both in the computer's memory and in transmission time.

➤ On the other hand, a texture map can save many polygons; this is a trade-off that many world designers make. They sacrifice geometric accuracy for visible accuracy, and use a texture map instead of 10,000 polygons. Seen in this light, texture maps can be a more efficient solution than explicit representation of an object.

Given these guidelines, it is possible to draw up a conception of the content of the "ideal" **LOD** node. It looks something like the following:

```
LOD {
        # Example using LOD with WWWInline
        # Low-resolution is explicit, others by reference
        # Each level has detail appropriate to its level

        range [ closest, close, further away, ..., far
➥of all ]
        center x_center y_center z_center

        # how it looks at its greatest level of detail
        # greater than 1000 polygons and/or texture maps
        WWWInline {
                name "http://www.foo.org/example/hirez.wrl"
                bboxSize x_size y_size z_size
                bboxcenter x_center y_center z_center
        }

        # how the object looks a bit closer still/medium
➥resolution
        # This object is probably between 100 - 1000 polygons
        # It might have a small, tiled texture map
        WWWInline {
                name "http://www.foo.org/example/medrez.wrl"
                bboxSize x_size y_size z_size
                bboxcenter x_center y_center z_center
        }

        ...etc...etc...etc...

        # how the object looks a bit closer/medium-low
➥resolution
        # This is probably between 10 - 200 polygons
        WWWInline {
                name "http://www.foo.org/example/lowmedrez.wrl"
                bboxSize x_size y_size z_size
                bboxcenter x_center y_center z_center
        }

        # explicit definition of the object at low resolution
        # A built-in primitive is an effective use of
➥bandwidth
```

```
# But if it has lots of polygons, it might be a wash
# So we'll use a cube rather than a sphere
Cube {
        # The cube has the approximate volume of the
➡object
        width cube_width
        height cube_height
        depth cube_depth
    }
}
```

There are a lot of trade-offs involved in the optimization of a VRML world; VRML-specific authoring tools will be able to generate part of the solution by themselves, but any large-scale project will always need a good dose of "hand tuning." The only way to accurately understand the relationship between rendering speed, transmission time, and browser behavior is by experimentation. Each VRML browser implements **LOD** slightly differently, and each of them have their own mechanisms for preserving a smooth feel to navigation within the world. This means that a solution that works well for one browser might be inappropriate in another. Unfortunately, there are no easy answers here— experimentation and experience are the best guides.

A large-scale VRML project could create a world with several hundred **WWWInline** statements. This means that many separate Web requests are required to create a complete view of the VRML world. The current, and rather unsophisticated, crop of VRML browsers perform these requests *synchronously*—one document is completely retrieved before the next transfer begins. HTML browsers such as Netscape Navigator can perform several simultaneous retrievals—several images on a single page can all load at the same time. It is reasonable to assume that this functionality will migrate into VRML browsers as well.

The VRML Web site administrator is faced with a dilemma: if there's a VRML world on the server with hundreds of inline objects, each time the world is loaded, several hundred transactions will take place. More and more of them will be occurring simultaneously, as VRML browsers implement multiple simultaneous file retrieval. This can place an inordinate strain on a single Web server, which might end up processing thousands of simultaneous transfers. What's good for a browser may not be good for a server.

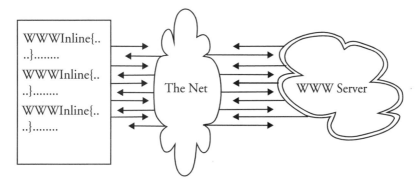

Figure 10.1

WWWInline can lead to an overwhelmed Web server.

Before an installation of a large-scale world is made to a major Web site, a detailed analysis of the VRML files that comprise the world must be made. From this, the administrator will be able to gain an understanding of the load burden associated with the files, and will be able to deposit them across an array of servers (if possible), or can reorganize the VRML documents, and so decrease the burden at any one time.

When reorganizing a VRML world, the site administrator needs to identify and place similar files—such as the group nodes in an **LOD** node—onto different hosts. Many browsers will load several levels of detail at once or, at best, sequentially. If the load burden for such a request can be spread across multiple machines, the users will experience much better performance, and the server load will remain more constant. In the case where the VRML files are arranged so that a large number of simultaneous requests are made to a single server, and that file is loaded into several VRML browsers simultaneously, a "cascade" effect could cause the server to become overloaded and suffer severe performance degradation.

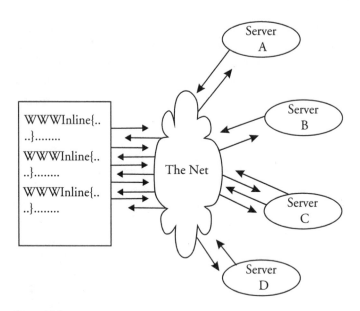

Figure 10.2

Spreading the WWWInline burden among an array of servers.

Object inlining will be even more prevalent in VRML than in HTML, so professional VRML publishing tools should conduct their own analysis of the load of any VRML document set, and generate a report of publishing recommendations for the site administrator. No tools like this exist at this writing, but some of the Web server analysis tools (most of which are written in PERL and freely available at major Web sites) can be adapted for use in VRML publishing.

Finally, file compression is an important issue in VRML. The VRML 1.0 specification makes no recommendation on a compression methodology. The VRML community, in a consensus process, has agreed that VRML 1.0 should be compressed using the GZIP algorithm. GZIP, part of the Free Software Foundation's GNU tools, is freely available in both source code and binaries for many platforms. Using GZIP alone, files can be reduced by as much as 80 percent in size.

WebSpace (Beta 2) will automatically "unzip" files that have been processed with GZIP. Some VRML browsers won't do that yet, so loading a compressed VRML file is a three-step process, as follows:

1. Save the compressed VRML file to the local disk.

2. Run GUNZIP or equivalent to decompress the VRML file.

3. Open the file within the VRML browser.

James Waldrop of Construct, Inc. developed a *datafat munger*, which examines the content of the VRML file and removes the "fat" from it by stripping excess precision from the numbers in the file. It appears to work well in most situations, and using it with GZIP can reduce file size by over 95 percent. The Interactive Media Festival used the munger to reduce a 2.5 megabyte file down to just 80 KB! Your actual mileage might vary, but it is possible to dramatically reduce file size—and decrease load time, if compression and munging are used judiciously. Your users will thank you. (Think about it—when was the last time you hesitated to download an 80 KB file? When was the last time you bothered to download a 2.5 MB file?)

The following is the PERL source for the munger, with thanks to James Waldrop:

```perl
#!/usr/bin/perl
#
# Written Fri May 19 11:48:25 PDT 1995 by
# James Waldrop (sulam@well.com)
#
# invoke like so:  scriptname foo1.wrl foo2.wrl
# produces output like foo1.wrl.new

for ($x=-1; $x++ < $#ARGV; ) {
    $file = $ARGV[$x];
    if (! (-e $file) ) {
        print "$file not found, skipping...\n";
        next;
    }
```

```
        &convert($file);
}

exit;

sub convert {
    local ($file) = @_;
    open (OLD, $file) |¦ die "Couldn't open $file: $!\n";
    open (NEW, ">$file.new") |¦ die "Couldn't open $file.new:
➥$!\n";

    while (<OLD>) {
        $line = $_;
        if (/Normal/) { while(<OLD>) { last if /}/; } $line =
➥""; }
        if (/normalIndex/) { while(<OLD>) { last if /[]]/; }
➥$line = ""; }
        $line =~ s/[-+]?[0-9]\.[0-9]+e[+-][0-9]+/0/g;
    ➥# makes an assumption
        $line =~ s/([0-9]+\.[0-9]{2})[0-9]+/$1/g;
➥# replace 2 with
        $line =~ s/0\.00/0/g;    # get rid of 0.00
➥# digits of precision
        $line =~ s/[ ]+/ /g;
        $line =~ s/[\t]+/ /g;
        $line =~ s/^ //g;
        print NEW $line;
    }
    close OLD;
    close NEW;
}
```

While tested, the munger might still have a few bugs; it's probably a good idea to run the munger after you've created a backup copy of your VRML documents. In addition, the data removed from this file is *probably* unimportant to your VRML browser, but it's always a good idea to test your VRML documents with several browsers. The fat in one document might be the essence of another.

Creating an effective and pleasing VRML site means using every trick in the book. Every step demands a quality-conscious approach—design, planning, meticulous attention to detail, and persistent monitoring of your finished product. You'll have to dispassionately evaluate the experience from the user's perspective. Is it fast enough? Does it load every time? Can I find my way around? Are the anchors live or dead? The reward is a VRML site that is easy to maintain and gets lots of visitors.

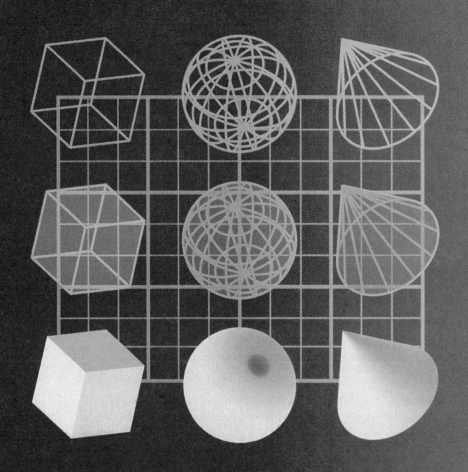

Chapter 11

How to Write a VRML Browser

The subject of the design of VRML browsers could fill entire books, but it is possible to detail the overall structure of a VRML browser in just a single chapter. The design of these browsers is evolving very rapidly; competition for usage is leading to increasing "featuritis" and a flowering of user interface paradigms. No single browser will be perfect for all situations, and many more technical individuals will opt to "roll their own" and create a VRML browser for a specific application or environment. New computers and operating systems are being invented all the time—we'll need VRML on new machines as well!

A browser has several essential components—a network interface, a VRML parser, a renderer, and a navigation interface. We'll touch on all of these in some detail.

VRML Parser

A VRML browser must have some way to get its data into the browser. There are two fundamental approaches to this—either the browser can be implemented as a helper application (launched and fed data by a Web browser, such as Netscape

Navigator), or it can be implemented as a stand-alone application. If the browser is implemented as a helper application, a set of interfaces to the Web browser must be implemented.

These interfaces, such as the *Client Communication Interface* (CCI), *Dynamic Data Exchange* (DDE), *Object Linking and Embedding* (OLE), and AppleScript, are decidedly non-trivial, and can take several weeks to months to design and implement. DDE, widely implemented on Microsoft Windows, exists nowhere else. OLE is implemented on the Macintosh and under Microsoft Windows, but is notoriously difficult to program and debug. CCI is common to most platforms, but is implemented in different ways on Unix, PC, and Macintosh platforms; one platform can't talk to the others using CCI. At this writing, there is no cross-platform standard for helper application communications, so each implementation will be quite different.

If a stand-alone application is desired, the browser will need to implement full Web functionality. Fortunately, the source code (mostly Unix platforms) for the World Wide Web networking libraries are freely available from NCSA (http://ncsa.uiuc.edu/) and the World Wide Web Consortium (http://w3.org/). A full-featured browser will need to implement the *Hypertext Transfer Protocol* (HTTP), *File Transfer Protocol* (FTP), and Gopher—all of which are available within the libraries. Implementation of any of these protocols is relatively easy, and the sources from the public domain libraries can be used as a guide.

Regardless of the data stream a VRML browser uses, it needs to be able to hand-off Web data types it does not understand. For example, a Web browser might know how to display an HTML document, but may not know how to play a QuickTime movie. For this reason, HTTP transactions begin with a declaration of the MIME type of the data; this is then used by the browser to determine how the data should be presented. A VRML browser is designed specifically to display data that has a MIME type

x-world/x-vrml; any other data type—for example, something linked to a book in a virtual environment—might not be representable within the VRML browser. The VRML browser, like an HTML browser, should be able to spawn helper applications to present this data. Often, the design will simply hand-off all unrepresentable data types to a companion HTML browser, but this leads into the implementation complexities outlined earlier. While there is no standard for telling a HTML browser to "go to this page," the VRML browser must implement that feature, or deal with all data types itself.

The VRML parser converts the VRML token stream from ASCII text into a form that the computer understands. The VRML browser receives data through its network interface and passes it along to the parser. The parser then "walks" the data within the VRML file, and converts this file into an internal representation, called a "parse tree." This parse tree is then *traversed*—its contents are examined, branch by branch, until the entire VRML file has been translated into a visible representation.

QvLib, the Quick VRML Parser (the source code for which is on the CD-ROM packaged with this book) written by Paul Strauss and Gavin Bell of SGI, is a public-domain library of source code that will convert VRML 1.0 files into a set of "C++" objects, which correspond to the nodes in the VRML file. Most VRML browsers— and all of the public domain ones—are built around QvLib. QvLib is pure "C++," and is very easy to transport to new computer systems, especially those that have a Unix flavor.

Rendering

As the parse tree is traversed, a visible representation is created. This representation must be *rendered*—that is, presented on the computer's display. There are a number of techniques for rendering, and we'll discuss two here—Silicon Graphics' OpenGL and Microsoft's Reality Lab.

OpenGL

OpenGL (graphics library) is a set of "C" language routines that can create a visible representation of a 3D environment from a set of commands. OpenGL is centered around the concept of the *display list*—that is, a set of OpenGL library calls that are made every time the image is to be rendered. If you use QvLib as your VRML parser, the parse tree that it builds must then be converted into a set of OpenGL commands. This is a non-trivial process. OpenGL is extremely flexible and full-featured; it's possible to build a VRML browser using OpenGL that could render the dinosaurs used in *Jurassic Park*. On the downside, OpenGL can be somewhat slower than other technologies used for rendering. WebSpace uses OpenGL.

Microsoft's Reality Lab

Microsoft's Reality Lab (which ships as a part of Windows 95, but is available for most other platforms) is one of a new class of software-accelerated 3D renderers. It uses the concept of "frames of reference," a concept similar to that used in physics. Each scene created in Reality Lab has a number of objects in it, each with its own frame of reference. The scene is maintained entirely by Reality Lab. Once the parse tree has been converted into Reality Lab objects—again, a non-trivial task—the programmer need do nothing more to the objects within the scene. Because the scene is managed internally by Reality Lab, rather than externally, as is the case with OpenGL, it is generally about 10 times faster than OpenGL. The trade-off for using this approach is a less flexible rendering solution, which may be fine for low to mid-range systems, but unacceptable for designers who want "Hollywood quality" real-time graphics. WorldView uses Reality Lab.

Criterion's RenderWare

The first of the software accelerated 3D renderers, Criterion RenderWare provides much of the same functionality as Microsoft's Reality Lab, and has the added advantage of being well-supported on a wide range of platforms, from Macintosh to

PC to SunOS to SGI. Again, very much like Reality Lab, a scene is created by RenderWare and maintained by it. WebFX uses RenderWare.

Hardware Accelerated Renderers

One of the most exciting prospects for VRML is the imminent availability of hardware to accelerate 3D graphics. Several companies, including Creative Labs, ATI, Diamond, and Radius, are designing plug-in cards for the PC and the Macintosh, which give them as much as 10 times an improvement in performance in their rendering speed. These cards support acceleration for OpenGL, Reality Lab, and RenderWare; this means that the addition of a graphics accelerator card will immediately accelerate most VRML browsers. These cards are relatively inexpensive, at about $300.

Navigation

Finally, the user has to be able to "walk" through the scene, examine objects, traverse links, and, in general, investigate the world. There are a number of approaches to this problem. WebSpace uses a "golf cart" metaphor that is very effective in producing the sense of driving through a scene, while its object manipulation mode works well for worlds composed of single objects. WorldView takes a different tack—its interface seems more closely related to CAD programs and 3D modelers than WebSpace, which seems more akin to Virtus Walkthough than AutoCAD.

Any navigator will have to implement the six degrees of freedom—movement in x, y, and z, and orientation in yaw, pitch, and roll. (These concepts are covered in Chapter 5, "3D Graphics Primer.") These are enough for simple browsers, but users like to have features like collision detection so they don't actually go through walls. VRML 1.0 provides no "hints" to the browser about which objects are solid and which are not, but a general collision detection feature isn't difficult to implement, and often produces a more realistic experience. Paragraph's Home Space Builder provides collision detection for users; rather than running through a wall, you "slide" along the length of it.

Collision detection is not difficult to implement; the browser must by nature know about the size and shape of any objects visible within it. From this, it is not difficult to calculate if any of these objects intersect with the scene's camera (your point of view). If any object does, it's a collision. What should happen during a collision (stop, go around, pass through) should be a user-configurable option.

Interfaces are a matter of taste; the first thing a developer should understand is that no 3D interface is right for everyone—except for the real world. This means that the design should incorporate several navigation paradigms—both WebSpace and WorldView do. VRML 1.*x* will include a set of guidelines for open navigation interfaces in VRML browsers. That means it won't be the job of the designers to come up with every possible navigation interface; people will be able to whip them up on their own, using whatever tools they have—C++, Visual Basic, Java, and so forth.

Anchors

The "right" way to display anchors in a virtual environment is an open question. Most people find that changing the cursor to a pointing hand is a polite way to indicate linkage. WebSpace "colors" anchors to highlight their presence when the cursor is placed over them. Some people really like this feature, but others find it hideous. As with navigation interfaces, it's a good idea to leave the user several options.

The main event loop of a VRML browser is very simple. It checks for user interface events, and then sends the appropriate commands to the renderer as the user navigates through the environment, or fires off the appropriate messages or network requests to get more data in response to a selection. The whole architecture looks like figure 11.1.

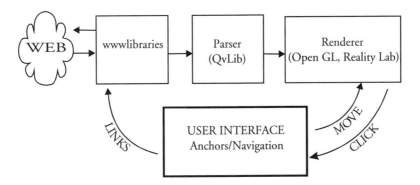

Figure 11.1
The architecture of a prototypical VRML browser.

Alternatively, if all of this is too much for you to do on your own, either due to time or inclination, Silicon Graphics and Template Graphics Software have Open Inventor libraries that implement full VRML 1.0 functionality. It often makes more sense to focus on the task at hand than the support infrastructure; using the Open Inventor toolkit, rapid development of VRML applications is almost easy.

Multiprocessing, Very Large Worlds, and Cyberspace Protocol

The constraints on most desktop computers—memory and processor speed—have limited the amount of information a VRML world can contain. The comfortable upper limit is about 10,000 polygons for any PC or Macintosh. Certainly, workstations can run much higher, but require huge amounts of memory and multiple processors to do the job really well. Multiprocessor desktop systems are still rare outside the Unix market, but with the widespread adoption of Windows NT, we'll see multiprocessor systems showing up in the office as well. A multiprocessor system lends itself well to a "threaded" execution environment—where the browser is performing a number of tasks simultaneously using the different processors.

A VRML browser with a multiprocessor design could run the network interface and the parser on one thread—as they are relatively synchronous—and the renderer on another thread. Because the renderer is the overwhelming determinant of the "quality" of the user's experience, priority should be given to the rendering task at all times. At the same time, another process could *cull* the environment—remove objects from the scene when they're no longer in view or far away—using VRML's level-of-detail features as a hint to aid in the culling process. Further-more, the browser should be intelligent, and should "look ahead" to understand what objects might need to be loaded in high-resolution descriptions. The browser can retrieve these objects through the Web (assuming they are **WWWInline**, that is), and have them ready to be loaded into the scene before they are required. This will give the browser a very smooth feeling, akin to Netscape Navigator's progressive GIF loading.

Cyberspace Protocol

Even with multiprocessing, VRML browsers will hit a performance wall beyond which they can not pass. While a multiprocessor browser can handle a world of 100,000 polygons effectively, the VRML model of San Francisco could well have 1,000 times more polygons (100,000,000 polygons). There's no computer in exist-ence that could handle a model that big. Nonetheless, people will want very large, continuous environments—shopping malls, concert halls, and conference spaces—where thousands or millions of different objects might reside. This is where VRML starts to become cyberspace—in the sense of the word as origi-nally coined by William Gibson—where a planetary model becomes a key feature of the data landscape. Worlds of this size and complexity will exist soon. How can VRML deal with such an eventuality?

Over the next year, VRML worlds will *fragment*; that is, they will become a set of constituent parts, organized and gathered up by where they are in cyberspace—by the volume of cyberspace they occupy. If I were viewing a VRML model of San Francisco, from the corner of Market and Second Streets, I'd only be interested in that part of the city that was proximally relevant—that is, closest to me. All I'd need to know is on which Web servers the VRML objects that describe the space around me are stored.

Enter *Cyberspace Protocol* (CP). Labyrinth, the proto-VRML scripting language and 3D Web interface, was invented to demonstrate Cyberspace Protocol. In 1991, I had a series of insights on how to create a perception of space within internetworks. After 30 months of math and programming, I had a workable version of CP, but it had a text-based interface! Except for a few mathematicians, no one could understand what kind of service it provided. In order to demonstrate CP to others, I built a 3D graphical interface to CP and connected it to the Web so I'd have a big pool of data with which I could link. The genesis of VRML lies within CP.

The VRML browser, using CP, understands where it is—and little else—then uses that information to get a list of hosts (Web servers) that define that volume of space. The conversation is a little like the following:

VRML Browser: Hey!

CP Server: Huh? Oh, yes... What can I do for you?

VB: I'm at the corner of Market and Second...

CPS: I see...well...you should get http://www.sf.ca.us/main_2nd_corner.wrl.

VB: Thanks!

The trick of all of this lies at the server end. If every server had to know where everything in cyberspace was, the system would soon collapse of its own weight. Instead, each server knows a little bit about all of cyberspace, but *knows who to ask to find out more* about any part of cyberspace. In a rough analogy to the "six degrees of separation" principle, one server asks another asks another asks another, until a pretty clear picture is developed. It turns the Internet into the computer equivalent of the hologram; each part contains the whole, but only in very fuzzy detail. Put the picture together and abrahadabra—the whole is quite clear.

A CP-compliant VRML browser is never quiescent; constantly exploring the virtual world (using CP to make queries and receiving replies), it progressively develops an increasingly accurate representation of the cyberspace around it. It's as if a Web browser could guess which page you were going to next, and could pre-load it for you. That's much easier to do in three dimensions because space is connected; being in one place at one moment means that it's likely you'll be in a place quite nearby in the next moment. CP exploits the continuity of space and human movement through it to produce a whole that's greater than the sum of its parts.

Cyberspace Protocol is analogous to the *Domain Name Service* (DNS) used to map host names (this.that.com) into IP addresses (xxx.yyy.zzz.www), but it operates in three dimensions. VRML browsers will implement CP—or something very much like it—as we move forward into a cyberspace that is unified, unique, and ubiquitous.

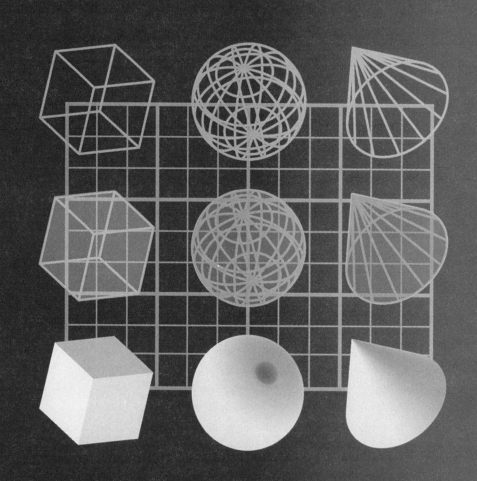

Chapter 12

The Cyberspace Style Guide

If cyberspace had been around for a few thousand years, we would expect that an entire *aesthetic electronic* would have developed around it. There would be a look and feel to cyberspace, just as Catholicism has a particular style, or Impressionism has a well-known look. Cultures and movements create and embody their own styles; that's part of culture and part of being human. Style is communication—cyberspace is only about communication.

But cyberspace is brand-new, just out of the box, barely unwrapped, and still wetting the bed. Just as we had to be taught to tie our own shoes, read a clock, and ride a bicycle, we'll need to teach ourselves how to build cyberspace. Cyberspace is the imagination—anything desired can be realized. But right now, we flounder around like infants unable to walk or talk; we can punch a few buttons and put up a few buildings, but the great maturing of our artistic nature in cyberspace is still ahead of us.

This chapter makes a loop through the real—the earliest failures and successes of cyberspace—into the speculative, where we will attempt to discern some guiding principles for the design of useful, beautiful, and meaningful virtual environments.

VR: The Unqualified Failure

Have you ever been in a fully immersive virtual reality system? Several years ago, when I first entered the field, I trotted over to the University of California at Berkeley. In the video game parlor at the UCB Student Center, called the The Underground, a pair of $70,000 *Virtuality* VR systems were installed, complete with a 12-pound head-mounted display, motion tracking, and a game called *Dactyl Nightmare*, where you spent time shooting at your opponent or getting munched by a big ol' Pterodactyl, straight out of *10 Million Years B.C.* The installation was a huge success, making TV and newspaper reports throughout the Bay Area. People waited upwards of three hours to pay five dollars for three minutes of fun. The first month, they couldn't move people through fast enough. But within six months, the machines stood idle 95 percent of the time, abandoned by the same cyber-freaks who'd blown their allowances to blow each other away in cyberspace. What happened?

Take the case of VPL. Jaron Lanier—the man who coined the phrase "virtual reality" and the founder of VPL, the first virtual reality company—found himself out of a business (and out of his basic patents) when the French firm Thomson CSF seized VPL and its assets as a form of debt repayment. Many people saw this as a maneuver by Thomson to monopolize the fledgling VR industry, but Thomson found itself with very little of any value. The patents—considered unenforceable among most experts in intellectual property law—amounted to almost nothing, and the technology—the *DataGlove, EyePhone,* and *BodyElectric* products—seemed plagued with fundamental problems. What happened?

Finally, Sega of America blew into the 1993 Winter Consumer Electronics Show in Las Vegas touting *Sega Virtua VR*, a fully immersive head-mounted display system that—they promised—would retail for under $200 and be on the market before Christmas of that year. Sega garnered enormous press, making the cover of *Popular Science*, and captured the imagination of every 14 year-old in the world who owned a Sega *Genesis* video gaming system. But the planned release suffered delay after delay. Christmas 1993 became Spring 1994 became Fall 1994, and suddenly Sega grew very silent about its VR product, never actually canceling the project, but never bringing it to market, either. What happened?

Designing Cyberspace

Cyberspace is unique. It represents an intersection between what we think and how we feel. Using it, we can exteriorize our imaginings, share our deepest feelings with others, and represent the stuff that dreams are made of. That's the potential of cyberspace, but, despite this, there are very few examples that actually manage to capitalize upon its potential as a new means of human expression—one that can give the mind and heart a voice *together*. There are many reasons for this, but perhaps the most important is that we aren't really taught how to move within an aesthetic mode of being. The arts are considered extracurricular in our culture, and get shunted aside before the requirements of business and society. Cyberspace is going to dramatically invert that situation. We'll need our aesthetic senses more than ever before—they will give form to the avalanche of information available to us through cyberspace, and will provide a pillar of sanity in the midst of a riot of factuality.

Beyond this, we need to understand that *cyberspace is not the end of the human body*. William Gibson's cyberpunk-cowboy hackers disdain what they call "the meat," but Gibson sees himself as a kind of late 20th century Henry Miller, conducting a novelistic discourse on the entombment of the soul in the sensual world. Physicality is good; it provides a corridor for experiences beyond the purely abstract. The concrete is always presented through manifestation rather than through evocation. You might get misty-eyed reading a poem about a flower, but the transcendental presence of the flower itself is the reality that gives birth to the poem.

Amputation or Communication?

All of this may seem like the wanderings of philosophy, but if we tie these observations together with our example VR disasters given at the beginning of this chapter, we start to comprehend why VR hasn't taken off in the way most of its boosters projected it would. The answer lies in our bodies and our feelings. VR was designed as an intellectually appealing assemblage of technologies—*it was a nice idea.* By and large, however, it was cold, unfriendly, and uncomfortable. How many people have donned the full VR head-mount/dataglove/body trackers more than once? Not many, and not just because the costs on these devices are prohibitive. They don't feel good, and people will not jump into experiences that are painful, unfeeling, or disorienting. The almost exclusively male cadre of VR programmers always quipped that women wouldn't wear head-mounted displays because "they're afraid it'll mess up their hair." Beyond the clearly implied chauvinism, this remark betrayed a complete misapprehension of the body and its feelings, which, it appears, have a more persistent connection in women. They wouldn't wear an HMD because it hurt them, and cut them off from their body's own feelings.

On the other hand, *CyberFin*, one of the most successful VR designs to date, lulled people into relaxation as they lay upon a heated "Vibrasonic" pad, hearing subsonic dolphin clicks pass through their torso, while watching a 3D television display of dolphins at play. When CyberFin debuted at SIGGRAPH '94, it soon sported a line about three hours long, yet it was the first VR installation *ever* to have more women pass through it than men. It seems that women are ready for VR, if they don't find the experience painful.

Furthermore, before the Web, women rarely bothered to surf the content of cyberspace. However, when sociologists and researchers began to examine MUDs (text-based cyberspaces), they found that thirty percent or more of the MUD users were women, a figure far greater than that of any other Internet service. Amy Bruckman, a researcher at the Massachusetts Institute of

Technology's Media Lab, found that women instinctively re-
sponded to the communicative richness of MUDs, which favor
interaction and role-playing. It's well known that women persis-
tently outscore men on verbal tests, while men score better in
spatial and mathematical areas of knowledge. Cyberspace—in
the sense of creating a three-dimensional environment—isn't
enough. Cyberspace must communicate itself and its content
through several modalities—text and shapes and images and
sound—to reach both sexes.

The Style Guide

The one thing that could kill VRML, and virtual reality in general,
is a continued ignorance of the aesthetic landscape that opens
to us as we enter cyberspace. In earlier years, Strunk and White
could define the *Elements of Style* to writers and editors, and
William Morris could explain the elements of visual composition
to a legion of graphic artists and designers. We have no equivalent style guide for cyberspace.

This chapter is an attempt to present a cyberspace style guide; its
brevity will one day be attributed to ignorance, but some basic
rules of thumb, imparted at the start of our creative efforts, will
help to engender a livable, human, warm environment for those
who will follow and articulate a more complete philosophy.

The Sacred and the Profane

Any discussion of cyberspace is a discussion about believing; if
cyberspace is the imagination, then cyberspace contains what we
believe it contains, nothing more, and nothing less. Put another
way, the only things we take into cyberspace are our preconceptions. These preconceptions can come in the form of prejudices,
tastes, or even spiritual beliefs. Each of these has a place in
cyberspace design.

In his book, *The Sacred and the Profane: The Nature of Religion*,
anthropologist Mircea Eliade analyzed the human desire to create

spaces or places where the religious or sacred event occurs. This sacred space—and there is always sacred space—serves as the foundation point for the world. It is the *axis mundi*, the center of the world, and acts as the absolute reference point for all other places or events. This reference point is the boundary between *how things happen* and *why things happen.*

The fact that the medieval town always had a church at its center says something fundamental about the human construction of the world. The placement of the television set as the 20th century's equivalent of the hearth—which was also sacred space—speaks volumes about the position it occupies in our beliefs.

Every cyberspace must have some design elements that have a sacred or religious character. In most cases, these elements should not dominate the content of a space, but they must serve as the reference point; without that reference, the space is condemned to be cold, inhuman, and lifeless.

George Lucas' *Star Wars* trilogy is an incredible example of how spiritual belief (The Force) can couple with a technical future to create a believable mythology. The sacred elements of the story support the other elements; in the same way, sacred design—created around what you know—can act as a springboard into the sublime.

The sacred can find many modes of expression; everything from a cathedral to a precious stone to the starry night sky can, in the right situation, be impossibly meaningful. The sacred enters cyberspace with us; we endow virtual objects with their sacred attributes. It's essential to create a design that has places in which visitors can exteriorize their imaginings, place the sacred within themselves into the space, and sanctify it.

Design to Avoid Disorientation

For some, the allure of cyberspace is the intense freedom experienced in a boundless, conceptual space. Any form imaginable is possible. Unfortunately, the private vision doesn't imply sensibility. Quite often, a cyberspace designer is so infatuated with the possibilities presented that his or her creation is confusing.

Humans have at least two distinct types of native aesthetic sensibility. The first, imposed upon us by our senses, conforms to the dictates of the physical universe—at least insofar as the physical universe conforms to the dictates of our senses! The second is a cultural sensibility, which, while never taught, is something one becomes acutely aware of when traveling in a foreign country. The dislocation of symbols in an alien culture is acutely disorienting. Imagine the feeling you'd have in a Beijing subway station, with no English symbols anywhere, and being *lost*. That's what a poorly designed cyberspace is like.

When designing public cyberspaces that are for everyday use, it is always best to *conform to expectation*—create a space that behaves as though it were real. When successful, a visitor to such a space will need no cues beyond those provided by enculturation to navigate through the environment.

Kevin Long, a designer at the *Internet Underground Music Archive* (IUMA) created an early VRML world, which he promptly nicknamed "The Sonic Lodge." The Lodge was quite simply a living room in cyberspace, with a couch, a coffee table with magazines (linked to various IUMA home pages), and a gigantic stereo system with floor-to-ceiling speakers that spanned one side of the room. Upon observation, the stereo looked very much like any other stereo you might have seen, with a tuner dial (a texture map), and a CD player with the normal row of iconographic buttons. If you pressed the "Play" button—wham! IUMA's "Song of the Week" would download and begin playing. Because the interface conformed to expectation, anyone could enter and use the IUMA space.

Ceilings and Floors

Although this may seem quite obvious, it's remarkable how many virtual worlds are simply an object floating in "black silence," as if suddenly burped out of the void. People are not used to being thrust into a space without gravity—which cyberspace doesn't have—and as a result, need ceilings and floors even more in cyberspace than in real space. These two tell the visitor "which way is up;" a clever arrangement of spacing between the two can create a feeling of claustrophobia or expansiveness. The floor can also be thought of as a guide; it can be studded with texture maps or other features that can serve as "markers" to help orient visitors.

Archetypes

In *Psyche and Symbol*, Carl Jung identified the *archetype* as the primal form of a symbol. There may be many expressions of a single archetype—the number of representations of the Earth Goddess or the Death/Rebirth cycle, for example—but all instances of an archetype express a common thread. Some of the most basic archetypes are simple geometric forms—the Platonic solids of tetrahedral, cube, and sphere. Others are more complex, like the petroglyphs of the Native Americans, or the hieroglyphics of the ancient Egyptians and Mayans.

Cyberspace researchers Brenda Laurel, Rachel Strickland, Rob Tow, and Sean White sowed the rich soil of the archetype in their *PLACEHOLDER* project. Designed as an immersive experience for two simultaneous participants, PLACEHOLDER asked its users to select one of four archetypal creatures that would be representative of their selves in cyberspace—a snake, signifying earth; a spider, signifying fire; a fish, signifying water; and a crow, signifying air. When one PLACEHOLDER participant looked at the other, the selected archetypal figure—represented as a texture map of an Anasazi glyph—would be seen. But PLACEHOLDER's designers went far beyond this visual representation; they encoded behaviors specific to the archetype into each characterization. Flap your arms as the crow and you would fly, wiggle around as the snake and you'd crawl! These actions conform to the archetypal expectations for each character, so PLACEHOLDER's users quite often would express actions appropriate to them.

PLACEHOLDER provides an important example for the VRML designer. A careful search through symbols—archetypes—will yield a set of concise representations that can be brought into the VRML environment and used as signs, glyphs, and pointers. If a virtual world is constructed entirely in archetypes, it's much easier for a visitor to explore, experiment, and experience; archetypes conform to expectation because archetypes are the primary forms of experience.

Explore Multiple Modalities

Space is in the eye, but place lies within the ear. In *Understanding Media: The Extensions of Man*, Marshall McLuhan identified the "global village" as the *sound* of a planetary community. While we have a history of 500 years of visual-literate organization within Western culture, that visual history sits on top of a global history of 500,000 years of aural-oral culture.

Cyberspace is deathly quiet today, but before long it will be a noisy place, filled with the bustle that comes naturally to inhabited spaces. Although our interface devices can only provide sound and vision conveniently—we're still some time away from effective and inexpensive force-feedback sensors—we must use both modalities together to produce the most sensually appealing and meaningful environment possible. Each of these senses has several sub-modalities—sculpture versus texture versus text; ambient versus foreground versus noise. The cross-fertilization of these techniques will create identifiable regions, areas of cyberspace that are linked through sensuality into the domain of understanding.

It's quite likely that future VRML worlds will be navigable by sound, by sight, by text, perhaps even by touch. By mixing these modes of experience and providing a wealth of choices, you can create a world that can be enjoyed by many people of different abilities and sensibilities.

Never Rely on Text

The Internet is an English language culture. Because the majority of the planet doesn't understand English, reliance on text in a virtual world restricts its utility unnecessarily. There is a large canon of international symbology developed to be language- and culture-independent, and these symbols are well-suited for inclusion within cyberspace environments. Furthermore, many visitors to cyberspace environments will be children who don't have the language skills that can be expected of adults.

It's permissible to use text within cyberspace, but it should always be de-emphasized, unless the text itself is a specific feature of the environment. For example, IUMA's "Sonic Lodge" has a "billboard" along one wall that is a texture map of IUMA's home page, complete with text and pictures. Its presence provides a link between the HTML and VRML views of IUMA.

It's almost always preferable to use symbols over language in a VRML environment—symbols have a near-universal appeal, and are generally more concise. Archetypal shapes for things like exits, directional arrows, and so forth can provide needed directional information, while maintaining a text-free environment. You may not be able to eliminate text from every world, but if you can keep it to a minimum, you open your doors wider to a real world of global visitors.

Leave a Place for Being

This guideline is a corollary to the observations about the necessity for sacred space. Cyberspace needn't be busy like a stock exchange, where activity and meaning crowds in so thoroughly that it all becomes a blur, each element washed out by the others into a gray goo possessing no differentiation or meaning. In its ideal form, cyberspace is a filter between information overload and our own personal maps of meaning. That means that there should be space and place—visually and aurally—to think, to experiment, or just zone out.

Architecture has a lot to teach us about the creative design of rich but comprehensible spaces. The great architects of the 19th and 20th centuries—Louis Sullivan, Frank Lloyd Wright, and Mies van der Rohe, to name but a few—will find their core tenets of design translated into cyberspace.

Design Emotionally, Implement Intellectually, Play Physically

Finally, cyberspace is integrative. The power to create an evocation lies in the ability to reach souls, and the path to the soul is not entirely or even primarily intellectual. A cyberspace design sensibility must not be purely conceptual—it has to reach and speak to other modes of being as much as it speaks to differing sensory modalities. The aesthetics of beauty differ from person to person, but everyone can tell that a space has been designed with aesthetic intent.

Design for cyberspace most closely resembles the production values and sensibility associated with film. You may have noticed that many VRML terms have been adopted from filmmaking. VRML worlds are often referred to as "scenes," and a scene is viewed with a "camera." A visitor to a VRML world thinks of it as a stage—set with props, and ready for action.

Several years ago, hypertext pioneer Theodor Holm ("Ted") Nelson quipped, "In the future, we'll all be filmmakers." The future has arrived, and so we need to study Griffith, Attenborough, Fellini, and Spielberg to understand the principles of emotion, ideal, and action in what will otherwise be a lofty but stale realm.

Listening to Others Speak about Design

My own comments are gathered from five years of observation, but they're far from complete. My background is in writing and networking, not architecture and visual design. I've invited three gifted individuals to contribute their insight and wisdom—*Clay Graham*, a virtual architect of broad vision; *Michael Gough*, a real architect who has tasted the first fruits of cyberspace; and *Mark Meadows*, an artist and designer with deep experience in VRML. Each will, in their own words, express principles to which they conform as they design for cyberspace. You will find echoes of my words in theirs; that's because they each have taught me how to see.

Mark Meadows

Mark Meadows, the Art Director of the 1995 Interactive Media Festival, has a fine arts background and a deep exposure to the guts of VRML. Before VRML browsers existed, he led a crew of fifteen volunteers (who nicknamed themselves the *Virtual Reality Modeling Nerds*—VRMN or "vermin") through the planning, design, and implementation of a fully realized VRML model of the Festival installation at Los Angeles' Variety Arts Center. His hands-on experience with VRML is equal to that of any individual in the world.

I asked Mark to develop a list of his recommendations to would-be VRML designers, artists, and architects. His comments, which begin with the precise and succinct "Ten Demandments," clearly quantify process, while the articulation of each of these ten points seeks to qualify a cyberspace aesthetic.

The Construction: Designing VRML as Touch

The Ten Demandments are as follows:

1. Decide what you have to say.

2. Prepare link strategy and all destination files in advance.

3. Consider the symbols and signs being used.

4. Maximize content.

5. Use HTML.

6. Use fewer than 10,000 polygons.

7. Work on no more than two machines.

8. Stay at or below 16-bit color depth.

9. Let the entire site mature as a photograph.

10. Proof the proof of your proof.

Designing and producing VRML is a balancing act. The following is an elaboration of Mark Meadows' Demandments:

1. Ask yourself, please, why you're doing this. There is an occasional lack of content on the Net because people enjoy delivering new protocols more than they enjoy delivering old ideas. Decide what it is that you have to say, why you want to say it, and how you want to go about doing it. Decide on an opinion, world-view, or context for things to happen. Every time you are building a new world, you are implicitly deciding what is important and what the laws of that reality are. One easy route is to simply model the real world as closely as possible. Consider other topics such as scales, navigation clues, and color palettes. These help give the participant a sense of familiarity rather than disorientation—place must be established.

2. If you have all of your links and destination files ready before you even begin the VRML itself, you'll be doing yourself and everyone you work with a large favor. This forces you to have a cogent vision of what the thing looks like and where it will link to before you ever pound a nail. Resolve all images, sounds, videos, inlines, texture maps, and HTML at the outset of the piece. Many more things will show up that you'll think are needed, and it's good to keep it simple and clean.

3. Recognize that a computer icon is an abstraction nested within an abstraction. If the designer is not careful, the maps soon are indistinguishable from the territories and navigation becomes impossible. The landscape is kaleidoscopic and differentiations cannot be found—this is very bad. Think about the placement of the arrow on the floor, the exit sign on the wall, the elevator button on the door, or

the stairs in the hall. Is it clear, necessary, appropriate? Decide what navigation structures (I mean stairs, doors, catwalks, elevators, etc.) you have available and how far from the "reality" of the situation you can afford to go.

4. We started with the concept that "everything is alive—everything links." This is a great idea, and one that is a logical fallout if we use the real world as our example. But it's an idea that, unfortunately, got overlooked by the good folks that wrote the browsers. As it stands today, browsers highlight the sections of the models that are hotlinked. The browsers should leave the models alone and change the icon instead of the models. The point here is that if you have the option, make the environment as rich and as interactive as possible. Include as many details and intricacies as possible that will increase the information given without detracting from the interactivity of the model. This is the primary design concern.

5. HTML is good for not only constructing your linking methodology, for keeping track of what is where, and for providing people assisting you with current information—it is also irreplaceable. VRML does not yet support text, but text has been around longer than even the printing press. Text is a tried and true interface that we have all come to know and love. And just as a picture is worth a thousand words, so too are some words worth a thousand pictures.

6. If there are more than 10,000 polygons used, you will find yourself with a choppy sideshow, not an interactive world. The rendering speed, file size, participation, and appearance of the model all get sacrificed and the final output is not only fat, but sloppy to navigate and impossible to enjoy. At present, the processor speed is crucial to these elements as well, so consider who your audience is as you're flying buttresses and adding sexy curvatures.

7. Keep the platforms you are using to a minimum. Move it into one environment and then *don't leave*. If you have one workstation that will fulfill all of the designing, modeling,

rendering, conversions, and proofing needs, do the work there and then keep it in that environment.

8. The number of colors is not crucial, but if texture maps are being used (texture maps generally make the files large and loading them a slow process), then make sure that the browser has as few elements as possible to sort out while rendering. This, like the number of polygons being used, is simply good etiquette. Somewhere, somehow, someone will grab this file and find themselves waiting five minutes to move one inch. This is definitely a sad state of affairs—we should not wait for the browsers to increase in speed; we should instead take proactive steps to produce trim and robust files. We'll soon see browsers that calculate the maximum number of frames per second for the respective computer that is running it.

9. Think of this thing as a garden or a photograph. It is better to let the ideas resolve themselves bilaterally, and to let them be reflected in the overall piece as such, rather than for there to be constricted parts that diverge from the overall look and feel of the site. If there are conceptual changes to the site, then it is important to keep that concept consistent throughout the site rather than having some files be of one extreme and others being the opposite. We made this mistake while building our site, and the end result was a bit schizophrenic.

10. Look the final product over and make sure it suits your needs. Check it to make sure it is VRML-compliant—*http://www.geom.umn.edu/~daeron/bin/checkvrml.cgi.*

The Imagination: Designing VRML as Thought

The power of VRML lies in its abilities to create a bridge between the two primary methods of human communication: cerebral imagination and visceral sensation. VRML is the closest manifestation we have to imagination that we are able to see. It functions like imagination in that there are no physical laws that constrain it, and no legal issues that bind it. It is sheer imagination that is articulated through a vision. This is interesting if we look at it as art, rather than as a publishing metaphor.

Maybe it could be said that cyberspace *is* imagination, and that it has been around much longer than we might first think. Maybe it could be said that all art has lived on the fringe of technology and that 3D publishing is, in its infancy, taking broad leaps into the world of the arts (whatever "art" is). Maybe it could be said that VRML has the capacity to become a new art form, and that its design needs to hold this nurturing process in the foreground of priorities. If so, then VRML is the new art, and imagination is the fuel for that artistic vehicle.

Hegel points to five different forms of art (music, dance, architecture, painting, and sculpture) that he thinks are significant because they each are taken in by one of the five senses and processed in the brain; once there, they spit back relations and images that the physical version may or may not contain. There is physical input that is resolved by a mental and non-physical consideration. So the painting is viewed, examined, and considered; then (after consideration), the relations and images that are contained on that canvas—within that illusion of space—are processed so that new relations evolve, so that new sights are seen, and so that the richness, content, and overall sensation of the work is actually electrified by our brain's added wattage. This is the point to thinking about things, as I understand it.

This is a bit strange if we look at it because the membrane of the virtual is somewhere punctured. Somewhere between the large glob of linseed oil and the small neural arcs that are firing deep in the brain is a relational image—an image that allows the actual to talk to the physical. VRML is a bit different—a bit more immediate and a bit less physical. It exists only within the computer and so the membrane that separates the actual from the virtual, or the imagined from the real, is torn open and strange images spill out. The image that the computer is capable of producing is so close to our mental proceedings that it seems we have finally struck something of an accord, a temporary cease-fire between the real and the virtual.

Because it has this ability to so closely replicate our thinking and mental wanderings, VRML provides us with the interesting opportunity to investigate strange new realms and places of which we might only dream. It offers us a complement to the world of the real with the world of the imagined. Networked VR, in spite of all of its hype and huff, is now able to provide us with consensual dreams, shared imaginings, and communal night-mares that were once only held in the imageless world of text and speech. We are now able to triangulate, to compare, to gain multi-perspectives, and to gather synthetic information on the world we live in and how we see it. This new method of commu-nication, while not terribly impressive as a methodology or technical advance, has deep meaning when it is in the proper hands of people considering its final use.

While designing a VRML site, it is thus important to consider these things, to look at what is being represented and how it is being used. If, indeed, VRML has the capabilities we are now considering, if indeed the things that lie ahead of us are possible, then we are going to see some beautiful and elaborate worlds emerging in the coming years.

You can contact Mark Meadows at pighed@well.sf.ca.us or pighed@construct.net. His home page is http://www.arc.org/who/ pighed/.

Michael Gough

A professional architect for almost twenty years, Michael Gough was the principal architect for the Interactive Media Festival's VRML efforts. Recreating the Festival from a set of blueprints, he discovered some of the joys of architecture in cyberspace: no physics, no building codes, and no budgets. It left such an im-pression on him that after the completion of the IMF project, he vowed to leave physical architecture behind for its virtual analog. His expressive yet concise architectural style allowed him to create a set of VRML models for the Festival that were simulta-neously rich and compact.

I asked Michael to comment on the architecture of cyberspace; he straddles the boundary between real and virtual constructions, as all architects have always done. In the following, he speaks from his years of experience about a newfound love:

1. In an apt reading of architectural history, Bernard Tschumi describes a "continuing transformation of buildings...from material to immaterial...from the heavy stones of the Egyptians to Roman vaults, then gothic arches, then iron construction, the curtain wall, structural glass, immaterial light screens, Albert Speer's Cathedral of Light, Holograms, and now virtual reality." (Bernard Tschumi, "Ten Points, Ten Examples," ANY, no. 3 (November-December 1993):41.

2. The medium of building is inherently cumbersome. The process is laborious, difficult, and generally unrewarding. The architect fights not only gravity, the elements, and natural disasters, but is set upon by cadres of lawyers and politicians, dead set on ensuring that the interests of a disinterested public are served—creating buildings that are safe, accessible, affordable, maintainable, and most importantly inoffensive. In the end, however, they are also devoid of expressive content.

3. Architects find themselves the guardians of arcane tradition, their efforts limited to optimizing projects within proscribed and cumbersome constraints. The greatest portion of the design effort is dedicated to satisfying the confusing demands of a changing client body, shrinking budgets, and restrictive schedules—leaving what little time remaining for the satisfaction of technical issues.

4. Today, architecture is 98 percent problem solving and 2 percent expression. Architecture in cyberspace reverses these percentages, dedicating most of the effort to expression, communication, or meaning. If architecture is measured as the superlative of mere building—considering the relative percentages given over to each—constructions in cyberspace have far more claim to the term architecture than anything built in the physical world today.

5. If the relative ease of construction (compared to building with steel and stones) allows some of these constructions to be unsophisticated or arbitrary or otherwise without merit, they will simply not be visited.

   Every construction will require at a minimum the potential for application, either usable or readable or both. A weight of responsibility will be placed on the would-be cyber architect that will come with the understanding that there are few excuses left in cyberspace—few external forces bearing on the activity. Their products, the objects, and the environments will be true representations of the designer's intentions. This should certainly help keep them honest.

6. As a result, cyberspace will be a far more intentional and objective space than anything in the physical environment. Here lies an invigorating opportunity to refocus architectural efforts, to strip the endeavor of its most mundane and limiting aspects, by focusing directly on the fashioning of experience itself.

7. The question then becomes, "What to make?"

8. In cyberspace, the concepts of space and time are collapsed and compressed beyond recognition, and so the concept of place requires redefinition. Is the communication or exchange occurring here on my screen, or there on yours, or some third electromagnetically generated place? Cyberspace is begging to be located, a place found where the interchange can be founded.

9. Cyberspace is a new "deep structure" for the human environment, an environment where information is processed, deals are consummated, and financial transactions occur. This is a "real" space, already a sub-space of our major urban environments, and increasingly, an international, unified, and unifying space.

10. Although its power lies in its limited dimension and speed, there is danger in its lack of corporeality. It is becoming everything, but it is nowhere, and that ineffability is

frightening. Like people who store their cash in pillowcases unless they find a bank that will allow them to occasionally visit and touch their money, the general public finds this single-dimensioned environment frightening.

11. VRML offers the opportunity for the reassurance of place, the comfort that comes from knowing with certainty that there is a *there* there because you have actually visited it.

12. This ephemeralization of commerce and culture has real costs. With the production of intangible commodities like digital movies and digital television and nano-second financial transactions carried through fiber spanning the breadth of the globe, a new elite has formed. This digital culture is the purview of the digital alchemist, the manipulators of bytes and bits. There has been an attendant disenfranchisement, however. In this bold new world, the visually or spatially oriented need not apply—until now, that is.

13. With the relatively minor introduction of a three-dimensional interface, those of us dependent on the thingness of things, uncomfortable with the wholly intangible or intellectual, can reach out and touch things in the digital environment. The poverty of the linear and numerical gives way to the rich world of the three-dimensional. We will go to the place where binary and hex do their dance, but we will see the familiar, and we will be less afraid. The intangible and incomprehensible is given form and it becomes touchable—explicable.

14. If place is the goal, then there are tools aplenty at the architect's disposal. But they will need to be used well to divorce the viewer from their comfortable chair in front of their screens in some other place. To truly make the cyberthere into the here and now will require the willing suspension of disbelief.

15. There are conditions to avoid in cyberspace. The creation of place, the ability to apprehend and inhabit will determine success of the medium. The difference between bas-relief extrusions of 2D content, little better than chamfered buttons or drop shadows, and convincing 3D experience is

the creation of a place that is compelling, pulling the voyeur past the barrier of the screen or proscenium and, like Alice stepping through the Looking Glass, to actually be there.

16. The cyber architect walks the line between architectural conventions and digital media-based conceits. If VRML reality is limited to representations of buildings or landscapes devoid of all the other sensual input of the real thing, it can only be hollow, empty, and unsatisfying. On the other hand, the lack of Newtonian constraints can lead to the creation of environments littered with arbitrary and unconvincing forms, unintelligible and of no value. For cyberspace to succeed in the short term, it will need to take visitors places they could not go otherwise, while maintaining enough convention to communicate a convincing sense of place.

17. Architecture in cyberspace is the architecture of cyberspace, creating the place for a new human intercourse. Here we are free to express changing intentions, interests, and thoughts without regard to more mundane concerns. It is possible that with time and continued advances, corresponding parts of the "real world" will give way to the digitally real— appreciated solely by eccentric connoisseurs or historians.

18. In cyberspace, there is no need for foundations, enclosure, or shelter. There will be lots of signs, however. Space is not the most important consideration; communication across space becomes paramount. This will require a language of symbol that replaces the architect's portfolio of form, and the introduction of time as an element where the architect's product has been static. These ideas are not new—Venturi found them while studying and subsequently venerating suburban landscapes.

19. There will be a typology, born of repetition and the limitations of the tools. There will be rationalists subordinating everything to technical imperatives and expressionists focusing on the subjective and the mythological. There will be the technological equivalent of local building traditions, based primarily on development platforms and tools.

20. Cyberspace has an episodic quality that recent architectural theory has proposed, but that real (meat) architecture has failed to realize. Through these episodes, a continuous narrative may be possible, but the wholeness or completeness that is the hallmark of quality in architectural experience will be unattainable in cyberspace, hampered as it is by screen size, frame rates, and limited senses. But this is entirely appropriate. Our (media)ted sense requires sound bytes, digestible moments that fracture the whole. There are interesting implications for meaning systems or the system of meaning. As the whole recedes in importance, fluctuation and change become the accepted system and meaning changes on the fly.

21. Although cyberspace does remove many constraints from the architect, it is not the elimination of constraints that makes virtual space so appealing. There remain constraints, whether perceptual or physical, which are as tangible and important for the cyber architect as they are in building in the physical world. These are the controls that design is figured against, and without them, there would be little distinction between arbitrary choices of alternatives. So, in cyberspace, gravity becomes orientation, the budget is measured in polygons rather than dollars, and the program for the effort is concerned far less with area or volume and far more with what needs to be communicated or accomplished.

22. In cyberspace, space is not contained or defined so much as driven. Given the constraints of the screen and resolution, and the lack of involvement of any sense other than sight, the interaction of figures create a clearer sense of extent and direction than the actual borders of figural space, and exert a stronger sense of influence. Spatial relations are effectively stirred up by objects, creating a more explicit connection between the space, or those objects that drive it, and the viewer. For example, a billboard device asserts some effect on the space adjacent to its face, orienting the space to that face and imposing a sense of orthogonality that is directly

related to the geometry of the face. It creates an expectation, which implies orientation, or more powerfully, address.

23.   The appeal of the medium is undeniable and its expressive power has yet to be explored. As with any emerging medium, much of the excitement surrounding the new technology focuses on the technology itself. As a result, most of the sites developed to date showcase the possible as opposed to the appropriate. With experience and patience, these first efforts will give way to a new creative activity that will, in the end, add considerably to the store of form. Freed of Newtonian constraints, the imagination will flourish. There is an opportunity here that is more conceptual and potentially paradigmatic than anything in conventional architecture. As a new way of seeing the world ("reality"), as a new means and effect of perception, as a new vision of what could or ought to be, the effects will be far reaching. A resensitizing process emerges as a possibility, where the jaded gravity bound dweller, media hyped and bereft of any appreciation of spatial or kinesthetic pleasure, is offered the opportunity to "do space" again, to make the most of senses and abilities that were developed thousands of years ago, and to appreciate anew the significance of place.

24.   There was no *there* there, but now it is emerging. We are starting with a cleaner slate than was ever possible in meat reality. Build well.

You can contact Michael Gough at bossarc@construct.net or visit his work at http://vrml.arc.org/.

Clay Graham

It's my personal opinion that Clay Graham will be remembered as the Louis Sullivan of cyberspace. One of the first virtual architects—that is, one of the first individuals to regard cyberspace as a domain of design and not just scientific visualization—he quickly established a visual style that suggests forms without fully articulating them.

Clay's evocative designs for meditative spaces, and use of transition spaces to connected disparate ideational domains will become fixtures in cyberspace's future worlds. As Silicon Graphics' VRML evangelist, he divides his time between helping customers and dreaming up new ways to use VRML.

I asked Clay to contribute some philosophical comments that can act as a very broad guide to the design of cyberspace. You will see a number of his spaces in this book; their unique look is due to the application of these principles.

Introduction

VRML holds unknown potential, enabling ordinary people to create unique places and share them with the world. Just as the artist uses the language of symbolism to communicate the stirrings of the soul, the new architect or designer will communicate through a sculptural and architectural language.

To illustrate the relationship between physical architecture and cyberspace architecture, I will discuss some of the primary pillars of architectural and sculptural theory: space, place, symbol, and sign.

Space

The archetypal elements of wall, floor, datum, and column exist in space to guide the user through the data. "Space" articulates the domain in which a particular query has taken place. The space also infers scale, so the architectural metaphor serves as a natural point of reference from which the user can read the data.

The architectural domain is created from spatial archetypes such as floor, roof, wall, and datum, and provides points of reference that distinguish the data from the space it resides within. By creating a space, the user intuitively knows that no data to be examined resides outside of the space. We all know that the words to a novel are *inside* the covers of the book; the same applies for the architecture of cyberspace.

Defining the Domain—Elements of Space

We'll now examine each of the basic forms of design in space: wall, floor, datum, column, and openness and closure. Each of these elements work with the others to create a coherent environment and a sensible cyberspace.

Wall

Wall is the primary bounding object; it also defines openness and closure of the space. At a human scale, the primary interaction occurs within spaces created by walls.

Floor

Floor is a secondary bounding object, defining the difference between the user, ground, and sky. The floor is the scale or yardstick for data that has depth.

Datum

Datum defines the scale of primary interaction.

Column

Column is the primary vertical element. Column is very good at describing the scale of interaction—columns give a sense of how big things are—while doing very little to the data. They are useful yardsticks.

Openness and Closure

The relationships between open and closed spaces form meaning. The figure and ground relationships between these identifiers creates a spatial element of its own.

In Chapter 8, "Advanced VRML and Server Scripts," Figure 8.7 is a space that shows how each of the elements described here can come together into a cogent architectural design for a cyberspace.

Scale and Texture

Experiments on human perception point to a strong relationship between scale and the perceived passage of time. One experiment determined that scale is directly proportional to the perception of time. If you perceived a 1/24th scale model as your reality, 75 seconds would seem like 30 minutes.

Other experiments with textures created similar results. It would seem that variable texture mapping would be a revolution in the control perception relativity. Such a simple premise has very profound implications under a virtual environment. If time becomes relative for our culture, based upon our abilities to manipulate scale and texture, then a true shift is on the horizon.

Guidelines for Successful Spaces

Follow these guidelines to successfully use spaces:

➤ Space defines the domain in which your application resides.

➤ Create relationships between the elements.

➤ Scale defines the density and traversal time through data.

Axis Mundi: Looking Inward to the Self

In *The Sacred and the Profane,* Mircea Eliade described spatial archetypes that relate to similar themes articulated by Carl Jung and Joseph Campbell. These archetypes communicate themes on a symbolic level, but are related to how humans understand space and place. His concept of "axis mundi" represents the connection between the heavens and earth. This "center of the world" provides spiritual orientation to humankind's place in the cosmos, the spiritual totem that supplies the waters of the soul.

Axis

Axis is the way to the light of goal. The theme of axis does not mean that the way is straight. Rather, axis infers a path or way in the physical journey to a goal. It can be seen in the rhythm of a colonnade symbolizing the path from the worldly culture to the way of God. This is the way to the place where sky and earth meet. It ends with the passage through the threshold, which is initiation.

Court

The court supplies both light of sky and green of earth. The ground becomes the focus of awareness. The court represents the connection between the heavens and earth. The passage into this place requires an initiation, or crossing of the threshold.

Interrelationship of Path and Place

The act of ritual in most spiritual endeavors is symbolized by path and goal. The process passed through the following archetypal spaces: the herald of change, the first threshold, the belly of the beast, the final threshold, and finally enlightenment (Campbell, *Hero of a Thousand Faces*). This path can be direct, as in Stonehenge, or indirect, as in the Cistercian plan.

Modality and Multi-Modality

It is possible to examine an object in cyberspace phenomenologically; that is, by how it is perceived. If we look at the modes of perception of any object, we might perceive a sound channel, a picture channel, a text channel, or a multitude of other channels beneath these, which are conduits for the perception of information.

Each mode of perception requires its own representation, and these modes must not be isolated; the perception of all modes should be equally available. If an object's representation is dynamic, then users should be able to select their favored modes of perception.

Symbol and Index

Jung defines a symbol to be "anything that represents more than itself." This concept is at the heart of indexing. Symbolism is the essence of the indexed pointer because it is the mechanism that enables people of different sensibilities to communicate effectively in a simulation space.

Indexing is the foundation of tokens. If I make a dictionary of everything that I know exists, describe it in the modalities of my choosing, and give each object a number, it then should be possible for other people to index that number to a representation in their dictionary.

The program that represents those indexes is a "client," and the computer that is telling that program what objects are there is "the server." This relationship creates a system where the server sends the client the current indexes, and the client represents those indexes with attributes.

For example, let's say Joe and Eddy exchange dictionaries online. Their exchange is a kind of "agreement" that a semantic relationship is valid for each party. It is a kind of "reality check."

Attribute Editing

The ability to edit and control the attributes of the representations of indexes will give the user the ability to tune to the modalities of choice. Once an object was described, it would be added to the user's dictionary.

The medium of virtual space would enable users to interact in the medium; the index, space, and place are referenced into the modality of their choosing. Proximity, size, position, and interaction all could be represented by attributes that the user has specified.

Implications for Disabled Users

The combined effects of multi-modal objects, object indexing, and attribute editing create an environment where processor power, output investment, and overall interaction can be focused to each user's needs.

If we have the bravery to perceive different things differently when they reference an instance, it could be possible for people of different modalities to communicate using semantic metaphors.

You can contact Clay Graham at cyber23@well.com

Experiment, Experience, Explain

All of this commentary—which ranges from the substantial to the sublime—is still based on only a tiny body of work. There isn't much in cyberspace yet, so the only thing that can be true is that we have a lot to learn. Even so, it can be seen that cyberspace inspires idealism and a search for the transcendental qualities of ideal and idea. These ideals, translated into ideas, will be subject to future experiments, which will yield experience. The explanation of these experiences will form the basis for a real aesthetics of cyberspace.

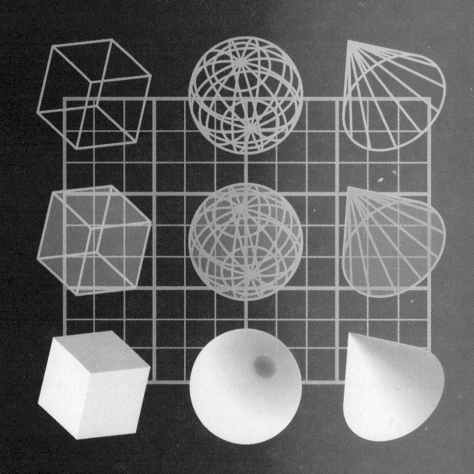

Chapter 13

VRML: The Next Generation

The *Virtual Reality Modeling Language* (VRML) is rapidly evolving. Although the first specification of the language is completed, day-to-day experience with VRML will drive new features into its specification. There are a number of features that didn't make it into the first specification. In many cases, the time to specify and implement these features made them prohibitive; in other cases, a lack of consensus caused VRML's developers to defer any decision on these features until more research had been performed.

In many ways, the VRML specification process reflects the archetypal evolution of a technical standard—continuous revision and feedback between developers and the user base. VRML wasn't handed down from on high, inscribed on tablets. From a solid foundation in Open Inventor, VRML was designed to grow to encompass the needs of its users as those users become more fluent in the implementation of VRML design, browsers, and authoring tools.

Each browser has its own preferences for the types of texture maps it likes. WebSpace uses the SGI-specific RGB format, while WorldView uses GIF and JPEG. Clearly, if we really want to see texture maps that work in a browser-independent manner, there's a need for some specifications on which types of texture maps must be supported within a VRML browser, and which others are optional.

Push Me—Pull You

The 1.1 release of Netscape Navigator added a very neat hack called *client-side pull*. Using client-side pull, it's possible to create an HTML document that reloads itself (or another HTML document) after a specified period of time. It's possible to create a Web page that, a few seconds after it loads, sends the browser somewhere else. This is great for guided tours of the Web, and even better for services like stock quotes, for which the browser can go fetch the latest updates from the server every few minutes.

Navigator also allows *server-side push*—this is a little more complicated. When the server responds to a browser's request for data, it replies, but keeps the connection to the browser open. (Normally, these connections are closed after the reply to the request.) Then, at a later time, the server can update the browser's data by sending more information through the connection. Again, the stock quote analogy works well; the server could send a continuous stream of data to a client browser, to reflect dynamic data, and turn this into a "stock market," where the financial information can be represented visibly, perhaps by changing the height or size of an object in the virtual world. Here the burden is on the server, not on the client, as it is in client-side pull. Both of these facilities will be added to VRML 1.*x*, making it much easier to create dynamic VRML worlds.

Scalability

Perhaps the most serious issue to be addressed in VRML 1.*x* is scale. The first VRML worlds are relatively small—a few tens of thousands of polygons—because any computer, no matter how powerful, will quickly become overburdened by a large VRML environment. While VRML files are quite often compact, the process of rendering them to the display is very memory- and processor-intensive; even with faster computers being developed continuously, we won't see truly gigantic VRML worlds on the desktop. The computers would choke, or worse, crash. (Try creating and loading a 100,000 polygon VRML file if you don't believe this.)

VRML 1.0 worlds are *monolithic*—all of a piece—and each world is an "island universe" unto itself. Clever use of level-of-detail can, in some limited sense, extend a single world endlessly. A scene can open up into another scene, and another, and another, but the VRML browser will still become overburdened with polygons if the browser doesn't "cull" polygons as new ones are loaded (*culling* means removing polygons from the renderer that aren't visible to it). So we're stuck with small worlds, strung together as islands in the Web, not much better off than we are today.

The Web, with its roots in the hyperspace of island universes, will need to transcend them in order to provide the three spatial principles required for a human-navigable environment: ubiquity, uniformity, and unity. There must be a single, infinitely large cyberspace—even if there are others—which is everywhere, continuous, and regular. When such a cyberspace exists, we can knit together our islands into a continuous whole. It doesn't mean that my house will be next to yours, but that if I travel from my house to yours, I travel through all of the intervening space. This is very important for the users of cyberspace—with a unified layout, people can remember where they are and what's around them. Without this, people will find cyberspace rather disorienting and discontinuous—something the real world is not. In a unified cyberspace, you can make maps, or stop somewhere and ask for directions.

Cyberspace Protocol, discussed in Chapter 11, "How to Write a VRML Browser," provides a protocol framework for very large cyberspaces in VRML. VRML itself, however, will have to change—or rather the behavior of the browsers will have to change—so that individual VRML objects can be sent to a browser from a server, in the context of a much larger scene.

Just as a VRML document can request objects that are not explicitly within the VRML document (this is known as *inline reference*), the VRML browser will be able to request objects based on where in cyberspace the browser's scene camera lies. In this kind of cyberspace, there are no more "worlds," just a truly gigantic set of objects, with well-known positions, distributed on computers all across the Internet.

VRML 1.*x* browsers will begin to use the Web as a *proximal cache*, requesting the VRML scene elements that have the greatest *proximal relevance*; that is, are closest to the user's location in cyberspace. This means that a VRML browser can retrieve and view the five or ten thousand most relevant (closest and most visible) objects, in the middle of a VRML universe containing hundreds of billions.

Audio, Video, and Data Streaming

The beginning of interactivity is the ability to deliver real-time data sources into an environment. VRML 1.*x* will be adding the capabilities of attaching a data stream to a VRML world. A *data stream* is exactly what the name implies—a continuous flow of data sent from a server to a browser. Data streams are quite different from server-side push because the push is occasional, not continuous. A telephone is a good example of a data stream—continuous audio data sent from a sender to a receiver. The most obvious examples of how this might be used in VRML are the addition of audio and video streaming within VRML worlds.

Audio support in VRML 1.*x* will extend the specification in two directions. VRML will add support for *spatialized audio*—sound that is digitally processed to create the illusion of emanating from a particular point in space—and support for the *Musical Instrument Digital Interface* (MIDI). Spatialized audio is a new VR technology that creates "localized sound;" that is, sound within the virtual world that appears to have a specific location within the virtual world. In reality, it's a sound source that is digitally processed to give the listener the impression that it is coming from a point in cyberspace.

MIDI is a well-established language of *control codes*—messages sent to a computer, giving it precise instructions on how to create and play sounds—and is a very powerful yet compact way to increase the sensual richness of a virtual environment. Most PCs and Macintoshes include support for MIDI, through hardware devices like Creative Labs' *SoundBlaster* accessory. A continuous soundscape of MIDI—creating a rich environment of ambient (background) music—uses only about 5 percent of the bandwidth on a 14.4 KB modem connection.

The possibilities for ambient sound and auditory "tours" through VRML worlds is enormous. Spatialized audio can be combined with MIDI to create localized music—within a particular room or a corner of a world—and can be used in conjunction with a regular audio stream, such as someone's voice, to produce the perception of objects in space emitting sound. In the same way that many Web pages have "backgrounds" (using Netscape HTML extensions), soon VRML spaces will have background audio within them, so that they can provide directions, two-way communication, or simply enhance the sensuality of the experience.

Video streaming, from desktop cameras and remote sensors, is another very promising technology. Most of the rendering technologies used in conjunction with VRML—including OpenGL and Microsoft's Reality Lab—can accept a video image as a texture map, and can "wrap" that texture map onto an object. When video texture mapping is combined with spatialized audio streaming, VRML 1.*x* will have all of the components to produce a convincing "conference room in cyberspace," or a chat room, or a rock concert.

CD-ROMs, Resource Naming, and Caching

VRML 1.0 is poorly adapted to the CD-ROM; this is true in general of the World Wide Web, which is great when describing a global cyberspace, but poorly equipped to reference data on your own CD-ROM drive. The problem lies in how CD-ROMs are used with computers. Every computer has a slightly different mechanism for connecting to its CD-ROM drive, so it's rarely possible to reference the data on it with a URL, which requires that the content of the CD-ROM drive be consistently available at the same location. That's not going to happen anytime soon, so VRML 1.*x* (and the Web in general) needs to adopt another approach.

The Internet community is on the threshold of creating a new type of Internet address, known as the *Universal Resource Name* (URN, sometimes called the Universal Resource Identifier). The URN provides a mechanism through which the Web can retrieve objects by their name. The current method, the URL, requires that you explicitly request an object by specifying a machine name and a file name; none of this is required with the URN. In the same way that "Mark D. Pesce" refers uniquely to me (as far as I know), the request, "Mad Hatter's Tea Cup" will soon translate into a VRML document that describes that teacup uniquely.

The URN leaves it to the Web to figure out how "Mad Hatter's Tea Cup" turns into a VRML document; there are several proposals before the Web community that address this issue. One of them will be adopted by the Internet community soon, and it will become the basis for a URN facility in VRML.

CD-ROMs, used in conjunction with VRML, will create a local URN resource; that is, a set of objects that can be referenced by their names, and can be found—very quickly—on the CD-ROM. This is one of the great leaps forward VRML will be making in the next year. Instead of having to wait a long time as various VRML object definitions download from the Internet across your modem, the VRML document will contain only the arrangement of a set of objects specified with URNs. If the URNs exist on a local CD-ROM—presto! The world appears very quickly. It's quite likely that as the online services offer VRML interfaces, they'll distribute this interface with a CD-ROM, and so provide rich, unique, and fast environments for their users.

Finally, VRML 1.*x* browsers will begin to incorporate caching. *Caching* sets aside a portion of the user's hard disk as a local store for objects. If a VRML world or object has been downloaded, a copy of it remains on the hard disk. If it is requested again, the browser checks with the server to see if the object has changed. If it hasn't, the local copy is used. This feature, found in Netscape Navigator and other HTML browsers, will be even more vital to VRML browsers; the real world (and cyberspace, too) is made up of basic objects, endlessly replicated. It's quite conceivable that a set of 10,000 basic objects could be used to define most VRML environments. Once these objects are stored locally, there's no need to explicitly send VRML object definitions—only their arrangements within scenes.

Universal Navigation Interfaces

One of the big design issues in 3D environments is *navigation*— how we get around within them. Because we can't actually walk through a VRML world—at least, not yet—we need to develop lots of different metaphors to compensate for the fact that our feet get lost when we enter cyberspace. Inventors and computer hackers are constantly developing new navigation widgets, like Logitech's *SpaceMan*, Virtual I/O's *i-glasses*, the Flogiston Chair, and many others. Browser developers are faced with a big problem: how do we develop and maintain interfaces to every new and cool navigation device that comes to market? And what about experimental devices designed to enable handicapped people? Clearly the job is too big for any one company, no matter what size.

For this reason, VRML 1.*x* will define a *Universal Navigation Interface* (UNI), which provides a standardized set of inputs to any VRML browser from any navigation device, hardware, or software. This way, the designer of the device can provide the appropriate interface components, taking the burden off the shoulders of the browser manufacturers. This is a great idea for two reasons: it means that creative people will be free to proto-type and test lots of different navigation devices, and it means that a wide array of navigation mechanisms will be available to users. There is no right way to navigate through cyberspace—or, if there is, we still don't know what it is—so the UNI provides an open-ended solution to an open-ended problem.

Planning for VRML 1.x

All of these issues are immediate, and are being addressed by the VRML community as this book is being written. It's very likely that a specification that covers the points addressed here will be developed into a specification to be completed before the end of 1995. There's significant commercial interest in VRML; this has helped to facilitate a coherent and non-partisan specification process—everyone in the VRML community needs these features, and needs them now. More than that, these issues must be cleared out of the way before planning can begin for VRML 2.0, as it will build upon VRML 1.x functionality, and grow from it into full interactivity.

VRML 2.0

Everyone is waiting for *real cyberspace*—an interactive, multiparticipant environment. VRML is now static—it never or only rarely changes, and doesn't lend itself to the kind of explora-tions that we can conduct in the real world. While the Web has succeeded despite a lack of interactivity, the real world is quite interactive (give someone a kiss and find out!); VRML, as a model of the real world, must conform to its behaviors. Furthermore, the real world has billions of people within it—we should be able to see and communicate with any of them, anywhere in cyberspace, at any time.

Many people call this type of cyberspace the *holy grail*, implying that it's a situation greatly to be desired, but never to be achieved.

There are a lot of obstacles to be overcome before we can create an environment with 100,000 or 100,000,000 participants, but creating an interactive, shared environment with five or ten people is not difficult. Ubique Corporation's *Virtual Places* is an excellent example of how multiparticipant interactivity can be achieved for as many as ten people simultaneously, and MUDs and MOOs (text-based cyberspaces) have been in use for years, providing interactive multiparticipant environments for hundreds of simultaneous users. VRML 2.0 can make baby steps into cyberspace; technologies like these prove that it's doable.

Technologies like SUN Microsystems' *Java* language provide another important component of cyberspace—the ability to create an object that behaves similarly on different computers. If you've used a computer running Microsoft Windows and one using Apple's Macintosh OS, you know that programs written for one computer do not run on the other—quite often you can't even use the same data files! Java creates an "abstraction layer;" that is, it creates a machine-within-the-machine, which can execute the same programs regardless of the computer's actual hardware or operating system. It's as if, within my PC, I have a software-based "Java computer" that talks to my PC's hardware. My Java programs run on my "Java computer," which is identical to a "Java computer" on a Macintosh, or a SUN SparcStation, or an SGI workstation, etc.

This means that I can create an object—perhaps a pen for writing—on my machine and hand it to you in cyberspace, and it'll still behave like a pen when you use it, regardless of what machines we're actually using. VRML 2.0 will need a technology very much like Java—perhaps even Java itself—to ensure that objects within VRML worlds are *interactive*—that is, they can express complex behaviors—on every computer platform. Without something like Java, VRML will remain static and lifeless.

There are many different approaches to a multiparticipant interactive cyberspace, each of which have their own advantages and liabilities—no one solution is right for all situations or applications. The requirements for a conference room with four or five people are very different from the requirements for a "rock concert in cyberspace" with 10,000 or more simultaneous participants. The network infrastructure and software requirements for each of these situations varies widely. The U.S. military has done significant work on a system known as *Distributed Interactive Simulation* (DIS), which it uses for war-gaming and other wide-area simulation tasks, but it requires a "perfect" Internet and large amounts of expensive hardware to create a shared simulation. On the other end of the scale, Worlds, Inc. *Worlds Chat* creates a multiparticipant cyberspace in which you can see others and participate in a text-based chat; Worlds Chat will run on almost any PC with a dial-up Internet connection.

As of this writing, there's a complete lack of consensus within the VRML community around any "right way" to begin solving these problems. That's one reason why there's no interactivity specification in VRML 1.0—every discussion invariably degenerated into "religious wars" about the right way to do things. That might be one of the best things that ever happened to VRML, because it left the door open to a great idea: why not leave VRML open to every possible model of multiparticipant interactivity?

In order to do this, VRML 2.0 will specify an *Application Program Interface* (API) for interactivity. This means that everyone will be free to "roll their own" behaviors and interactivity, without affecting the browser. Instead, there will be a standard methodology (the API) through which interactivity takes place within the VRML browser, but this will be done without specifying how the interactivity occurs. That will be handled in a "sidecar" application, which will be talking to the VRML browser, in much the same way that WebSpace talks to Netscape Navigator. It will even be possible to support multiple behavior engines and interaction models—they'll talk to each other across the API.

This solution is admittedly incomplete, but keeps VRML open enough to accommodate a wide range of solutions to very difficult problems. In situations like this, it's often best to grow a solution from a range of possible candidates, rather than mandating one. This is a little risky—there's some chance that the VRML community will fragment into a Babel of different standards that don't work with each other—but it also stands a chance of producing a range of "right" ways to implement cyberspace.

Marching Toward the Matrix

The next generations of VRML features will start appearing in VRML browsers before the end of 1995. I hope that in subsequent editions of this text, this section is replaced with chapters that specifically address the features of VRML 1.x and 2.0. As we extend the capabilities of VRML into the areas defined in this chapter—and into regions we haven't yet thought of—we'll retain the core capabilities as the essential elements within a larger sea of possibilities. VRML is a precarious balance between openness and chaos; in that region, creativity and vitality will give us room to design the global cyberspace.

Even if it were possible to provide a holy grail cyberspace immediately, most of us wouldn't know what to do with it—except perhaps to play games—and fewer of us would know how to design for it. We can expect to see a rapid evolution in tools that create interactive objects; these will be the foundation stones of Gibson's Matrix, which we skitter toward in tiny footsteps, like children learning to walk. By the time we're done, we'll be striding into a new medium of communication, conscious of its power, and capably equipped to use it.

Afterword:
The World-song

There is another world—you can see it in the distance. Turn your sturdy craft around and begin to tack toward it. As you move closer, you can see more of this world; its features become familiar to you. From far above, weather systems are white pinwheels, but you move in. Diving closer...closer...closer. Finally, you ride the rows in a forest of corn, swooping in like an eagle. Seeing everything.

Then a plaza where all roads cross and the highways have their end. This place is crowded and bubbling and alive with speech and human presence. People are selling, "Things to-buy to-day!" and people are saying, "I'll buy that thing to-day." The space where all meet, display their wares, nourish friendships, transmit secrets, and listen to the noise of five billionanity.

And a room—improbably long and impossibly high—dense with shelves and books. In this room, all human things are kept, every memory or fragment of knowledge or wisdom or truth or scientific fact or creation or prayer or great word spoken. You glide through the room, and as you do, it changes—listening to what you say, conforming to your need.

Last, a place that is no space, but a feeling and a sound of a voice opened up and shared; every voice within—there and next door and the world around, being in here, in song, as one.

Mark Pesce

June—July 1995

Los Angeles, Boston, and San Francisco

Appendixes

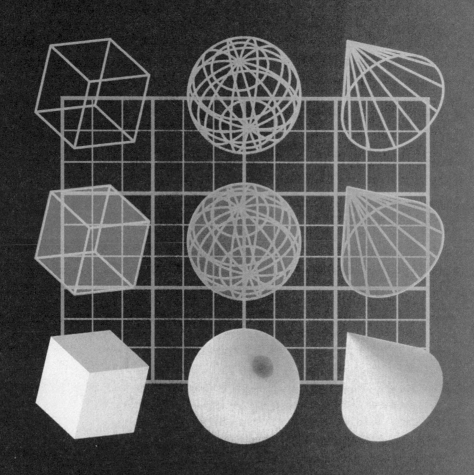

Appendix

VRML: The Virtual Reality Modeling Language Version 1.0 Specification

Gavin Bell, Silicon Graphics, Inc.

Anthony Parisi, Intervista Software

Mark Pesce, VRML List Moderator

Acknowledgments

I want to thank three people who have been absolutely instrumental in the design process: Brian Behlendorf, whose drive (and disk space) made this process happen; and Tony Parisi and Gavin Bell, the final authors of this specification, who have put in a great deal of design work, ensuring that we have a satisfactory product.

My hat goes off to all of them, and to all of you who have made this process a success.

Mark Pesce

I would like to add a personal note of thanks to Jan Hardenbergh of Oki Advanced Products for his diligent efforts to keep the specification process on track, and his invaluable editing assistance. I would also like to acknowledge Chris Marrin of Silicon Graphics for his timely contributions to the final design.

Tony Parisi

Revision History

First Draft—November 2, 1994

Second Draft—May 8, 1995

Third Draft—May 26, 1995

Table of Contents

Introduction

➤ VRML Mission Statement

➤ History

➤ Version 1.0 Requirements

Language Specification

➤ Language Basics

➤ Coordinate System

➤ Fields

➤ Nodes

➤ Instancing

➤ Extensibility

➤ An Example

Browser Considerations

➤ File Extensions

➤ MIME Types

Introduction

The *Virtual Reality Modeling Language* (VRML) is a language for describing multi-participant interactive simulations—virtual worlds networked via the global Internet and hyperlinked with the World Wide Web. All aspects of virtual world display, interaction, and internetworking can be specified using VRML. It is the intention of its designers that VRML become the standard language for interactive simulation within the World Wide Web.

The first version of VRML allows for the creation of virtual worlds with limited interactive behavior. These worlds can contain objects that have hyperlinks to other worlds, HTML documents, or other valid MIME types. When the user selects an object with a hyperlink, the appropriate MIME viewer is launched. When the user selects a link to a VRML document from within a correctly configured WWW browser, a VRML viewer is launched. VRML viewers are thus the perfect companion applications to standard WWW browsers for navigating and visualizing the Web. Future versions of VRML will allow for richer behaviors, including animations, motion physics, and real-time multiuser interaction.

This document specifies the features and syntax of Version 1.0 of VRML.

The VRML Mission Statement

The history of the development of the Internet has had three distinct phases—first, the development of the TCP/IP infrastructure, which allowed documents and data to be stored in a proximally independent way; that is, the Internet provided a layer of abstraction between data sets and the hosts that manipulated them. While this abstraction was useful, it was also confusing; without any clear sense of "what went where," access to the Internet was restricted to the class of sysops/Net surfers who could maintain internal cognitive maps of the data space.

Next, Tim Berners-Lee's work at CERN, where he developed the hypermedia system known as the World Wide Web, added another layer of abstraction to the existing structure. This abstraction provided an "addressing" scheme, a unique identifier (the *Universal Resource Locator*), which could tell anyone "where to go and how to get there" for any piece of data within the Web. While useful, it lacked dimensionality; there's no *there* there within the Web, and the only type of navigation permissible (other than surfing) is by direct reference. In other words, I can only tell you how to get to the VRML Forum home page by saying, "http://www.wired.com/," which is not human-centered data. In fact, I need to make an effort to remember it at all. So, while the World Wide Web provides a retrieval mechanism to complement the existing storage mechanism, it leaves a lot to be desired, particularly for human beings.

Finally, we move to "perceptualized" Internetworks, where the data has been sensualized—that is, rendered sensually. If something is represented sensually, it is possible to make sense of it. VRML is an attempt to place humans at the center of the Internet, ordering its universe to our whims (how successful this attempt is, only time and effort will tell). In order to do that, the most important single element is a standard that defines the particularities of perception. Virtual Reality Modeling Language is that standard, designed to be a universal description language for multi-participant simulations.

These three phases—storage, retrieval, and perceptualization—are analogous to the human process of consciousness, as expressed in terms of semantics and cognitive science. Events occur and are recorded (memory), inferences are drawn from memory (associations) and from sets of related events, and maps of the universe are created (cognitive perception). What is important to remember is that the map is not the territory, and we should avoid becoming trapped in any single representation or world-view. Although we need to design to avoid disorientation, we must always work creatively and intelligently to broaden the domain of experience we can bring into manifestation!

This document is the living proof of the success of a process that was committed to being open and flexible, responsive to the needs of a growing Web community. Rather than reinvent the wheel, we have adapted an existing specification (Open Inventor) as the basis from which our own work can grow, saving years of design work and perhaps many mistakes. Our real work can now begin—that of rendering our noospheric space.

History

VRML was conceived in the spring of 1994 at the first annual World Wide Web Conference in Geneva, Switzerland. Tim Berners-Lee and Dave Raggett organized a *birds-of-a-feather* (BOF) session to discuss virtual reality interfaces to the World Wide Web. Several BOF attendees described projects already underway to build three-dimensional graphical visualization tools that interoperate with the Web. Attendees agreed on the need for these tools to have a common language for specifying 3D scene description and WWW hyperlinks—an analog of HTML for virtual reality. The term *Virtual Reality Markup Language* (VRML) was coined, and the group resolved to begin specification work after the conference. The word "Markup" was later changed to "Modeling" to reflect the graphical nature of VRML.

Shortly after the Geneva BOF session, the www-vrml mailing list was created to discuss the development of a specification for the first version of VRML. The response to the list invitation was overwhelming: within a week, there were over a thousand members. After an initial settling-in period, list moderator Mark Pesce of Labyrinth Group announced his intention to have a draft version of the specification ready by the WWW Fall 1994 conference, a mere five months away. There was general agreement within the list that, while this schedule was aggressive, it was achievable provided that the requirements for the first version were not too ambitious and that VRML could be adapted from an existing solution. The list quickly agreed upon a set of requirements for the first version, and began a search for technologies that could be adapted to fit the needs of VRML.

The search for existing technologies turned up several worthwhile candidates. After much deliberation, the list came to a consensus: the Open Inventor ASCII File Format from Silicon Graphics, Inc. The Inventor File Format supports complete descriptions of 3D scenes with polygonally rendered objects, lighting, materials, ambient properties, and realism effects. A subset of the Inventor File Format, with extensions to support networking, forms the basis of VRML. Gavin Bell of Silicon Graphics has adapted the Inventor File Format for VRML, with design input from the mailing list. SGI has publicly stated that the file format is available for use in the open market, and has contributed a file format parser into the public domain to bootstrap VRML viewer development.

Version 1.0 Requirements

VRML 1.0 is designed to meet the following requirements:

➤ Platform independence

➤ Extensibility

➤ Ability to work well over low-bandwidth connections

As with HTML, the preceding are absolute requirements for a network language standard; they should need little explanation here.

Early on, the designers decided that VRML would not be an extension to HTML. HTML is designed for text, not graphics. Also, VRML requires even more finely tuned network optimizations than HTML; it is expected that a typical VRML scene will be composed of many more "inline" objects and served up by many more servers than a typical HTML document. Moreover, HTML is an accepted standard, with existing implementations that depend on it. To impede the HTML design process with VRML issues and constrain the VRML design process with HTML compatibility concerns would be to do both languages a disservice. As a network language, VRML will succeed or fail independent of HTML.

It was also decided that, except for the hyperlinking feature, the first version of VRML would not support interactive behaviors. This was a practical decision intended to streamline design and implementation. Design of a language for describing interactive behaviors is a big job, especially when the language needs to express behaviors of objects communicating on a network. Such languages do exist; if we had chosen one of them, we would have risked getting into a "language war." People don't get excited about the syntax of a language for describing polygonal objects; people get very excited about the syntax of real languages for writing programs. Religious wars can extend the design process by months or years. In addition, networked inter-object operation requires brokering services such as those provided by CORBA or OLE, services that don't exist yet within WWW; we would have had to invent them. Finally, by keeping behaviors out of Version 1, we have made it a much smaller task to implement a viewer. We acknowledge that support for arbitrary interactive behaviors is critical to the long-term success of VRML; they will be included in Version 2.

Language Specification

The language specification is divided into the following sections:

➤ Language basics

➤ Coordinate system

➤ Fields

➤ Nodes

➤ Instancing

➤ Extensibility

➤ An example VRML document

Language Basics

At the highest level of abstraction, VRML is just a way for objects to read and write themselves. Theoretically, the objects can contain anything—3D geometry, MIDI data, JPEG images, and so forth. VRML defines a set of objects useful for doing 3D graphics. These objects are called *nodes.*

Nodes are arranged in hierarchical structures called *scene graphs.* Scene graphs are more than just a collection of nodes; they define an ordering for the nodes. The scene graph has a notion of state—nodes earlier in the scene can affect nodes that appear later in the scene. For example, a Rotation or Material node will affect the nodes after it appears in the scene. A mechanism is defined to limit the effects of properties (Separator nodes), allowing parts of the scene graph to be functionally isolated from other parts.

A node has the following characteristics:

➤ **The kind of object it is.** A node might be a cube, a sphere, a texture map, a transformation, and so forth.

➤ **The parameters that distinguish this node from other nodes of the same type.** For example, each Sphere node might have a different radius, and different texture maps nodes will certainly contain different images to use as the texture maps. These parameters are called *fields.* A node can have zero or more fields.

➤ **A name to identify this node.** Being able to name nodes and refer to them elsewhere is very powerful; it enables a scene's author to give hints to applications using the scene about what is in the scene, and creates possibilities for very powerful scripting extensions. Nodes do not have to be named; if they are named, however, they can have only one name. Names do not have to be unique—several different nodes can be given the same name.

➤ **Child nodes.** Object hierarchy is implemented by allowing some types of nodes to contain other nodes. Parent nodes traverse their children in order during rendering. Nodes that may have children are referred to as *group nodes*. Group nodes can have zero or more children.

The syntax chosen to represent these pieces of information is straightforward, as follows:

```
DEF objectname objecttype { fields children }
```

Only the object type and curly braces are required; nodes may or may not have a name, fields, and children. Node names must not begin with a digit, and must not contain spaces or control characters, single or double quote characters, backslashes, curly braces, the plus character, or the period character.

For example, the following file contains a simple scene defining a view of a red cone and a blue sphere, lit by a directional light:

```
#VRML V1.0 ascii
 Separator {
        DirectionalLight {
              direction 0 0 -1  # Light shining from viewer
➥into scene
        }
        PerspectiveCamera {
              position   -8.6 2.1 5.6
              orientation -0.1352 -0.9831 -0.1233  1.1417
              focalDistance      10.84
        }
        Separator {   # The red sphere
              Material {
                   diffuseColor 1 0 0   # Red
              }
              Translation { translation 3 0 1 }
              Sphere { radius 2.3 }
```

```
            }
            Separator {  # The blue cube
                Material {
                        diffuseColor 0 0 1  # Blue
                }
                Transform {
                        translation -2.4 .2 1
                        rotation 0 1 1  .9
                }
                Cube {}
            }
```

General Syntax

For easy identification of VRML files, every VRML file must begin with the following characters:

```
#VRML V1.0 ascii
```

Any characters after these on the same line are ignored. The line is terminated by either the ASCII newline or carriage-return characters.

The "#" character begins a comment; all characters until the next newline or carriage return are ignored. The only exception to this is within string fields, where the "#" character is part of the string.

Comments and white space may not be preserved; in particular, a VRML document server might strip comments and extraneous white space from a VRML file before transmitting it. Info nodes should be used for persistent information, such as copyrights or author information. Info nodes could also be used for object descriptions.

Blanks, tabs, newlines, and carriage returns are white-space characters wherever they appear outside of string fields. One or more white-space characters separates the syntactical entities in VRML files, where necessary.

After the required header, a VRML file contains exactly one VRML node. That node can of course be a group node, of course, containing any number of other nodes.

Coordinate System

VRML uses a Cartesian, right-handed, three-dimensional coordinate system. By default, objects are projected onto a two-dimensional device by projecting them in the direction of the positive z axis, with the positive x axis to the right and the positive y axis up. A camera or modeling transformation can be used to alter this default projection.

The standard unit for lengths and distances specified is meters. The standard unit for angles is radians.

Fields

There are two general classes of fields—fields that contain a single value (where a value may be a single number, a vector, or even an image), and fields that contain multiple values. Single-valued fields all have names that begin with "SF," and multiple-valued fields have names that begin with "MF." Each field type defines the format for the values it writes.

Multiple-valued fields are written as a series of values separated by commas, all enclosed in square brackets. If the field has zero values, then only the square brackets ([]) are written. The last may optionally be followed by a comma. If the field has exactly one value, the brackets can be omitted and just the value written. For example, all of the following are valid for a multiple-valued field containing the single integer value 1:

```
1
[1,]
[ 1 ]
```

SFBitMask

A single-value field that contains a mask of bit flags. Nodes that use this field class define mnemonic names for the bit flags. SFBitMasks are written to file as one or more mnemonic enumerated type names, in the following format:

```
( flag1 ¦ flag2 ¦ ... )
```

If only one flag is used in a mask, the parentheses are optional. These names differ among uses of this field in various node classes.

SFBool

A field containing a single boolean (true or false) value. SFBools can be written as 0 (representing FALSE), 1, TRUE, or FALSE.

SFColor

A single-value field containing a color. SFColors are written to file as an RGB triple of floating-point numbers in standard scientific notation, in the range 0.0 to 1.0.

SFEnum

A single-value field that contains an enumerated type value. Nodes that use this field class define mnemonic names for the values. SFEnums are written to file as a mnemonic enumerated type name. The name differs among uses of this field in various node classes.

SFFloat

A field that contains one single-precision, floating-point number. SFFloats are written to file in standard scientific notation.

SFImage

A field that contains an uncompressed two-dimensional color or grayscale image.

SFImages are written to file as three integers representing the width, height, and number of components in the image, followed by width*height hexadecimal values representing the pixels in the image, separated by white space. A one-component image will have one-byte hexadecimal values representing the intensity of the image. For example, 0xFF is full intensity, and 0x00 is no intensity. A two-component image puts the intensity in the first (high) byte and the transparency in the second (low) byte.

Pixels in a three-component image have the red component in the first (high) byte, followed by the green and blue components (so 0xFF0000 is red). Four-component images put the transparency byte after red/green/blue (so 0x0000FF80 is semi-transparent blue). A value of 1.0 is completely transparent, and 0.0 is completely opaque. Each pixel is actually read as a single unsigned number, so a three-component pixel with value "0x0000FF" can also be written as "0xFF" or "255" (decimal). Pixels are specified from left to right, bottom to top. The first hexadecimal value is the lower left pixel of the image, and the last value is the upper right pixel.

For example, 1 2 1 0xFF 0x00 is a one-pixel wide by two-pixel high grayscale image, with the bottom pixel white and the top pixel black.

```
2 4 3 0xFF0000 0xFF00 0 0 0 0 0xFFFFFF 0xFFFF00
```

The preceding is a two-pixel wide by four-pixel high RGB image, with the bottom left pixel red, the bottom right pixel green, the two middle rows of pixels black, the top left pixel white, and the top right pixel yellow.

SFLong

A field containing a single long (32-bit) integer. SFLongs are written to file as an integer in decimal, hexadecimal (beginning with "0x"), or octal (beginning with "0") format.

SFMatrix

A field containing a transformation matrix. SFMatrices are written to file in row-major order as 16 floating-point numbers separated by white space. For example, a matrix expressing a translation of 7.3 units along the x axis is written as follows:

```
1 0 0 0  0 1 0 0  0 0 1 0  7.3 0 0 1
```

SFRotation

A field containing an arbitrary rotation. SFRotations are written to file as four floating-point values separated by white space. The four values represent an axis of rotation, followed by the amount of right-handed rotation about that axis, in radians. For example, a 180-degree rotation about the y axis is the following:

```
0 1 0  3.14159265
```

SFString

A field containing an ASCII string (sequence of characters). SFStrings are written to file as a sequence of ASCII characters in double quotes (optional if the string doesn't contain any white space). Any characters (including newlines) may appear within the quotes. To include a double quote character within the string, precede it with a backslash. For example, the following are all valid strings:

```
Testing
"One, Two, Three"
"He said, \"Immel did it!\""
```

SFVec2f

A field containing a two-dimensional vector. SFVec2fs are written to file as a pair of floating-point values separated by white space.

SFVec3f

A field containing a three-dimensional vector. SFVec3fs are written to file as three floating-point values separated by white space.

MFColor

A multiple-value field that contains any number of RGB colors. MFColors are written to file as one or more RGB triples of floating-point numbers in standard scientific notation. When more than one value is present, all of the values must be enclosed in square brackets and separated by commas. For example, the following line represents the three colors red, green, and blue:

```
[ 1.0 0.0 0.0, 0 1 0, 0 0 1 ]
```

MFLong

A multiple-value field that contains any number of long (32-bit) integers. MFLongs are written to file as one or more integer values, in decimal, hexadecimal, or octal format. When more than one value is present, all the values are enclosed in square brackets and separated by commas, as follows:

```
[ 17, -0xE20, -518820 ]
```

MFVec2f

A multiple-value field that contains any number of two-dimensional vectors. MFVec2fs are written to file as one or more pairs of floating-point values separated by white space. When more than one value is present, all of the values are enclosed in square brackets and separated by commas, as shown in the following:

```
[ 0 0, 1.2 3.4, 98.6 -4e1 ]
```

MFVec3f

A multiple-value field that contains any number of three-dimensional vectors. MFVec3fs are written to file as one or more triples of floating-point values separated by white space. When more than one value is present, all of the values are enclosed in square brackets and separated by commas, as follows:

```
[ 0 0 0, 1.2 3.4 5.6, 98.6 -4e1 212 ]
```

Nodes

VRML defines several different classes of nodes. Most of the nodes can be classified into one of three categories—shape, property, or group. *Shape nodes* define the geometry in the scene. Conceptually, they are the only nodes that draw anything. *Property nodes* affect the way shapes are drawn. *Grouping nodes* gather other nodes together, allowing collections of nodes to be treated as a single object. Some group nodes also control whether or not their children are drawn.

Nodes can contain zero or more fields. Each node type defines the type, name, and default value for each of its fields. The default value for the field is used if a value for the field is not specified in the VRML file. The order in which the fields of a node are read is not important; for example, "Cube { width 2 height 4 depth 6 }" and "Cube { height 4 depth 6 width 2 }" are equivalent.

Here are the 36 nodes grouped by type. The first group contains the shape nodes:

➤ AsciiText

➤ Cone

➤ Cube

➤ Cylinder

➤ IndexedFaceSet

➤ IndexedLineSet

➤ PointSet

➤ Sphere

The second group contains the geometry and material nodes:

➤ Coordinate3

➤ FontStyle

➤ Info

➤ LOD

➤ Material

➤ MaterialBinding

➤ Normal

➤ NormalBinding

➤ Texture2

➤ Texture2Transform

➤ TextureCoordinate2

➤ ShapeHints

The third group contains the transformation nodes:

➤ MatrixTransform

➤ Rotation

➤ Scale

➤ Transform

➤ Translation

The fourth group contains the camera nodes:

➤ OrthographicCamera

➤ PerspectiveCamera

The fifth group contains the lighting nodes:

➤ DirectionalLight

➤ PointLight

➤ SpotLight

These are the group nodes:

➤ Group

➤ Separator

➤ Switch

➤ TransformSeparator

➤ WWWAnchor

Finally, the WWWInline node does not fit neatly into any category.

AsciiText

This node represents strings of text characters from the ASCII-coded character set. The first string is rendered with its baseline at (0,0,0). All subsequent strings advance y by –(size * spacing). See FontStyle for a description of the size field. The justification field determines the placement of the strings in the x dimension. LEFT (the default) places the left edge of each string at x=0. CENTER places the center of each string at x=0. RIGHT places the right edge of each string at x=0. Text is rendered from left to right and top to bottom in the font set by FontStyle. The width field defines a suggested width constraint for each string. The default is to use the natural width of each string. Setting any value to 0 indicates that the natural width should be used for that string.

The text is transformed by the current cumulative transformation and is drawn with the current material and texture.

Textures are applied to 3D text as follows. The texture origin is at the origin of the first string, as determined by the justification. The texture is scaled equally in both S and T dimensions, with the font height representing one unit. S increases to the right. The T origin can occur anywhere along each character, depending on how that character's outline is defined.

```
JUSTIFICATION

        LEFT    Align left edge of text to origin

        CENTER  Align center of text to origin

        RIGHT   Align right edge of text to origin

FILE FORMAT/DEFAULTS

    AsciiText {
                string          ""    # MFString
                spacing         1     # SFFloat
                justification   LEFT  # SFEnum
                width           0     # MFFloat
        }
```

Cone

This node represents a simple cone whose central axis is aligned with the y axis. By default, the cone is centered at (0,0,0) and has a size of –1 to +1 in all three directions. The cone has a radius of 1 at the bottom and a height of 2, with its apex at 1 and its bottom at –1. The cone also has two parts: the sides and the bottom.

The cone is transformed by the current cumulative transformation and is drawn with the current texture and material.

If the current material binding is PER_PART or PER_PART_INDEXED, the first current material is used for the sides of the cone, and the second is used for the bottom. Otherwise, the first material is used for the entire cone.

When a texture is applied to a cone, it is applied differently to the sides and bottom. On the sides, the texture wraps counterclockwise (from above) starting at the back of the cone. The texture has a vertical seam at the back, intersecting the yz plane. For the bottom, a circle is cut out of the texture square and applied to the cone's base circle. The texture appears right side up when the top of the cone is rotated toward the –z axis.

```
PARTS

        SIDES       The conical part

        BOTTOM      The bottom circular face

        ALL         All parts

FILE FORMAT/DEFAULTS

        Cone {
                parts           ALL     # SFBitMask
                bottomRadius    1       # SFFloat
                height          2       # SFFloat
        }
```

Coordinate3

This node defines a set of 3D coordinates to be used by a subsequent IndexedFaceSet, IndexedLineSet, or PointSet node. This node does not produce a visible result during rendering; it simply replaces the current coordinates in the rendering state for subsequent nodes to use.

```
FILE FORMAT/DEFAULTS

        Coordinate3 {

                point  0 0 0  # MFVec3f

        }
```

Cube

This node represents a cuboid aligned with the coordinate axes. By default, the cube is centered at (0,0,0) and measures 2 units in each dimension, from –1 to +1. The cube is transformed by the current cumulative transformation and is drawn with the current material and texture.

If the current material binding is PER_PART, PER_PART_INDEXED, PER_FACE, or PER_FACE_INDEXED, materials will be bound to the faces of the cube in this order: front (+z), back (–z), left (–x), right (+x), top (+y), and bottom (–y).

Textures are applied individually to each face of the cube; the entire texture goes on each face. On the front, back, right, and left sides of the cube, the texture is applied right side up. On the top, the texture appears right side up when the top of the cube is tilted toward the camera. On the bottom, the texture appears right side up when the top of the cube is tilted toward the –z axis.

FILE FORMAT/DEFAULTS

```
Cube {

        width   2     # SFFloat

        height  2     # SFFloat

        depth   2     # SFFloat

}
```

Cylinder

This node represents a simple capped cylinder centered around the y axis. By default, the cylinder is centered at (0,0,0) and has a default size of –1 to +1 in all three dimensions. The cylinder has three parts: the sides, the top (y = +1), and the bottom (y = –1). You can use the radius and height fields to create a cylinder with a different size.

The cylinder is transformed by the current cumulative transformation and is drawn with the current material and texture.

If the current material binding is PER_PART or PER_PART_INDEXED, the first current material is used for the sides of the cylinder, the second is used for the top, and the third is used for the bottom. Otherwise, the first material is used for the entire cylinder.

When a texture is applied to a cylinder, it is applied differently to the sides, top, and bottom. On the sides, the texture wraps counterclockwise (from above) starting at the back of the cylinder. The texture has a vertical seam at the back, intersecting the yz plane. For the top and bottom, a circle is cut out of the texture square and applied to the top or bottom circle. The top texture appears right side up when the top of the cylinder is tilted toward the +z axis, and the bottom texture appears right side up when the top of the cylinder is tilted toward the –z axis.

PARTS

  SIDES The cylindrical part

  TOP The top circular face

  BOTTOM The bottom circular face

  ALL All parts

FILE FORMAT/DEFAULTS

```
Cylinder {
        parts   ALL   # SFBitMask
        radius  1     # SFFloat
        height  2     # SFFloat
    }
```

DirectionalLight

This node defines a directional light source that illuminates along rays parallel to a given three-dimensional vector.

A light node defines an illumination source that may affect subsequent shapes in the scene graph, depending on the current lighting style. Light sources are affected by the current transformation. A light node under a separator does not affect any objects outside that separator.

```
FILE FORMAT/DEFAULTS

        DirectionalLight {
                        on          TRUE        # SFBool
                        intensity   1           # SFFloat
                        color       1 1 1       # SFColor
                        direction   0 0 -1      # SFVec3f
                }
```

FontStyle

This node defines the current font style used for all subsequent
AsciiText. Font attributes only are defined. It is up to the browser
to assign specific fonts to the various attribute combinations. The
size field specifies the height (in object space units) of glyphs
rendered and determines the vertical spacing of adjacent lines
of text.

```
FAMILY

        SERIF       Serif style (such as TimesRoman)

        SANS        Sans Serif Style (such as Helvetica)

        TYPEWRITER  Fixed pitch style (such as Courier)

STYLE

        NONE        No modifications to family

        BOLD        Embolden family

        ITALIC      Italicize or Slant family

FILE FORMAT/DEFAULTS

        FontStyle {
                        size    10      # SFFloat
                        family  SERIF   # SFEnum
                        style   NONE    # SFBitMask
                }
```

Group

This node defines the base class for all group nodes. Group is a node that contains an ordered list of child nodes. This node is simply a container for the child nodes and does not alter the traversal state in any way. During traversal, state accumulated for a child is passed on to each successive child and then to the parents of the group (Group does not push or pop traversal state as separator does).

FILE FORMAT/DEFAULTS

```
Group {
      }
```

IndexedFaceSet

This node represents a 3D shape formed by constructing faces (polygons) from vertices located at the current coordinates. IndexedFaceSet uses the indices in its coordIndex field to specify the polygonal faces. An index of –1 indicates that the current face has ended and the next one begins.

The vertices of the faces are transformed by the current transformation matrix.

Treatment of the current material and normal binding is as follows:

➤ The PER_PART and PER_FACE bindings specify a material or normal for each face.

➤ PER_VERTEX specifies a material or normal for each vertex.

➤ The corresponding _INDEXED bindings are the same, but use the materialIndex or normalIndex indices.

➤ The DEFAULT material binding is equal to OVERALL.

➤ The DEFAULT normal binding is equal to PER_VERTEX_INDEXED; if insufficient normals exist in the state, vertex normals will be generated automatically.

Explicit texture coordinates (as defined by TextureCoordinate2) can be bound to vertices of an indexed shape by using the indices in the textureCoordIndex field. As with all vertex-based shapes, if there is a current texture, but no texture coordinates are specified, a default texture coordinate mapping is calculated using the bounding box of the shape. The longest dimension of the bounding box defines the S coordinates, and the next longest defines the T coordinates. The value of the S coordinate ranges from 0 to 1, from one end of the bounding box to the other. The T coordinate ranges between 0 and the ratio of the second greatest dimension of the bounding box to the greatest dimension.

Be sure that the indices contained in the coordIndex, materialIndex, normalIndex, and textureCoordIndex fields are valid with respect to the current state, or errors will occur.

FILE FORMAT/DEFAULTS

```
IndexedFaceSet {
            coordIndex          0  # MFLong
            materialIndex      -1  # MFLong
            normalIndex        -1  # MFLong
            textureCoordIndex  -1  # MFLong
    }
```

IndexedLineSet

This node represents a 3D shape formed by constructing polylines from vertices located at the current coordinates. IndexedLineSet uses the indices in its coordIndex field to specify the polylines. An index of −1 indicates that the current polyline has ended and the next one begins.

The coordinates of the line set are transformed by the current cumulative transformation.

Treatment of the current material and normal binding is as follows:

➤ The PER_PART binding specifies a material or normal for each segment of the line.

➤ The PER_FACE binding specifies a material or normal for each polyline.

➤ PER_VERTEX specifies a material or normal for each vertex.

➤ The corresponding _INDEXED bindings are the same, but use the materialIndex or normalIndex indices.

➤ The DEFAULT material binding is equal to OVERALL.

➤ The DEFAULT normal binding is equal to PER_VERTEX_INDEXED; if insufficient normals exist in the state, the lines will be drawn unlit. The same rules for texture coordinate generation as IndexedFaceSet are used.

FILE FORMAT/DEFAULTS

```
IndexedLineSet {
        coordIndex        0  # MFLong
        materialIndex    -1  # MFLong
        normalIndex      -1  # MFLong
        textureCoordIndex -1 # MFLong
}
```

Info

This class defines an information node in the scene graph. This node has no effect during traversal. It is used to store information in the scene graph, typically for application-specific purposes, copyright messages, or other strings.

```
Info {
        string   "<Undefined info>"    # SFString
}
```

LOD

This group node is used to allow applications to switch between various representations of objects automatically. The children of this node typically represent the same object or objects at varying levels of detail, from highest detail to lowest.

The specified center point of the LOD is transformed by the current transformation into world space, and the distance from the transformed center to the world-space eye point is calculated. If the distance is less than the first value in the ranges array, then the first child of the LOD group is drawn. If between the first and second values in the ranges array, the second child is drawn, and so on. If there are N values in the ranges array, the LOD group should have N+1 children. Specifying too few children will result in the last child being used repeatedly for the lowest levels of detail; if too many children are specified, the extra children will be ignored. Each value in the ranges array should be less than the previous value, otherwise results are undefined.

FILE FORMAT/DEFAULTS

```
LOD {
           range [ ]     # MFFloat
           center 0 0 0  # SFVec3f
}
```

Material

This node defines the current surface material properties for all subsequent shapes. Material sets several components of the current material during traversal. Different shapes interpret materials with multiple values differently. To bind materials to shapes, use a MaterialBinding node.

FILE FORMAT/DEFAULTS

```
Material {
           ambientColor    0.2 0.2 0.2    # MFColor
           diffuseColor    0.8 0.8 0.8    # MFColor
           specularColor   0 0 0          # MFColor
           emissiveColor   0 0 0          # MFColor
           shininess       0.2            # MFFloat
           transparency    0              # MFFloat
}
```

MaterialBinding

This node specifies how the current materials are bound to shapes that follow in the scene graph. Each shape node may interpret bindings differently. The current material always has a base value, which is defined by the first value of all material fields. Because material fields may have multiple values, the binding determines how these values are distributed over a shape.

The bindings for faces and vertices are meaningful only for shapes that are made from faces and vertices. Similarly, the indexed bindings are only used by the shapes that allow indexing.

When multiple material values are bound, the values are cycled through, based on the period of the material component with the most values. For example, the following table shows the values used when cycling through (or indexing into) a material with two ambient colors, three diffuse colors, and one of all other components in the current material (the period of this material cycle is 3), as follows:

Material	Ambient color	Diffuse color	Other
0	0	0	0
1	1	1	0
2	1	2	0
3 (same as 0)	0	0	0

BINDINGS

DEFAULT	Use default binding
OVERALL	Whole object has same material
PER_PART	One material for each part of object
PER_PART_INDEXED	One material for each part, indexed

```
        PER_FACE              One material for each face of object

        PER_FACE_INDEXED     One material for each face, indexed

        PER_VERTEX            One material for each vertex of object

        PER_VERTEX_INDEXED One material for each vertex, indexed

FILE FORMAT/DEFAULTS

        MaterialBinding {
                    value  DEFAULT        # SFEnum
            }
```

MatrixTransform

This node defines a geometric 3D transformation with a 4 by 4 matrix. Note that some matrices (such as singular ones) might result in errors.

```
FILE FORMAT/DEFAULTS

        MatrixTransform {
                    matrix  1 0 0 0        # SFMatrix
                            0 1 0 0
                            0 0 1 0
                            0 0 0 1
            }
```

Normal

This node defines a set of 3D surface normal vectors to be used by vertex-based shape nodes (IndexedFaceSet, IndexedLineSet, PointSet) that follow it in the scene graph. This node does not produce a visible result during rendering; it simply replaces the current normals in the rendering state for subsequent nodes to use. This node contains one multiple-valued field that contains the normal vectors:

```
FILE FORMAT/DEFAULTS

     Normal {
                         vector   0 0 1 # MFVec3f
          }
```

NormalBinding

This node specifies how the current normals are bound to shapes that follow in the scene graph. Each shape node may interpret bindings differently.

The bindings for faces and vertices are meaningful only for shapes that are made from faces and vertices. Similarly, the indexed bindings are used only by the shapes that allow indexing. For bindings that require multiple normals, be sure to have at least as many normals defined as are necessary; otherwise, errors will occur.

```
BINDINGS
```

DEFAULT	Use default binding
OVERALL	Whole object has same normal
PER_PART	One normal for each part of object
PER_PART_INDEXED	One normal for each part, indexed
PER_FACE	One normal for each face of object
PER_FACE_INDEXED	One normal for each face, indexed
PER_VERTEX	One normal for each vertex of ➥object
PER_VERTEX_INDEXED	One normal for each vertex, indexed

```
FILE FORMAT/DEFAULTS

     NormalBinding {
```

```
                        value   DEFAULT        # SFEnum
            }
```

OrthographicCamera

An orthographic camera defines a parallel projection from a viewpoint. This camera does not diminish objects with distance, as a PerspectiveCamera does. The viewing volume for an orthographic camera is a rectangular parallelepiped (a box).

By default, the camera is located at (0,0,1) and looks along the negative z axis; the position and orientation fields can be used to change these values. The height field defines the total height of the viewing volume.

A camera can be placed in a VRML world to specify the initial location of the viewer when that world is entered. VRML browsers will typically modify the camera to enable a user to move through the virtual world.

Cameras are affected by the current transformation, so you can position a camera by placing a transformation node before it in the scene graph. The default position and orientation of a camera is at (0,0,1) looking along the negative z axis.

FILE FORMAT/DEFAULTS

```
    OrthographicCamera {
                position        0 0 1          # SFVec3f
                orientation     0 0 1 0        #
➥SFRotation
                focalDistance   5              # SFFloat
                height          2              # SFFloat
            }
```

PerspectiveCamera

A perspective camera defines a perspective projection from a viewpoint. The viewing volume for a perspective camera is a truncated right pyramid.

By default, the camera is located at (0,0,1) and looks along the negative z axis; the position and orientation fields can be used to change these values. The heightAngle field defines the total vertical angle of the viewing volume.

See more on cameras in the OrthographicCamera description.

FILE FORMAT/DEFAULTS

```
        PerspectiveCamera {
                     position        0 0 1        # SFVec3f
                     orientation     0 0 1 0      #
➡SFRotation
                     focalDistance   5            # SFFloat
                     heightAngle     0.785398     # SFFloat
                 }
```

PointLight

This node defines a point light source at a fixed 3D location. A point source illuminates equally in all directions; that is, it is omni-directional.

A light node defines an illumination source that may affect subsequent shapes in the scene graph, depending on the current lighting style. Light sources are affected by the current transformation. A light node under a separator does not affect any objects outside that separator.

FILE FORMAT/DEFAULTS

```
        PointLight {
                     on          TRUE    ,    # SFBool
                     intensity   1            # SFFloat
                     color       1 1 1        # SFColor
                     location    0 0 1        # SFVec3f
                 }
```

PointSet

This node represents a set of points located at the current coordinates. PointSet uses the current coordinates in order, starting at the index specified by the startIndex field. The number of points in the set is specified by the numPoints field. A value of –1 for this field indicates that all remaining values in the current coordinates are to be used as points.

The coordinates of the point set are transformed by the current cumulative transformation. The points are drawn with the current material and texture.

Treatment of the current material and normal binding is as follows:

➤ PER_PART, PER_FACE, and PER_VERTEX bindings bind one material or normal to each point.

➤ The DEFAULT material binding is equal to OVERALL.

➤ The DEFAULT normal binding is equal to PER_VERTEX.

➤ The startIndex is also used for materials or normals when the binding indicates that they should be used per vertex.

```
FILE FORMAT/DEFAULTS

    PointSet {
                startIndex  0 # SFLong
                numPoints   -1         # SFLong
        }
```

Rotation

This node defines a 3D rotation about an arbitrary axis through the origin. The rotation is accumulated into the current transformation, which is applied to subsequent shapes:

```
FILE FORMAT/DEFAULTS

    Rotation {
                rotation  0 0 1  0    # SFRotation
        }
```

See the rotation field description for more information.

Scale

This node defines a 3D scaling about the origin. If the components of the scaling vector are not all the same, this produces a non-uniform scale.

```
FILE FORMAT/DEFAULTS

    Scale {
                scaleFactor  1 1 1    # SFVec3f
        }
```

Separator

This group node performs a push (save) of the traversal state before traversing its children and a pop (restore) after traversing them. This isolates the separator's children from the rest of the scene graph. A separator can include lights, cameras, coordinates, normals, bindings, and all other properties.

Separators can also perform render culling. *Render culling* skips over traversal of the separator's children if they are not going to be rendered, based on the comparison of the separator's bounding box with the current view volume. Culling is controlled by the renderCulling field. These are set to AUTO by default, allowing the implementation to decide whether or not to cull.

```
CULLING ENUMS

        ON    Always try to cull to the view volume

        OFF   Never try to cull to the view volume
```

```
AUTO  Implementation-defined culling behavior
```

FILE FORMAT/DEFAULTS

```
Separator {
            renderCulling    AUTO      # SFEnum
    }
```

ShapeHints

The ShapeHints node indicates that IndexedFaceSets are solid, contain ordered vertices, or contain convex faces.

These hints allow VRML implementations to optimize certain rendering features. Optimizations that can be performed include enabling backface culling and disabling two-sided lighting. For example, if an object is solid and has ordered vertices, an implementation may turn on backface culling and turn off two-sided lighting. If the object is not solid, but has ordered vertices, it may turn off backface culling and turn on two-sided lighting.

The ShapeHints node also affects how default normals are generated. When an IndexedFaceSet has to generate default normals, it uses the creaseAngle field to determine which edges should be smoothly shaded and which ones should have a sharp crease. The *crease angle* is the angle between surface normals on adjacent polygons. For example, a crease angle of .5 radians (the default value) means that an edge between two adjacent polygonal faces will be smooth shaded if the normals to the two faces form an angle that is less than .5 radians (about 30 degrees). Otherwise, it will be faceted.

VERTEX ORDERING ENUMS

```
UNKNOWN_ORDERING    Ordering of vertices is unknown

CLOCKWISE           Face vertices are ordered clockwise

                                  (from the outside)
```

```
          COUNTERCLOCKWISE    Face vertices are ordered
➡counterclockwise


                                  (from the
➡outside)

SHAPE TYPE ENUMS

     UNKNOWN_SHAPE_TYPE  Nothing is known about the shape

     SOLID               The shape encloses a volume

FACE TYPE ENUMS

     UNKNOWN_FACE_TYPE   Nothing is known about faces

     CONVEX              All faces are convex

FILE FORMAT/DEFAULTS

     ShapeHints {
                    vertexOrdering  UNKNOWN_ORDERING      #
➡SFEnum
                    shapeType       UNKNOWN_SHAPE_TYPE    #
➡SFEnum
                    faceType        CONVEX                #
➡SFEnum
                    creaseAngle     0.5                   #
➡SFFloat
          }
```

Sphere

This node represents a sphere. By default, the sphere is centered at the origin and has a radius of 1. The sphere is transformed by the current cumulative transformation and is drawn with the current material and texture.

A sphere does not have faces or parts. Therefore, the sphere ignores material and normal bindings, using the first material for the entire sphere and using its own normals. When a texture is applied to a sphere, the texture covers the entire surface, wrapping counterclockwise from the back of the sphere. The texture has a seam at the back on the yz plane.

FILE FORMAT/DEFAULTS

```
Sphere {
            radius   1      # SFFloat
    }
```

SpotLight

This node defines a spotlight light source. A spotlight is placed at a fixed location in 3D-space and illuminates in a cone along a particular direction. The intensity of the illumination drops off exponentially as a ray of light diverges from this direction toward the edges of the cone. The rate of drop-off and the angle of the cone are controlled by the dropOffRate and cutOffAngle fields.

A light node defines an illumination source that might affect subsequent shapes in the scene graph, depending on the current lighting style. Light sources are affected by the current transformation. A light node under a separator does not affect any objects outside that separator.

FILE FORMAT/DEFAULTS

```
SpotLight {
            on            TRUE      # SFBool
            intensity     1         # SFFloat
            color         1 1 1     # SFVec3f
            location      0 0 1     # SFVec3f
            direction     0 0 -1    # SFVec3f
            dropOffRate   0         # SFFloat
            cutOffAngle   0.785398 # SFFloat
    }
```

Switch

This group node traverses one, none, or all of its children. One can use this node to switch on and off the effects of some properties or to switch between different properties.

The whichChild field specifies the index of the child to traverse, where the first child has index 0.

A value of –1 (the default) means do not traverse any children. A value of –3 traverses all children, making the switch behave exactly like a regular group.

FILE FORMAT/DEFAULTS

```
    Switch {
                whichChild  -1        # SFLong
        }
```

Texture2

This property node defines a texture map and parameters for that map. This map is used to apply texture to subsequent shapes as they are rendered.

The texture can be read from the URL specified by the file-name field. To turn off texturing, set the file-name field to an empty string ("").

Textures can also be specified inline by setting the image field to contain the texture data. Specifying both a URL and data inline will result in undefined behavior.

WRAP ENUM

```
        REPEAT   Repeats texture outside 0-1 texture coordinate
    ➥range

        CLAMP    Clamps texture coordinates to lie within 0-1
    ➥range
```

```
FILE FORMAT/DEFAULTS

    Texture2 {
                filename    " "        # SFString
                image       0 0 0      # SFImage
                wrapS       REPEAT     # SFEnum
                wrapT       REPEAT     # SFEnum
        }
```

Texture2Transform

This node defines a 2D transformation applied to texture coordinates. This affects the way textures are applied to the surfaces of subsequent shapes. The transformation consists of (in order) a non-uniform scale about an arbitrary center point, a rotation about that same point, and a translation. This enables a user to change the size and position of the textures on shapes.

```
FILE FORMAT/DEFAULTS

    Texture2Transform {
                translation  0 0      # SFVec2f
                rotation     0        # SFFloat
                scaleFactor  1 1      # SFVec2f
                center       0 0      # SFVec2f
        }
```

TextureCoordinate2

This node defines a set of 2D coordinates to be used to map textures to the vertices of subsequent PointSet, IndexedLineSet, or IndexedFaceSet objects. It replaces the current texture coordinates in the rendering state for the shapes to use.

Texture coordinates range from 0 to 1 across the texture. The horizontal coordinate, called S, is specified first, followed by the vertical coordinate, T.

```
FILE FORMAT/DEFAULTS

        TextureCoordinate2 {
                point  0 0     # MFVec2f
        }
```

Transform

This node defines a geometric 3D transformation consisting of (in order) a (possibly) non-uniform scale about an arbitrary point, a rotation about an arbitrary point and axis, and a translation.

```
FILE FORMAT/DEFAULTS

        Transform {
                translation      0 0 0       # SFVec3f
                rotation         0 0 1  0    #
➡SFRotation
                scaleFactor      1 1 1        # SFVec3f
                scaleOrientation 0 0 1  0    #
➡SFRotation
                center           0 0 0        # SFVec3f
        }
```

The transform node...

```
Transform {
        translation T1
        rotation R1
        scaleFactor S
        scaleOrientation R2
        center T2
}
```

...is equivalent to the following sequence:

```
Translation { translation T1 }

Translation { translation T2 }

Rotation { rotation R1 }
```

```
Rotation { rotation R2 }

Scale { scaleFactor S }

Rotation { rotation -R2 }
Translation { translation -T2 }
```

TransformSeparator

This group node is similar to the separator node in that it saves
state before traversing its children and restores it afterwards. It
saves only the current transformation, however; all other states
are left as unchanged. This node can be useful for positioning a
camera, because the transformations to the camera will not affect
the rest of the scene, even through the camera will view the scene.
Similarly, this node can be used to isolate transformations to light
sources or other objects.

FILE FORMAT/DEFAULTS

```
TransformSeparator {

}
```

Translation

This node defines a translation by a 3D vector.

FILE FORMAT/DEFAULTS

```
Translation {
        translation  0 0 0    # SFVec3f
}
```

WWWAnchor

The WWWAnchor group node loads a new scene into a VRML
browser when one of its children is chosen. Exactly how a user
"chooses" a child of the WWWAnchor is up to the VRML browser;
typically, clicking on one of its children with the mouse will result

in the new scene replacing the current scene. A WWWAnchor with an empty ("") name does nothing when its children are chosen. The name is an arbitrary URL.

WWWAnchor behaves like a Separator, pushing the traversal state before traversing its children and popping it afterwards.

The description field in the WWWAnchor allows for a friendly prompt to be displayed as an alternative to the URL in the name field. Ideally, browsers will allow the user to choose the description, the URL, or both to be displayed for a candidate WWWAnchor.

The WWWAnchor's map field is an enumerated value that can be either NONE (the default) or POINT. If it is POINT, then the object-space coordinates of the point on the object the user chose will be added to the URL in the name field, with the syntax "?x,y,z."

```
MAP ENUM

        NONE  Do not add information to the URL

        POINT Add object-space coordinates to URL

FILE FORMAT/DEFAULTS

  WWWAnchor {
            name ""         # SFString
            description "" # SFString
            map NONE        # SFEnum
    }
```

WWWInline

The WWWInline node reads its children from anywhere in the World Wide Web. Exactly when its children are read is not defined; reading the children may be delayed until the WWWInline is actually displayed. A WWWInline with an empty name does nothing. The name is an arbitrary URL.

The effect of referring to a non-VRML URL in a WWWInline node is undefined.

If the WWWInline's bboxSize field specifies a non-empty bounding box (a bounding box is *non-empty* if at least one of its dimensions is greater than zero), then the WWWInline's object-space bounding box is specified by its bboxSize and bboxCenter fields. This allows an implementation to view-volume cull or LOD switch the WWWInline without reading its contents.

FILE FORMAT/DEFAULTS

```
WWWInline {
        name ""                 # SFString
        bboxSize 0 0 0          # SFVec3f
        bboxCenter 0 0 0        # SFVec3f
}
```

Instancing

A node may be the child of more than one group. This is called *instancing* (using the same instance of a node multiple times, called *aliasing* or *multiple references* by other systems), and is accomplished by using the "USE" keyword.

The DEF keyword both defines a named node, and creates a single instance of it. The USE keyword indicates that the most recently defined instance should be used again. If several nodes were given the same name, then the last DEF encountered during parsing "wins." DEF/USE is limited to a single file; there is no mechanism for USEing nodes that are DEFed in other files.

A name goes into scope as soon as the DEF is encountered, and does not go out of scope until another DEF of the same name or end-of-file are encountered. Nodes cannot be shared between files (you cannot USE a node that was DEFed inside the file to which a WWWInline refers).

For example, rendering this scene will result in three spheres being drawn. Both of the spheres are named "Joe"; the second (smaller) sphere is drawn twice, as follows:

```
Separator {
        DEF Joe Sphere { }
        Translation { translation 2 0 0 }
        Separator {
                DEF Joe Sphere { radius .2 }
                Translation { translation 2 0 0 }
        }

        USE Joe    # radius .2 sphere will be used here
```

Extensibility

Extensions to VRML are supported by supporting self-describing nodes. Nodes that are not part of standard VRML must write out a description of their fields first, so that all VRML implementations are able to parse and ignore the extensions.

This description is written just after the opening curly brace for the node, and consists of the keyword "fields" followed by a list of the types and names of fields used by that node, all enclosed in square brackets and separated by commas. For example, if Cube was not a standard VRML node, it would be written like this:

```
Cube {
        fields [ SFFloat width, SFFloat height, SFFloat depth ]
        width 10 height 4 depth 3
```

Specifying the fields for nodes that *are* part of standard VRML is not an error; VRML parsers must silently ignore the field specification.

Is-a Relationships

A new node type may also be a superset of an existing node that is part of the standard. In this case, if an implementation for the new node type cannot be found, the new node type can be safely treated as the existing node it is based on (with some loss of functionality, of course). To support this, new node types can define an MFString field called "isA," containing the names of the types of which it is a superset.

For example, a new type of Material called "ExtendedMaterial" that adds index of refraction as a material property can be written as the following:

```
ExtendedMaterial {

  fields [ MFString isA, MFFloat indexOfRefraction,
                    MFColor ambientColor, MFColor
➥diffuseColor,
                    MFColor specularColor, MFColor
➥emissiveColor,
                    MFFloat shininess, MFFloat transparency]
      isA [ "Material" ]
      indexOfRefraction .34
      diffuseColor .8 .54 1
```

Multiple is-a relationships may be specified in order of preference; implementations are expected to use the first for which there is an implementation.

An Example VRML Document

This is a longer example of a VRML scene. It contains a simple model of a track light consisting of primitive shapes, plus three walls (built out of polygons) and a reference to a shape defined elsewhere, both of which are illuminated by a spotlight. The shape acts as a hyperlink to some HTML text.

```
#VRML V1.0 ascii

Separator {

      Separator {      # Simple track-light geometry:
            Translation { translation 0 4 0 }
```

```
Separator {
        Material { emissiveColor 0.1 0.3 0.3 }
        Cube {
                width   0.1
                height  0.1
                depth   4
        }
}
Rotation { rotation 0 1 0  1.57079 }
Separator {
        Material { emissiveColor 0.3 0.1 0.3 }
        Cylinder {
                radius  0.1
                height  .2
        }
}
Rotation { rotation -1 0 0  1.57079 }
Separator {
        Material { emissiveColor 0.3 0.3 0.1 }
        Rotation { rotation 1 0 0  1.57079 }
        Translation { translation 0 -.2 0 }
        Cone {
                height  .4
                bottomRadius .2
        }
        Translation { translation 0 .4 0 }
        Cylinder {
                radius  0.02
        }
}
}
SpotLight {       # Light from above
        location 0 4 0
        direction 0 -1 0
        intensity       0.9
        cutOffAngle     0.7
}
Separator {      # Wall geometry; just three flat
➥polygons
        Coordinate3 {
                point [
```

```
                                     -2 0 -2, -2 0 2, 2 0 2, 2 0 -2,
                                     -2 4 -2, -2 4 2, 2 4 2, 2 4 -2]
                    }
                    IndexedFaceSet {
                         coordIndex [ 0, 1, 2, 3, -1,
                                      0, 4, 5, 1, -1,
                                      0, 3, 7, 4, -1
                                      ]
                    }
               }
               WWWAnchor {   # A hyperlinked cow:
                    name "http://www.foo.edu/CowProject/
➡AboutCows.html"
                    Separator {
                         Translation { translation 0 1 0 }
                         WWWInline {   # Reference another
➡object
                              name "http://www.foo.edu/
➡3DObjects/cow.wrl"
                         }
                    }
               }
          }
```

Browser Considerations

This section describes the file-naming and MIME conventions
to be used in building VRML browsers and configuring WWW
browsers to work with them.

File Extensions

The file extension for VRML files is .wrl (for world). If a VRML
document is compressed using GZIP, the file extension should
become .wrl.gz (world gzipped).

MIME

The MIME type for VRML files is defined as follows:

x-world/x-vrml

The MIME major type for 3D world descriptions is x-world. The MIME minor type for VRML documents is x-vrml. Other 3D world descriptions, such as oogl for The Geometry Center's Object-Oriented Geometry Language, or iv, for SGI's Open Inventor ASCII format, can be supported by using different MIME minor types.

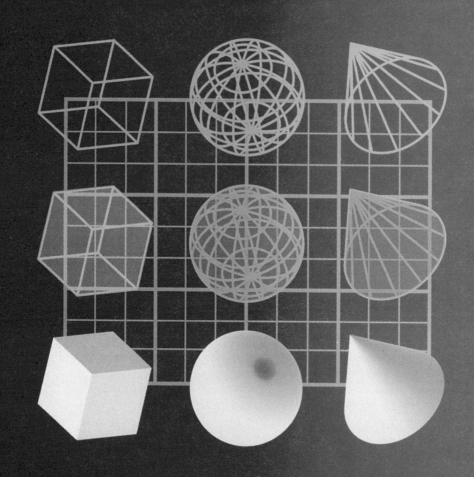

Appendix B

VRML Resources and Sites

Here's a list of the resources mentioned in this book. Some of them are the contact information for companies committed to bringing VRML products to market—a few of these are on the CD-ROM included with this book.

In addition, we've provided a small but significant list of pointers to VRML sites within the Web. From these selections, you should be able to find almost anything in the VRML universe.

The VRML Mailing List
send mail to info-rama@wired.com
no subject, message body
subscribe www-vrml <your@email.address.here>

VRML.ORG
The official VRML standards site
http://vag.vrml.org/

The Official VRML Repository (at the San Diego Supercomputing Center)
http://sdsc.edu/vrml/

A Small Selection of Popular VRML sites in the World Wide Web
WIRED's VRML Forum Page http://vrml.wired.com/
NCSA http://www.ncsa.uiuc.edu/General/VRML/
VRMLHome.html
Organic Online http://www.organic.com/vrml/
Virtual Vegas http://virtualvegas.com/vrml/vrml.html
Clay Graham's Worlds http://reality.sgi.com/employees/clay/
WaxWeb http://bug.village.virginia.edu/
CyberSamhain http://hyperreal.com/~mpesce/circle.wrl

Caligari Corporation
1955 Landings Drive
Mountain View, CA 94043
(415)390-9755 (fax)
http://www.caligari.com/

Enterprise Integration Technologies
800 El Camino Real
Menlo Park, CA 94025
(415)617-8000
info@eit.com
http://www.eit.com/

The Interactive Media Festival
448 Bryant Street
San Francisco, CA
(415)357-0100
info@arc.org
http://www.arc.org/
http://vrml.arc.org/

Intervista Software, Incorporated
45 Liberty Street
San Francisco, CA
(415)648-2749
info@intervista.com
http://www.intervista.com/

Netscape Communications Corporation
501 East Middlefield Road
Mountain View, CA 94043
info@netscape.com
http://www.netscape.com/

Paper Software, Incorporated
4 Deming Street
Woodstock, NY 12498
(914)679-2440
http://www.paperinc.com/

ParaGraph Corporation
1688 Dell Avenue
Campbell, CA 95008
(408)364-7726
info@paragraph.com
http://www.paragraph.com/

Silicon Graphics, Incorporated
Mountain View, CA 94043
info@sgi.com
http://www.sgi.com/

Syndesis Corporation
235 South Main Street
Jefferson, WI 53549
(414)674-5200
syndesis@beta.inc.net
http://www.webmaster.com/syndesis/

Template Graphics Software
9920 Pacific Heights Blvd. Suite 200
San Diego, CA 92121
(619)457-5359
info@tgs.com
http://www.tgs.sd.com/~template

Virtus Corporation
118 MacKenan Drive, Suite 250
Cary, NC 27511
(919)467-9700
info@virtus.com
http://www.virtus.com/

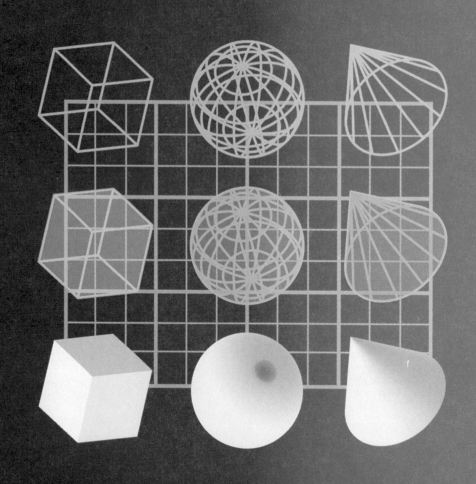

Appendix C

The VRML CD

The CD-ROM included with this book has copies of several of the programs described and used in this book—you can be browsing the VRML web within minutes of putting the CD-ROM into your drive.

The contents are described in the following sections.

Virtus Walkthrough VRML

This tool enables you to create rich scenes quickly and save them as VRML files. The installation comes with a set of sample object libraries. Using these libraries, you can construct a cyberspace living room in minutes. The "Project 188" Virtus file, 188CCC.VWT, is also on the CD-ROM. You can see how we built our virtual home. This tool is a bit different from Virtus Walkthrough Pro (which we used to construct Project 188); it doesn't enable you to apply texture maps. You can bring in texture-mapped models from Virtus Walkthrough Pro or Virtus VR, however, and convert them to VRML using this tool.

Paragraph Home Space Builder

Home Space Builder is a tool designed for 3D novices. Using a straightforward point-and-click drawing interface—documented in Chapter 9, "Homesteading Cyberspace"—you can quickly create simple, but visually rich, VRML spaces. You can even bring in your own favorite images and place them into your creations.

Caligari trueSpace 2.0 Demo

trueSpace is the much-acclaimed professional 3D object design tool from Caligari Corporation. This demo version shows what can be done with trueSpace; you'll find the interface intuitive and appealing. Used in conjunction with the WCVT2POV.EXE tool (save your trueSpace objects as DXF files to convert them), Caligari trueSpace is an easy route to creating complex shapes for your VRML projects.

InterVista Software's WorldView VRML Browser

Tony Parisi helped create VRML and has also helped create one of the most popular VRML browsers: WorldView. WorldView enables standard PCs and 14.4 modems to run real-time VRML apps.

Paper Software WebFX

WebFX, by Paper Software, is a component VRML browser that runs inside of QMosaic, Netscape, and other HTML browsers. You can page back and forth between HTML and VRML documents using WebFX running under a Web browser.

WCTV2POV.EXE 3D to VRML Conversion Utility

This freeware file converter, developed by Keith Rule, runs under Microsoft Windows and can be used to convert existing 3D models (from Wavefront, 3D Studio, AutoCAD DXF, and others) into VRML 1.0 files. These files can then be used as is or in WWWInline references. If you can't find a file type you need for your work, try exporting the 3D model in DXF format. This tool will read in DXF format and will write out VRML!

QvLib—The Quick VRML Parser Library in "C++"

For you hackers, we've included the complete source code to the Quick VRML Library, written by Paul Strauss and Gavin Bell of SGI, and placed into the public domain by SGI. Using this library (which compiles under G++ on Unix, CodeWarrior on Macintosh, and Microsoft Visual C++ under Windows (32-bit) systems), you can create your own VRML browser or other sophisticated VRML applications. If you want more information about QvLib, point your Web browser at *http://sdsc.edu/vrml/*.

Code Samples

All VRML code samples used in Chapters 6, 7, 8, and 10 can be found on the CD-ROM. Each of them has been tested with WebSpace; they should work in WorldView and WebFX as well, but they haven't been tested in these environments. The PERL code for the VRML orrey, ORREY.PL, is also included, as is James Waldrop's *datafat munger*, DFMUNGER.PL. If you need to get a copy of PERL to run the sample, you can easily download it from the Web. The YAHOO PERL site, which has links to a great deal of information about PERL, is at *http://www.yahoo.com/Computers/Languages/Perl/*.

Models

There are several VRML models included on the CD-ROM, designed to give you a feel for the kind of work people are doing in VRML. The New College vrmLab, VRMLLAB.WRL, designed by Jeff Sonstein, shows how much is possible with just a few basic objects. The World, WORLD.WRL, shows the Earth in good detail with links to high resolution maps of selected areas of North America. A tryptophan molecule, TRYPT.WRL, provides a decent example of the educational and scientific applications of VRML. Finally, we've got the VRML logo in VRML, courtesy of Kevin Hughes.

The VRML 1.0 Specification

The complete text of the HTML version of the VRML 1.0 specification is also provided. The VRML logo image at the head of the document links to the VRML logo!

Planet 9 Studio .wrl Files

Planet 9 Studios of San Francisco, under the leadership of architect and software developer David Colleen, is creating Virtual SOMA: San Francisco in VRML! Included here are two .wrl files, one of Planet 9 Studio's offices, the other from the Virtual SOMA project.

Recommended Reading

Each of the books in this list has made a profound contribution to my understanding of cyberspace, the Internet, and the creation of culture in the construction of meaning. Taken together, they provide a strong background in the fundamentals of cyberspace theory.

Artificial Reality II
Myron W. Krueger
1991, Addison-Wesley Publishing Company
Reading, MA
ISBN 0-201-52260-8

Computer Graphics: Principles and Practice
Foley, van Dam, Feiner, and Hughes
1990, Addison-Wesley Publishing Company
Reading, MA

Computers as Theatre
Brenda Laurel
1994, Addison-Wesley Publishing Company
Reading, MA
ISBN 0-201-51048-0

Cyberspace: First Steps
Michael Benedikt, ed.
1991, MIT Press
Cambridge, MA
ISBN 0-262-02327-X

The Inventor Mentor
Josie Wernecke
1994, Addison-Wesley Publishing Company
Reading, MA
ISBN 0-201-62495-8

The Inventor Toolmaker
Josie Wernecke
1994, Addison-Wesley Publishing Company
Reading, MA
ISBN 0-201-62493-1

Internetworking with TCP/IP
Douglas E. Comer
1991, Prentice-Hall, Incorporated
Englewood Cliffs, NJ
ISBN 0-13-468505-9

Neuromancer
William Gibson
1984, Ace Books, New York
ISBN 0-441-00068-1

OpenGL Programming Guide
Open GL Architecture Review Board
1993, Addison-Wesley Publishing Company
Reading, MA
ISBN 0-201-63274-8

Programming Perl
Larry Wall and Randal L. Schwartz
1991, O'Reilly and Associates, Incorporated
Sebastopol, CA
ISBN 0-937175-64-1

The Sacred and the Profane: The Nature of Religion
Mircea Eliade
1959, Harcourt Brace and Company, New York

Understanding Media: The Extensions of Man
Marshall McLuhan
1964, McGraw-Hill Book Company, New York

Virtual Reality
Howard Reingold
1991, Summit Books, New York
ISBN 0-671-69363-8

Glossary

3D—*Three-dimensional.*   Used to refer to fancy buttons with shadows, to the 3D "eye" optical illusions done with random dot stereograms and 3D rendering.

3D rendering   The process of turning 3D geometrically defined objects into pictures that give the illusion of depth. The major rendering techniques are ray tracing (start from eye), radiosity (start from lights), and geometry-based rendering, sometimes referred to as "real-time" or interactive 3D graphics. The latter technique forms the basis of almost all interactive 3D graphics.

Alpha blending   Alpha is an abstract value, associated with the color of a pixel (the A in RGBA), which determines what percentage of a new pixel in the resulting image is determined by this pixel when it is blended into the image. This is mostly for transparency and per primitive antialiasing.

Ambient light   An approximation to the illumination caused by the reflection of light from all objects in the scene. Outside the computer graphics industry, this is usually referred to as "diffuse light." One must be careful to distinguish diffuse light from diffuse reflection. Ambient light does not enter into the diffuse lighting calculations. In VRML, the browser can either implement an ambient light source or not.

Anchor   A hyperlink (hot link) from one VRML scene to another (or other Web document). This is implemented by the WWWAnchor node.

Antialiasing   The most common aliasing artifacts are "jaggies," or jagged edges that appear along edges of objects and lines. The alias is a given pixel that represents many points along the mathematical line. The attempt to reduce the effects of aliasing is known as antialiasing.

Aperture   The area or volume to be searched during picking.

API—*Application Programming Interface.*   A specific library with documented calling conventions to which an application program can be linked in order to create an executable program. OpenGL, renderWare, Reality Labs, and BRender are APIs.

ARPAnet—*Advanced Research Projects Agency Network.*   A research network funded by ARPA (later DARPA), a government agency, and built by BBN, Inc. in 1969. It was the first packet-switching network and served as the central Internet backbone for many years.

Aspect ratio   The ratio of the width to the height.

Backface   A portion of a surface primitive whose geometric normal, when transformed to the camera coordinate system, has a negative z-axis component. A backfacing polygon may be culled.

Bps—*bits per second.*   A measure of the rate of data transmission.

Buffer   A storage area used to hold input or output data.

Bump mapping   The rendering technique of grabbing a surface normal from a lookup table and recalculating the lighting on a per-pixel basis. This can be used to simulate the dimples on an orange more simply than modeling them geometrically.

Camera   In VRML, there are two nodes that define camera: OrthographicCamera and PerspectiveCamera. The position, orientation, and other attributes can be specified. The browser will provide a default camera.

Camera position   The position in space at which the eye or virtual camera is located. This is also known as the viewpoint, eye point, eye position, or viewing position.

Clipping   The process of determining whether a graphics object is wholly or partially outside some defined boundary. Portions of primitives that are outside the boundary are discarded and said to be clipped. In VRML, this means objects may be partially drawn when they are only partially visible.

Color   A color in VRML is specified as a *red, green, blue* (RGB) triplet. In addition, colors in texture maps can be grayscale (from black to white), RGBA (color with a transparency value), and RGB values.

Connection   A logical path between two protocol modules that provides a reliable delivery service.

Coordinate system   A system of axes and units that is used to define the position of objects. In VRML, all objects are defined in a local object space, including the camera.

Culling   The process of removing backfacing surfaces or frontfacing surfaces from the rendering pipeline; this may improve performance. It also removes bright spots on the silhouettes of dark sides, where the backface pokes through.

Depth cue   To blend the color of an object with the background color based on its distance from the viewing position. This gives an additional clue as to the depth of an object.

Diffuse reflection   A reflection from the surface of an object that bounces in all directions and, hence, is independent of viewing position. The amount of diffuse reflection depends on the amount of light striking that portion of the object and how directly the surface faces the light or lights.

Directional light   A light source, assumed to be at infinity, that is defined with a direction vector and a light color. Also referred to as a vector light or an infinite light.

DNS—*Domain Name System.*   A distributed database system used to map IP addresses to their system names. DNS also provides the location of mail exchangers.

DNS name servers   The servers that contain information about a portion of the DNS database.

DOF—*Degree of Freedom.*   Represents the ability of a parameter to vary. A body free to be anywhere in space has three degrees of freedom for position and three degrees of freedom for orientation. A flat object on the floor has three degrees of freedom; it can spin (one DOF) and move in two directions on the floor (two DOF).

Domain name space   The database structure used by DNS.

Double-buffering   The process of using two image buffers to achieve smoother or flicker-free graphics generation. One buffer is used for the generation of an image, while the other one is displayed. When the image is complete, the two buffers can be conceptually swapped to display the generated image. The process may be repeated to support smooth animation sequences.

Face   *See facet.*

Facet   A planar portion of a surface primitive. Some output primitives already contain portions that are planar.

Facet color   The color associated with a facet. Some output primitives allow facet colors to be passed along with the geometry information.

Facet normal   The geometric normal associated with a facet. Some output primitives allow facet normals to be passed along with the other geometry information. Facet normals are used in culling and lighting operations. If not provided explicitly, a facet normal may be computed using the vertices of the facet.

Flat shading   A shading technique in which the lighting is calculated once per facet and a single shade of color is used for the whole facet.

FQDN—*Fully Qualified Domain Name.*   A combination of the host name and domain name.

FTP—*File Transfer Protocol.*   A high-level protocol that supports file copying between systems. Requires client and server components.

Gateway   A computer that attaches multiple TCP/IP networks for the purpose of routing or delivering IP packets between them. Used interchangeably with IP router.

Glyph   The definition of a simple image, typically of a character or symbol.

Gouraud shading   Henri Gouraud invented Gouraud shading in 1971. It interpolates colors between vertices of a facet. In other words, the lighting calculation is done once per vertex, and then the resulting colors are blended smoothly from one vertex to the others.

Graphics pipeline   The series of steps representing the process of rendering; turning geometry and properties into pixels.

Group node   A class of VRML nodes that contains a group of other nodes. They organize a scene. The Separator node is the most common.

Host   Any computer system or device attached to the internetwork.

Host ID   The portion of an IP address that identifies the host in a particular network. Used in conjunction with network IDs to form a complete IP address.

IndexedFaceSet   In VRML, a shape node made of polygons specified as sets of indices into a list of coordinate values.

Inline   Referencing an object by specifying its URL. This is a handy way to create a scene by using and reusing other objects.

internet   A collection of packet-switching networks connected by IP routers and appearing to users as a single network.

Internet   The world's largest collection of networks that reaches universities, government research labs, business organizations, and military installations in many countries.

IP—*Internet Protocol.*   Along with TCP, one of the most fundamental protocols in TCP/IP networking. IP is responsible for addressing and sending datagrams across an internet.

IP address   The 32-bit address assigned to hosts that identifies a node on the network and specifies routing information on an internetwork.

Light, light source   A mathematical approximation of a light. Different types of light sources in VRML include DirectionalLight, PointLight, and SpotLight. They emulate sunlight, a naked light bulb, and a spot light, respectively. A browser may also provide an ambient light source.

Lighting   The process of computing the amount of light that strikes a surface and the amount and type of light that bounces off. Depending on the type of shading, this may be done once per facet, once per vertex, or once per pixel.

LOD   Short for *level of detail*, this VRML group node allows for different representations of an object to be used, depending upon the level of detail desired.

Material   In VRML, a node that determines the reflectivity of subsequent surfaces. It has fields for ambient, diffuse, and specular reflection. In addition, it governs surface transparency.

Matrix   In VRML, a 4-by-4 (doubly indexed) array of floating point numbers used to represent a transformation from one orientation and position to another orientation and position. It can also scale objects up or down. Also known as a transform or transformation matrix.

Name resolution   The process of mapping a computer name to an IP address. DNS and DHCP are two tools for resolving names.

Node   In VRML, a node is the basic building block of a scene graph. The three basic categories are shape, group, and property nodes.

Normal   A unit vector perpendicular to a plane. There are facet normals and vertex normals.

Normalized   An adjective, mostly for vectors, meaning to be of unit length.

NSFnet—*National Science Foundation Network.*   A network that serves as part of the current Internet backbone funded by the NSF.

Orientation   How an object is oriented. This can be specified as yaw, pitch, and roll; rotations in x, y, and z; with Euler Angles (azimuth, altitude, and twist); or a direction vector and an up vector.

Packet   The unit of protocol data sent across a packet-switching network.

Painter's algorithm   A hidden surface removal method that involves sorting all primitives based on their z-values and then rendering them in order from farthest to closest. The result is that primitives farther away will be "painted over" by primitives that are closer.

Palette   A table of color values that converts 8-bit pseudocolor values into RGB values that can be displayed. Also called a color lookup table.

Phong shading   The process of interpolating the surface normal over the surface and recalculating the lighting on a per pixel basis. Named for Phong Bui-Toung for an algorithm published in 1975. This is different from the Phong lighting model, which is used in most "real-time" 3D rendering.

Picking   The act of searching the graphics database for shapes that are within the pick aperture and meet other requirements. This is how objects are selected in 3D.

Pitch   The slant of a boat or plane from back to front.

Pixel   Short for a picture element. It is a single dot on the computer screen whose color is determined by the pixel value.

Point cloud   A collection of points [x,y,z] with no geometric relation between its members.

Point light   A type of light source that is defined with a position and a color. Light spreads in all directions as if it were a naked light bulb.

Polygon   A series of vertices that, when connected, define the boundary of a planar surface. The last vertex in the list is always implicitly connected to the first vertex in the list.

PPP—*Point-to-Point Protocol.*   An industry standard protocol for data transfer across serial links. It allows for several protocols to be multiplexed across the link.

Protocol   A set of rules used to govern the transmission and receiving of data.

Pseudocolor   A color display type that interprets pixels composed of an index value, which can be used as an index into a palette.

Radiosity   A lighting technique in which the amount of energy from each light source is distributed to the scene. Each object of the scene is then considered a light source because it is reflecting light. The technique iterates distributing light energy from surface to surface until some threshold energy value (or number of iterations) is reached.

Reflection   The mathematical approximation of the amount of light that bounces off the surface of an object, allowing it to be seen. There are three types of reflection in VRML: ambient, diffuse, and specular.

RGB   The color space in which colors are identified by red, green, and blue intensity values.

Roll   The side-to-side movement of a boat or plane. In computer graphics, the angle of rotation about the lengthwise axis.

Route   The path that network traffic takes from its source to its destination.

Router   A computer responsible for deciding the routes network traffic will follow, and then sending traffic from one network to another.

Shading   The part of rendering that deals with the conversion of color information into displayable color values. The most common techniques are flat, Gouraud, and Phong.

Shape node   The VRML nodes that contain geometry. Sometimes referred to as primitives.

SLIP—*Serial Line Internet Protocol.*   A simple protocol used to transmit datagrams across a serial line.

Smooth shading   *See Gouraud shading.*

Solid modeling   A modeling technique in which objects are considered "solid." Various properties such as mass are inherent in the database. This is especially useful in *computer aided design* (CAD).

Specular reflection   A mirror-like reflection of varying degree that is caused by light reflecting directly from a light source off the surface in the direction of the viewer. The amount of specular reflection depends on the camera position and orientation.

Spot light   A light source that is defined with a position, a direction vector, a drop-off angle, a spread angle, and a color. This creates a cone of light defined by the spread angle. Within the cone, the light is brightest directly along the direction vector and then drops off as the angle from the direction vector increases, as governed by the dropOffRate.

Surface   Any shape that defines an area, but has no volume. Surfaces can be faceted surfaces (indexed face set) or parametric surfaces, which are defined using splines.

Surface normal   A vector perpendicular to the given surface at a given point on the surface.

TCP—*Transmission Control Protocol.*   Along with IP, one of the most fundamental protocols in TCP/IP networking. TCP is a connection-based protocol that provides reliable, full duplex data transmission between a pair of applications.

Telnet   Remote terminal protocol that allows a terminal attached to one host to log in to other hosts, as if directly connected to the remote machine.

Texture map   An image used as the source for texture mapping.

Texture mapping   The technique of rendering a surface with colors from an image to give it the appearance of texture or to simulate a printed surface. Instead of shading (or in addition to it), a color value is selected from the texture map on a per-pixel basis. This can create a visual richness while maintaining simple geometry.

Transparency   A mathematical approximation of the effect of transmitting light through a non-opaque (translucent) surface. In VRML, this is controlled by the transparency field in the Material node.

Vertex   A point at the "corner" of a face or line set. Vertices connect edges.

View   *See Camera.*

Voxel   Similar to pixel, except it is the smallest unit of a volume rendering.

Wireframe   A rendering technique in which surface facets are drawn as outlines. Because no lighting or shading is done, this can be very fast, but confusing.

Yaw   The spinning of a boat or plane about its vertical axis.

Z-buffer   A hidden surface removal algorithm that maintains a depth or z-value for each pixel that is rendered. Pixel values are only overwritten if the object being rendered is closer to the viewing position than the z-value already written for that pixel.

Index

X-Y-Z

PLUG YOURSELF INTO...

THE MACMILLAN INFORMATION SUPERLIBRARY™

Free information and vast computer resources from the world's leading computer book publisher—online!

FIND THE BOOKS THAT ARE RIGHT FOR YOU!

A complete online catalog, plus sample chapters and tables of contents give you an in-depth look at *all* of our books, including hard-to-find titles. It's the best way to find the books you need!

- **STAY INFORMED** with the latest computer industry news through our online newsletter, press releases, and customized Information SuperLibrary Reports.

- **GET FAST ANSWERS** to your questions about MCP books and software.

- **VISIT** our online bookstore for the latest information and editions!

- **COMMUNICATE** with our expert authors through e-mail and conferences.

- **DOWNLOAD SOFTWARE** from the immense MCP library:
    - Source code and files from MCP books
    - The best shareware, freeware, and demos

- **DISCOVER HOT SPOTS** on other parts of the Internet.

- **WIN BOOKS** in ongoing contests and giveaways!

TO PLUG INTO MCP: →

GOPHER: gopher.mcp.com

FTP: ftp.mcp.com

WORLD WIDE WEB: **http://www.mcp.com**

GET CONNECTED
to the ultimate source of computer information!

The MCP Forum on CompuServe

Go online with the world's leading computer book publisher! Macmillan Computer Publishing offers everything you need for computer success!

Find the books that are right for you!
A complete online catalog, plus sample chapters and tables of contents give you an in-depth look at all our books. The best way to shop or browse!

➤ Get fast answers and technical support for MCP books and software

➤ Join discussion groups on major computer subjects

➤ Interact with our expert authors via e-mail and conferences

➤ Download software from our immense library:

  ▷ Source code from books
  ▷ Demos of hot software
  ▷ The best shareware and freeware
  ▷ Graphics files

Join now and get a free CompuServe Starter Kit!

To receive your free CompuServe Introductory Membership, call **1-800-848-8199** and ask for representative #597.

The Starter Kit includes:
➤ Personal ID number and password
➤ $15 credit on the system
➤ Subscription to *CompuServe Magazine*

Once on the CompuServe System, type:

GO MACMILLAN

for the most computer information anywhere!

MACMILLAN
COMPUTER
PUBLISHING

WANT MORE
INFORMATION?

CHECK OUT THESE RELATED TOPICS OR SEE YOUR LOCAL BOOKSTORE

CAD and 3D Studio

As the number one CAD publisher in the world, and as a Registered Publisher of Autodesk, New Riders Publishing provides unequaled content on this complex topic. Industry-leading products include AutoCAD and 3D Studio.

Networking

As the leading Novell NetWare publisher, New Riders Publishing delivers cutting-edge products for network professionals. We publish books for all levels of users, from those wanting to gain NetWare Certification, to those administering or installing a network. Leading books in this category include *Inside NetWare 3.12*, *CNE Training Guide: Managing NetWare Systems*, *Inside TCP/IP*, and *NetWare: The Professional Reference*.

Graphics

New Riders provides readers with the most comprehensive product tutorials and references available for the graphics market. Best-sellers include *Inside CorelDRAW! 5*, *Inside Photoshop 3*, and *Adobe Photoshop NOW!*

Internet and Communications

As one of the fastest growing publishers in the communications market, New Riders provides unparalleled information and detail on this ever-changing topic area. We publish international best-sellers such as *New Riders' Official Internet Yellow Pages, 2nd Edition*, a directory of over 10,000 listings of Internet sites and resources from around the world, and *Riding the Internet Highway, Deluxe Edition*.

Operating Systems

Expanding off our expertise in technical markets, and driven by the needs of the computing and business professional, New Riders offers comprehensive references for experienced and advanced users of today's most popular operating systems, including *Understanding Windows 95*, *Inside Unix*, *Inside Windows 3.11 Platinum Edition*, *Inside OS/2 Warp Version 3*, and *Inside MS-DOS 6.22*.

Other Markets

Professionals looking to increase productivity and maximize the potential of their software and hardware should spend time discovering our line of products for Word, Excel, and Lotus 1-2-3. These titles include *Inside Word 6 for Windows*, *Inside Excel 5 for Windows*, *Inside 1-2-3 Release 5*, and *Inside WordPerfect for Windows*.

Orders/Customer Service **1-800-653-6156**   Source Code **NRP95**

New Riders Publishing   201 West 103rd Street ◆ Indianapolis, Indiana 46290 USA

REGISTRATION CARD

VRML—Browsing and Building Cyberspace

Name _____ Title _____

Company _____ Type of business _____

Address _____

City/State/ZIP _____

Have you used these types of books before? ☐ yes ☐ no

If yes, which ones? _____

_____

How many computer books do you purchase each year? ☐ 1–5 ☐ 6 or more

How did you learn about this book? _____

Where did you purchase this book? _____

Which applications do you currently use? _____

_____

Which computer magazines do you subscribe to? _____

_____

What trade shows do you attend? _____

_____

Comments: _____

_____

_____

Would you like to be placed on our preferred mailing list? ☐ yes ☐ no

☐ **I would like to see my name in print!** You may use my name and quote me in future New Riders products and promotions. My daytime phone number is: _____

New Riders Publishing   201 West 103rd Street ◆ Indianapolis, Indiana 46290 USA

Fax to **317-581-4670**   Orders/Customer Service **1-800-653-6156**   Source Code **NRP95**

- Fold Here -

‖‖‖‖

NO POSTAGE
NECESSARY
IF MAILED
IN THE
UNITED STATES

BUSINESS REPLY MAIL
FIRST-CLASS MAIL PERMIT NO. 9918 INDIANAPOLIS IN
POSTAGE WILL BE PAID BY THE ADDRESSEE

**NEW RIDERS PUBLISHING
201 W 103RD ST
INDIANAPOLIS IN 46290-9058**